The Samuel & Althea Stroum Lectures in Jewish Studies

The Samuel & Althea Stroum Lectures in Jewish Studies

The Yiddish Art Song
   Performed by Leon Lishner, basso, and Lazar Weiner, piano
   (stereophonic record album)

The Holocaust in Historical Perspective
   Yehuda Bauer

Zakhor: Jewish History and Jewish Memory
   Yosef Hayim Yerushalmi

Jewish Mysticism and Jewish Ethics
   Joseph Dan

The Invention of Hebrew Prose:
Modern Fiction and the Language of Realism
   Robert Alter

Recent Archaeological Discoveries and Biblical Research
   William G. Dever

Jewish Identity in the Modern World
   Michael A. Meyer

I. L. Peretz and the Making of Modern Jewish Culture
   Ruth R. Wisse

The Kiss of God:
Spiritual and Mystical Death in Judaism
   Michael Fishbane

Gender and Assimilation in Modern Jewish History:
The Roles and Representation of Women
   Paula E. Hyman

Portrait of American Jews:
The Last Half of the 20th Century
   Samuel C. Heilman

Judaism and Hellenism in Antiquity:
Conflict or Confluence?
   Lee I. Levine

Imagining Russian Jewry:
Memory, History, and Identity
   Steven L. Zipperstein

PORTRAIT
OF AMERICAN
JEWS The Last Half of the 20th Century

Samuel C. Heilman

University of Washington Press / *Seattle & London*

Library of Congress Cataloging-in-Publication Data
Heilman, Samuel C.
Portrait of American Jews: the last half of the twentieth century /
Samuel C. Heilman
p. cm.—(The Samuel and Althea Stroum lectures in Jewish
studies)
Includes bibliographical references and index.
ISBN 0-295-97470-2(cloth: alk. paper).
ISBN 0-295-97471-0 (pbk.: alk. paper)
I. Jews—United States—Cultural assimilation. 2. Judaism—United
States. 3. Judaism—20th century. I. Title. II. Series.
E184.J5H5345   1995   95-13360
305.892'4073—DC20   CIP

SAMUEL STROUM, BUSINESSMAN, COMMUNITY LEADER, AND philanthropist, by a major gift to the Jewish Federation of Greater Seattle, established the Samuel and Althea Stroum Philanthropic Fund.

In recognition of Mr. and Mrs. Stroum's deep interest in Jewish history and culture, the Board of Directors of the Jewish Federation of Greater Seattle, in cooperation with the Jewish Studies Program of the Henry M. Jackson School of International Studies at the University of Washington, established an annual lectureship at the University of Washington known as the Samuel and Althea Stroum Lectureship in Jewish Studies. This lectureship makes it possible to bring to the area outstanding scholars and interpreters of Jewish thought, thus promoting a deeper understanding of Jewish history, religion, and culture. Such understanding can lead to an enhanced appreciation of the Jewish contributions to the historical and cultural traditions that have shaped the American nation.

The terms of the gift also provide for the publication from time to time of the lectures or other appropriate materials resulting from or related to the lectures.

For Dora Levy

Born and still living in America,
witness to and taking part in more than
100 years of Jewish life here.

Contents

Preface   xi

Prologue   3

1 / Starting Over: *Acculturation
and Suburbia, the Jews of the 1950s*
    8

2 / The Emergence of Two Types of Jews:
Choices Made in the 1960s and 1970s
    47

3 / Quality versus Quantity:
The Challenge of the 1980s and 1990s
    101

Notes   165

Index   187

Preface

WHEN PROFESSOR HILLEL J. KIEVAL, HEAD OF THE JEWISH Studies Program at the University of Washington, first extended to me an invitation to offer the eighteenth annual Samuel and Althea Stroum Lecture in Jewish Studies, I was sincerely honored. To join a list of some of the most distinguished personalities in Jewish studies, including such people as Irving Howe, Yehuda Bauer, Yosef Yerushalmi, Jacob Rader Marcus, Aharon Appelfeld, Robert Alter, Ruth Wisse, Michael Meyer, Michael Fishbane, Moshe Idel, and Paula Hyman—to name but a few—however also filled me with a kind of dread. Those were hard acts to follow, as the many fine volumes to come out of this series attest. To add to my anxiety was the realization that I would be the first sociologist in the series. Sociologists tend to deal with subjects that most people think they know at least as well as the so-called experts.

In his invitation, Professor Kieval, a distinguished historian, suggested that given we were approaching the turn of a century and a millennium, I might offer some sort of review of the contemporary condition of American Jewry. While the coming end of the millennium is not really a benchmark of Jewish significance—"the year of our Lord" 2001 will after all simply be 5761 for the Jews, whose count comes from another God—even among Jews these times nevertheless have aroused an inclination for stocktaking. Undoubtedly, the coming into middle age of the generation born in the post–World War II era (people like Professor Kieval and me), the palpable sense of a political watershed at the recent end of the cold war that leaves America as the victorious society and land of greatest promise, the profound ferment and change that have marked the last fifty years of Jewish life, as well as the oft-repeated questions about Jewish continuity and what Jewish life will be like in the year 2000, have all contributed to this current motivation to look backward and forward at American Jewry. I did not have to ask Professor Kieval why he made his suggestion; I grasped its impetus immediately. Still, the question was how to frame my observations.

From the outset, I did not imagine or presume that my presentation would or could review the entire gamut of what has transpired for American Jewry during the years since 1950, the period to which I have turned my attention. I was after all largely a captive of the data available, collected mostly by others. Neither did I expect I could provide the definitive reading of what so many others have found; nor did I hope to unerringly prophesy what lies ahead. "Since the destruction of the Holy Temple," remarked the talmudic sage Rabbi Yochanan, "prophecy has been taken from the prophets and given to fools." In order not to seem the fool, I could only offer my own meditations, a sociological reflection on what I have learned.

As for the title, I realized, as I collected my thoughts, that what seemed more than anything else to tie the experience of American Jewry together during the last four and a half decades was that, for all of them, being Jewish was no longer simply a matter of birth or, more precisely, a matter of irrevocable destiny. In the open society of America, being Jewish had become a matter of choice. Judaism was now a religious *persuasion,* and even the matter of Jewish ethnicity seemed something people could decide to emphasize or deny. Thus, if I was going to deal with Jews in America, I was going to be focusing attention essentially on those who were "choosing to be Jews." That therefore became the title of the lecture series.

Although most of my published work has been in the domain of social anthropology and the ethnography of Jewish life and has emerged out of my own field studies and original research, for years I have taught courses and lectured before lay audiences on the general sociology of American Jewry. What my teaching (to say nothing of my personal experience) has made clear to me is the tumultuous character of American Jewish life during most of my lifetime, its promise and its deficiencies. Yet lectures have an evanescent quality; words once spoken melt into the air, retrievable only in the not always reliable memory of listeners. The Stroum Lectures would allow me to collect my thoughts and then write them down in an ordered fashion.

Why begin in 1950? Born in the shadow of the Holocaust and the dawn of the new State of Israel, my generation was always advised by our forebears that the truly important events in the history of Jewish life in the twentieth century occurred in its first half. While no one would deny the consequence of American Jewish events in the earlier years of this century—the mass migrations and organizational establishment certainly stand out—my generation and I, as baby boomers, have always been persuaded that what has happened since we were born has been no less crucial for understanding American Jewry. In a sense, the pages that follow constitute my argument for that proposition.

Although for a historian, four and a half decades, the approximate period covered in these pages, are hardly more than a drop in the long stream of Jewish experience, for a sociologist like me, they are an enormous flood of events and trends. That is precisely why I make no claim to be exhaustive in the facts I have chosen to present and discuss. Sociologists, after all, deal with the ephemera of contemporaneity, analyzing events almost simultaneously with their unfolding. Unlike historians, we have neither the luxury of passing time to allow events to fall into place nor the profound perspectives of hindsight from which to make our generalizations. We have to see the structure and direction of the world around us, being insiders and outsiders at once. This is not always easy; some would argue it is not always possible.

This being said, I admit from the outset that while I have tried to be analytically descriptive, there may be times when my perspective runs the risk of being prescriptive. Writing or speaking about Jews, I cannot always maintain the strict value neutrality that is supposed to characterize my discipline. Moreover, to point out certain trends and neglect others, to select certain facts as significant and leave others unnoted, to see the dark side rather than the light side of Jewish life in America, as I sometimes do, necessarily place me beyond the purely sociological. As a conscientious academic I regret these biases. As an American Jew, with a stake in my people's future, I am pleased not to have completely obliterated my personal perspective. In all honesty, I believe that there are no completely neutral facts in the matter of American Jewry. Clearly, I come down in favor of Jewish continuity, and where I have seen trends and facts that speak to this issue I have emphasized them.

Thus, the pages that follow, while aiming analytically to detail American Jewry from the 1950s through the beginning of the 1990s, should at best be seen as a portrait, actually a diptych, drawn in a kind of intellectual free hand, rather than a snapshot or a graph. If the statistics and data nevertheless make what I have done look like a photo, that is true only for those who look cursorily at what I have to say; a closer look will reveal the sweep of the brush strokes in my double portrait. In a sense, these pages are my analogue to the marvelous self-portrait by artist Max Ferguson that I have selected for this book's cover; it only looks like a photo.

In his diptych, Ferguson, this Jew with the Ellis Island–inspired last name, has painted a double picture of himself, which he has entitled *Ralph Lauren's Worst Nightmare*. In my reading of this painting I see two alternative representations of a Jew. In one, the clean-shaven and bareheaded, assimilated American Jewish Ferguson is neatly attired in the style epitomized by the contemporary fashions of a designer who, although raised as Ralph Lifshitz in the Bronx, today as Ralph Lauren sets the standard for American fashion. In the other panel of this double portrait, however, the same Ferguson is bearded, wearing the fedora associated with Lubavitcher Hasidim and wrapped in a *talis*. No longer projecting the Lauren look, he is explicit and unmistakable in his Jewish identity. This he implies is "Ralph Lauren's worst nightmare," the nightmare of a Jew who thinks the move to change his appearance and pass as the American standard is forever but who discovers there are those Jews who abandon that look and choose to revert to the old and distinctive ways. To underscore this message, each panel of the self-portrait is accompanied by a caption (one in Yiddish and one in English) telling the joke of the hunchback who, like the assimilated Jew, has fooled himself into thinking that he has successfully escaped who he is. Reading the diptych from left to right (as one reads in America), one moves from the clearly identifiable Jew to the assimilated one, while reading from right to left (as one does in Hebrew), one begins with the assimilated American and ends up with the bearded Jew. In a sense, this diptych captures the two faces and orientations of American

Jewry during the last forty years, which my written portrait will try to reflect from a sociological viewpoint as well.

The reaction to these lectures was extraordinary. Each of the three talks was attended by an overflow audience obviously engaged by the topic. Into Kane Hall at the University of Washington came students and faculty, laypeople and rabbis, those fully involved in Jewish life and those on its periphery. They listened; they asked; they argued; one woman even asked to hug me at the end of the series—it was all a professor could ask for. The reactions were not so much a response to me, I think, but instead an affirmation that the subject was important to my listeners. They too were ready to take stock and to deal with the question of choosing to be Jewish in America.

Although there are more words in these pages than actually were spoken during the three lectures, I have in the main resisted the temptation to reorganize or heavily recast what I said during those two weeks of April 1993. Instead, I offer for those who listened, as well as those who might have listened, a written record of my reflections on what choosing to be Jewish in America since 1950 means.

No preamble to this book would be complete without a word of thanks to my hosts at the University of Washington. In particular, I wish publicly to thank Hillel and Patty Kieval, Marty and Leslie Jaffee, Joel and Marcy Migdal, Naomi Sokoloff, Peter and Ruth Medding, and Dorothy and Jerry Becker for not only providing an excellent academic environment but perhaps even more importantly creating an atmosphere that made my wife and me feel at home. The foresight and generosity of Samuel and Althea Stroum in creating and sustaining this lecture series stand as a testament to their Jewish commitment. We all are in their debt. Their kindnesses to me I shall not soon forget.

Special thanks must go to Uzi Rebhun of the Hebrew University, who, although at a crucial stage in the writing of his doctoral dissertation, was of enormous help in interpreting and retrieving data from the 1990 National Jewish Population Survey. I have learned enormously from the work of my colleagues Sergio DellaPergola, Calvin Goldscheider, Barry Kosmin, and Bethamie Horowitz and of course of my longtime fellow teacher at the City University of New York Steven M. Cohen; his writing on American Jewry, as well as his recent move to Israel, has taught me much. The fine work of the staff at the University of Washington Press and especially of Naomi Pascal and Pamela Bruton is deeply appreciated. Finally, as always, to my first and most loyal critic, my life partner, Ellin, I give my most profound thanks.

Portrait of American Jews: *The Last Half of the 20th Century*

Prologue

Our vision of the end of days has often been clearer
than our vision of this day.—Leonard Fein, *Where Are We?*
The Inner Life of America's Jews

IN JANUARY OF 1950, THE START OF THE SECOND HALF OF THE twentieth century, I was a passenger on the United States Navy transport ship *General Stuart Heintzelman*. For four years, my parents, survivors of the concentration camps, had lived in Karlsruhe, Germany, where I was born after the war. We had lived in relative luxury during those four years because my father had been appointed by the American occupation forces as an overseer of a large textile factory. But, as historian Lucy Dawidowicz has put it, "America beckoned with the future."[1] Now on board this floating refugee camp, along with approximately 1,100 other "displaced persons," most of them Holocaust survivors, my parents and I, having left behind a large apartment, maids, and all the comforts that the factory provided, were on our way to America to begin a new life. Arriving on Friday the thirteenth, we would join about 100,000 other DPs who had already immigrated since that first transport in May of 1946, hoping somehow to reconstruct ourselves and our people in what seemed at the time the most secure haven for Jews in the Diaspora.[2] With the destruction of nearly all of European Jewry, who in 1933 had constituted 46 percent of the world's Jews, America now indisputably had become the new center of Diaspora Jewry. My father was hopeful, my mother in trauma, and I had no idea what to expect.

To be sure, the two-year-old State of Israel also beckoned many Jews like us. By 1950, its reality had already begun to modify the perspective and activities of American Jewry. Indeed, on the very day of our arrival, the *New York Times* headlined a plea from the former president of the Zionist Organization of America demanding support for the fledgling Jewish state and announced that Henry Morganthau Jr., chairman of the United Jewish Appeal (UJA), had flown to Tel Aviv to confer with Prime Minister David Ben Gurion about the anticipated financial backing that American Jews were expected to provide. Two days later Mayor O'Dwyer of New York declared a general "Mobilization Day for the Zionist Organization of America" and called on Jews in New York to affiliate themselves with it; similar drives were held throughout the country.

But for many of the war-scarred like my parents, Israel was not attractive; the thought of having to struggle for life in a new and poor country in a land that, although promised by God to our people, was still very much contested by a hostile Arab population was overwhelming and therefore inconceivable. Instead, they chose to abandon Europe and come here, where they believed that behind the protective cover of American might and in the secure embrace of its democracy and its economic opportunity, we could once again find life. Had they read the newspaper a week later, they would have seen a report confirming their decision to turn toward America rather than Israel. Visiting some of Israel's immigration camps, the American chairman of the UJA proclaimed himself "shocked" by the poor conditions of immigrants there, while in America the headlines noted: "D.P.'s Quick to Catch Tempo of America, Survey Shows."[3] Indeed, in a 19 January 1950 dispatch on the DPs, a *New York Times* reporter asserted: "Those who are acquainted with the new adult immigrants say that once the English problem is solved, nobody will be able to distinguish them from any other American."[4]

At three and half years old, I was too young to understand any of this at the time, but when I watched my father leave for work on the bus to go to his job as a seventy-five-cent-an-hour shipper rather than seeing him driven to the factory by his chauffeur as in Germany, I recall asking him why we had given up so much to come to Boston, where we now lived. His answer, which he repeated throughout the years as I continued to query his decision to come to America, was simply: "I did not want you to be the only Jewish child in the school." He believed America would preserve and protect our family's Jewish future, and for that he had been ready to start all over again.

But what was Jewish life in America like in the 1950s, when we arrived? And, was my father correct in deciding to turn toward Boston rather than Jerusalem? What has happened to American Jewry during the last half of the twentieth century? Has this been a place that has preserved and protected Jewish life, or did those who chose to go to Israel make the right turn? Was Elliot Cohen, the first editor of *Commentary* magazine, correct when he wrote in its first issue in November 1945 that American Jews "will evolve new patterns of living, new modes of thought, which will harmonize heritage and country into a true sense of at-home-ness in the modern world?"[5] Does America safeguard the Jewish future?

In the course of these sociological reflections, my purpose will be to explore these general questions by taking a retrospective view of American Jewry since the 1950s. However tumultuous the first half of this century was for Jewry in general—with its mass migrations, socioeconomic changes, two world wars, pogroms and Holocaust, and the remarkable and miraculous reestablishment of the ancient Jewish homeland in Israel—the last four and half decades have been no less decisive.

Inexorably, the events that have allowed Jews to live in relative security have presented them with perhaps an even greater challenge than did the adversity and upheaval of the years leading up to 1950. The new haven in America, with its myriad of new possibilities and absence of organized anti-Semitism, made the membrane of Jewish life almost completely permeable. The core began to shrink while the periphery was pulled ever farther away. American Jews became no less American than any other group; some might argue they became more American than any other group. In the reorganization of America in this last half of the century, the Jews jumped into the thick of things and were caught up in the whirlwind.

Some might argue that Dickens's famous opening lines in his *Tale of Two Cities* best capture the Jewish experience in America during these last years:

> It was the best of times, it was the worst of times, it was the age of wisdom, it was the age of foolishness, it was the epoch of belief, it was the epoch of incredulity, it was the season of Light, it was the season of Darkness, it was the spring of hope, it was the winter of despair, we had everything before us, we had nothing before us.[6]

This is a time when American Jews experience a minimum of prejudice, when almost all domains of life are open to them, but it is also a time of extraordinary assimilation, of swelling rates of

intermarriage, and of large numbers of people simply ignoring their
Jewishness completely. This is a time when, in America, the physical safety of Jews is unparalleled in history (except perhaps for those
few ultra-Orthodox who still live in inner-city neighborhoods like
Crown Heights, Brooklyn), but Jewish cultural integrity seems more
precarious than ever before. This is a time when the Jewish population of America is steadily diminishing in numbers, certainly relative
to the general American population; in the last forty years, while
America grew by over two-thirds, American Jewry grew by only a
fifth. Moreover, as the 1990 National Jewish Population Survey demonstrates, the number of people who fill everyone's definition of a
Jew has actually shrunk to about 4.4 million.[7] This is a time when
Jews have no trouble building synagogues, but they have all sorts of
trouble filling them. This is a time when the quality of Jewish education is perhaps higher than ever before in history and when the
output of Jewish scholarship, whether in the yeshivas or in university
Jewish studies programs, is overwhelming in its scope and ampli-
tude. Never before in America has so much Judaica been published.
But it is also a time when most American Jews receive the most minimal level of such education, a time when a majority of "the people
of the book" do not read the great books of Jewish life, and even if
they wanted to, most could neither read nor comprehend the great
corpus of Jewish literature in its Hebrew (or Aramaic) original. The
many cultural islands populated by prodigious Jewish scholars are
surrounded by a sea of those who are Jewish illiterates. This is a time
in America when there is no shame in being a Jew and yet fewer
American Jews seem to know what being a Jew means. This is a time
when American Jews can and do marvel at the accomplishments of a
Jewish state in Israel but when fewer than half of them have ever visited it and practically none of them would even entertain the thought
of living there. This is a time when Jewish wealth and power reach
into the corridors of American power and influence, when Jewish
money endows symphony orchestras, art museums, and major universities, but when the number of those who work for the Jewish
community or give to Jewish causes shrinks daily. This *is* the best of
times and the worst of times.

How did all this come to be? What does it portend for the Jewish future? Do the facts of the last four and a half decades leave us with hope for the prospects of American Jewry, or do they force us to re-evaluate what American Jewry has become? I am not certain I can fully answer these questions, but I am certain that they will guide all that follows.

1 Starting Over:
Acculturation and Suburbia, the Jews of the 1950s

THIS STORY OF CONTEMPORARY JEWRY BEGINS IN A DE-cade that for a long time was overshadowed by its far more tumultuous predecessor and successor decades. Compared to the 1940s and 1960s, the 1950s seemed a lull between two storms. Although far from placid, as those who lived through those ten years will attest, the fifties were apparently a calm enough time for planting or, more precisely, replanting Jewish life in America. The harvest of those seeds would come later.

America in the Fifties

To understand the circumstances of the Jews during the decade, we must first of all understand the America in which they were situated. During the fifties, it seemed as if America's twentieth century was—after its false starts of world wars, economic depression, and culture shock—starting over. People wanted to forget the past. The returning soldiers came home to bring their lives back to normal, get an education and a job, and start families, leading to the now famous postwar baby boom. Although economic growth was not as massive as during the war years, the decade of the fifties saw the gross national product grow by 38 percent. President Truman's Fair Deal and Congress's Full Employment Act promised people a chance for a higher quality of life. The GI bill made it possible for many of the veterans to buy homes, go to college, and rebuild themselves and America at the same time. As a result, Americans flowed into the expanding and increasingly prosperous middle class. "During the 1950s a combination of government expenditures, private investment, consumer borrowing, and a nearly 30 percent expansion of the population allowed the United States, which represented only 6 percent of the world's people, to produce and consume approximately 33 percent of the world's economic output."[1] America was once again the land of promise.

The Housing Act of 1949 helped stimulate building starts. Between 1946 and 1951, a Jew from Brooklyn named William J. Levitt turned 1,200 acres of land on Long Island into 17,450 homes with a population of 35,000. By the late fifties, that number had doubled, and he had built another Levittown in Pennsylvania. Soon other tract suburbs like them, which offered affordable homes, nearby shopping districts, a calm and quiet residential zone, and no slums, were becoming the preferred form of housing for young couples who wanted a protected environment to shape their new lives and raise their new families.

The suburbs even seemed to leave behind the problem of old age. As demographer Alvin Chenkin noted in 1956, "the movement to the suburbs consist[s] largely of families in the most fertile age groups."[2] Grandma and Grandpa stayed behind in the city, in the apartment blocks in the old neighborhood. Indeed, the flow of Sunday traffic between the suburbs of Long Island and the old neighborhoods of the Bronx in New York City became a kind of choreography of this residential pattern.

To be sure, many young couples and families saw life in the suburbs as a chance to move out of their parents' homes or crowded apartments, a reflection of the ethos of mobility that was overtaking America, or they saw it as an opportunity to gain the personal satisfaction of having more control over their neighborhoods. They had seen the stress of their parents' lives in the city and shared the "belief that life can be lived with less personal strain and effort in suburbia."[3]

On the other hand, significant numbers were simply running away from what would become the rising crime in the cities, something increasingly associated with matters of race. Some saw the suburbs as nothing short of a white haven. In the metropolitan New York region, for example, while nonwhites increased by over 41 percent between 1950 and 1957 and the white population decreased by nearly 52 percent, Nassau County on Long Island saw an increase of over 75 percent in its white population. The suburbs obviously grew as a by-product of white flight.

New roads and affordable automobiles, along with plentiful and still cheap gasoline no longer subject to rationing, helped make life in these suburban peripheries conceivable. People began to speak of living within a suburban "commuting distance" of the cities, and a new style of American life blossomed. "Between 1948 and 1958, twelve million Americans moved to the suburbs"; between 1950 and 1955, suburbs grew seven times as fast as America's central cities.[4]

Before the postwar era, the basic culture patterns of America had not fundamentally changed since the industrial revolution and the rise of urban America. "If the Old American culture was rooted in small towns and the countryside, and the New in the cities of the East, the third culture," declared sociologist Morton Keller, "has its prototypical home in the suburbs."[5] As regions of new beginnings, the suburbs were places without history. The people who flooded into them cared nothing about yesterday and everything about tomorrow. Although the suburbs were not completely undifferentiated and within fifteen or twenty years would become as stratified by class and ethnicity as the urban neighborhoods that preceded them as areas of settlement, at the start they were relatively open places. In this new suburban cultural milieu, it seemed at first that "older issues of social organization, notably group distinctions and the question of 'cultural pluralism or melting pot,' " were no longer of significance.[6] Of course, they were irrelevant because nearly everyone in those early years of suburban development was white and middle class, or else they made themselves appear that way.

Although putatively built for the sake of the children, this new suburban culture actually placed intense pressures on the nuclear family. In the suburbs, this family, left pretty much on its own in the splendid isolation of the one-family home, was commonly separated from the support structures of relatives and the plethora of institutions that remained in the old neighborhoods of the city or that were dispersed throughout several suburbs. And even if the American city of the fifties was no longer a supportive environment of intimate neighborhoods and institutions but was characterized instead by what David Riesman called "the lonely crowd," life in the new suburbs was often just as lonely; along with the gains came some "deep feelings of loss" and even vulnerability.[7] People were too mobile to feel a part of any sort of crowd. During the day suburbanites were all off early on their separate tracks. The children went to school and the commuter husband/father left for work in town—a state of affairs that in time gave the suburbs the appellation "bedroom communities." "My husband seldom sees the children during the week," one suburban mother lamented. "He has to rush off to the office early in the morning. When he gets home the children have usually had their dinner and are already doing their homework."[8]

Women, left behind in the house, were expected to obtain all their satisfaction from a primary career as wife and mother. They were expected to decorate, supply, sustain, and remain within the protected boundaries of hearth and home during the fifties, to "drive the cars, do the shopping, transport the children to and from school and take them to keep dentist and other appointments," and to serve as anchors of the nuclear family.[9] But as the decade went on, for many it became harder and harder to find meaning in a life that left them with more time but less to do in the suburbs. With fewer children and with devices that made the tasks of homemaker less time-consuming or engrossing, women often felt "kind of isolated and lonely."[10] Some women reacted by focusing on friendships, especially with other women. Still others did volunteer work, in hospitals, libraries, schools, or other (predominantly women's) organizations. Some women, continuing trends begun by the exigencies of wartime, worked outside the home in the 1950s, but those who did so were generally expected to "retire" upon the birth of their first child. Suburban working mothers of the fifties were viewed as anomalies, and their incomes, almost always smaller than those of their male counterparts, were used to hire people to take care of their homes and families while they were at work.[11] In general, the suburban wife and mother of the fifties was expected to "devalue most social roles outside of the family."[12] The unacceptability of this pattern would become apparent only by the end of the next decade, when the revolutions of the sixties had culminated in a new women's movement.

As noted, the children of the fifties, thrown into a kind of splendid isolation with their suburban parents, could escape to school, but they were always sources of endless concern and satisfaction to their parents. Given that so much of the suburban experience was ideologically based on the notion of the importance of the children, parents (perhaps no group more so than the family-oriented Jews) often focused enormous (some might argue, excessive) hopes and dreams on the accomplishments of their children. By the end of the next decade, however, the focus of this concern had often left to live at college, sometimes leaving the parents—and especially the mothers, whose energies had been so wrapped up in child-rearing—with a feeling of abandonment (which nevertheless had to be camouflaged under the expressed pride of having children in college).

As for the evening hours, although suburbanites discovered they could "walk virtually anywhere at night," few places that were worth walking to were open after dark, and thus these same suburbanites were increasingly closed in together in their homes, often settled around the television, their electronic window on the world, which turned them into passive observers of life rather than actors in it.[13] In the suburbs, what family life went on outside occurred in everyone's own backyard, commonly on the weekends.

In this little house in the suburbs, both the television in the living room and the car (and soon two) in the garage were key vehicles of an increasingly desirable escape. In a sense the mass-produced, affordable car symbolized the living ideals of American life: the independence of the individual, democracy, and mobility. Indeed, for many of those who would grow up in the suburbs, getting a driver's license (and, for the wealthy among them, getting the car to go with it) would in time become as (if not more) important a rite of passage as bar mitzvah or confirmation.[14] "Can I have the keys to the car?" was probably one of the most universally asked questions of their parents by those who came of age in suburbia.

As for the television, it became increasingly a part of suburban America, for it gave people a view of life in the wider world from the protective precincts of their own homes. From the first small black-and-white portholes to the wide-screen visions in "living color" that were available by the mid-1960s, television offered views that confirmed suburban America in its conception of itself. It entertained the people with an enhanced mirror image of their own white, essentially Christian, middle-class world. After all, what the "tube" showed viewers of the fifties was what life in America was *supposed* to be like. With its *Father Knows Best* ethos of the male-dominated suburban nuclear family, where the mother stayed at home to take care of the house and family, where the children went to school and never broke the law but tried hard to please, where all problems could be solved, and where all families were supposed to be more or less alike, television helped in the homogenization of American society. Voices of discontent and deviant images were by and large not broadcast. As for the crime shows, they all showed the violence and trouble to be back there in the city, which the nightly newscasts would continue to confirm.

Perhaps in part as an explosive reaction to being so much the focus of their parents' attention, hopes, and dreams, or as a backlash to the sterile conventionality of the social order of the suburb that put them at the center, the young embraced the idea of their own importance and celebrated a youth culture that not only emphasized the dominance of the young over the old but also created models of existence that excluded their parents' generation. Probably nothing epitomized this more than the popular music that the young embraced and that their parents could not understand, let alone appreciate. Elvis was not just a new kind of singer, nor was rock and roll simply a new style of music. Both were symbolic expressions of the dawn of a new age in which the young would break with all the conventions of the past. This new age would be given full expression in the next decade, when Bob Dylan told "mothers and fathers throughout the land don't criticize what you can't understand; your sons and your daughters are beyond your command," but its seeds began to germinate during the last years of the fifties.

Although some ambivalence was certainly felt about the strains suburban behavior patterns put on family life, the new suburbanites of the fifties—especially young, new parents—accepted this pattern of life as inevitable and even desirable in the pursuit of the American dream. We know now that this suburban life-style only *appeared* to be beneficial for the family. In fact, it emphasized the individual pursuit of happiness and competitive achievement above all else. "Keeping up with the Joneses" was something every member of the family was forced to do. Individuals had to rely on themselves or their nuclear family resources, even when these were insufficient or overly taxed.

The suburb and the ethic of individual achievement also often led to a diminished set of ties to the local community. Of course, this did not make the identity of the suburb irrelevant: people cared about where they lived, especially about the quality of the schools in the neighborhood (for schools guaranteed individual improvement). Typically, one would choose a particular suburb in which to live because of the quality of its schools, and most of its taxes went to supporting them. Not surprisingly, participation in Parent-Teacher Associations (PTAs) was often the only community-oriented activity. But unlike real communities, PTAs were temporary and single-issue organizations; as children grew up, parent participation in the associations waned. And as each individual pursued his or her own goals, loyalty to place and community became secondary. People ceased to expect to remain forever in the place where they grew up: moving up meant moving out. (In time, even retirement would stimulate a move away.) Satisfying or not, this arrangement became normative by the early years of the sixties, when American people moved on average once every five years. Loyalty to neighborhood or place or past became an increasing irrelevancy—a not inconsequential fact for people like Jews, for whom such loyalties were key to their historic survival.

Although in the hindsight of history, the fifties seemed a time when Americans celebrated the routine—so welcome after the extreme ups and downs of the First World War, the Roaring Twenties, the depression of the thirties, and the Second World War—all was not really calm and peaceful. In the political domain, the decade saw the beginnings of the cold war and the dramatic growth of anticommunist fervor. Following closely upon the perjury conviction in January 1950 of State Department official Alger Hiss, who denied he had passed information to a Soviet agent, and the 1953 execution of Ethel and Julius Rosenberg on Soviet espionage charges came the emergence of McCarthyism, which culminated in often reckless accusations of sedition and blacklists. Television also brought this into the American home via the McCarthy-Army hearings in 1954.

Paralleling the anxious anticommunism were the nuclear arms race and its accompanying apprehensions of universal annihilation in a war between the emergent superpowers or even as a result of accident. These anxieties were nurtured by the repeated air-raid drills that trained youngsters in school to "duck and cover" in the event of a nuclear attack. Americans were living under what John F. Kennedy would in 1961 call "a nuclear sword of Damocles."[15] The idea that a world so painstakingly reconstructed could in a flash be wiped out invaded the American mind. Although the world situation exploded most dramatically into national consciousness during the 1962 Cuban missile crisis, topics such as bomb tests, lost bombers, nuclear fallout, and strontium 90–contaminated milk seemed always to enter people's conversations, indicating a general perception of calamity lurking in the background and threatening the promise of the future.

But the 1950s, and 1954 in particular, were not only a time of McCarthyism and nascent cold-war nuclear anxiety. The year 1954 was also the year of the landmark *Brown v. Board of Education of Topeka* Supreme Court decision, which revoked the opinion that separate was equal in matters of civil and minority rights, ushering in what would be decades of change that moved America away from the notion that only white Christians of European ancestry were entitled to full civil and social rights in this country. In the years ahead, America would gradually but inexorably move toward both a greater ethnic diversity and laws that legitimated that diversity as genuinely American. Yet in the 1950s the underlying theme of the Brown decision—as indeed of the times—was that democracy was a cherished American value and that, as a consequence, no one should be excluded from the mainstream.

At the outset, many took this to mean that diversity had to be resolved into homogeneity. The aim of the Supreme Court decision was a fuller integration of black and white, which in 1954 still meant giving blacks (and all others) a chance to be assimilated into white Christian America. There was no mistaking the fact that in this postwar period, although democracy was the ideal, the "established pattern" of American life was, as Ben Seligman put it, "dominated by the mentality [and politics] of white, Protestant, middle-class, native Americans." [16] That was what the melting pot meant: a chance to be white, Protestant-like, and middle class. After all, at the start of the civil rights struggle the trend was to get everyone into what had been all-white institutions and neighborhoods. No one spoke then, as they would forty years later, about maintaining the integrity of, say, black institutions or neighborhoods.

In fact, "a national style of conformity emerged in the 1950s as Americans self-consciously strove for similarity and shunned difference." [17] The controversial, nonconformist was out; "an unthinking faith in shared assumptions" was in. [18] In a sense, even McCarthy-

ism can be understood as a misguided and often sinister effort to
make everyone alike: is not the dark side of an assimilatory aspira-
tion nothing other than xenophobia and prejudice toward those who
appear not to share the common values, heritage, and goals of the
majority? All this was embraced because of a general yearning for
the appearance of normalcy. *But what did all this mean for Jews?*

The Jewish Experience of the Fifties

No Longer Outsiders

To Jews ready to escape the stigma of a pariah people and the status
of outsider, America offered a welcome opportunity to move away
from the old ethnic ties and patterns and to identify with the dominant culture, and they did so in great numbers. In the 1950s, before the anxieties of assimilation and of the loss of Jewish identity
had entered American Jewish consciousness, social integration into
American culture was still a highly valued goal, not only for the immigrant displaced persons (DPs) but also for those whose parents
or grandparents had come to these shores. American culture was in-
viting because it was ubiquitous, accessible, and offered advantages
to those who embraced its norms and values. In the emergent social
order of postwar America (what today we label the "meritocracy"),
the identity one held as a consequence of birth (what sociologists
called "ascribed status") mattered little if at all. What counted was
what a person achieved by dint of his or her own efforts and accomplishments. And since being Jewish was an ascribed status—a matter
of birth rather than achievement—it became less and less salient. In
answer to the question "Who are you?" more and more Jews were
answering, "Here is what I do." And what they did had little, if any,
connection to their being Jewish. In this new America, where everyone seemed to be starting again, Jews did not have to be outsiders.
And they *wanted* to be like everyone else.

Rabbi Morris Kertzer, president of the Jewish Chaplains Organization, was asked in June 1952 to answer the question "What
is a Jew?" for the readers of *Look* magazine, one of the widest-
circulation weeklies in America, claiming a circulation of almost
eight million. Reprinted in the August 1952 *Readers Digest,* another
mass-circulation magazine, Kertzer's article addressed such ques-

tions as "Do Jews believe that Judaism is the only true religion?" "On what points do Christians & Jews agree?" and "Is an American Jew's first loyalty to Israel or America?" His answers (tacitly endorsed by the mass-circulation publications, which printed and reprinted them —and have even reprinted them in the 1990s as a paperback book) stressed that *American Jews were really not different from the white, middle-class Christians around them*. They were tolerant, democratic, and unabashedly American. "Jews do not presume to judge the honest worshiper of a faith," he wrote. Moreover, Kertzer explained: "Both [Jews and Christians] share the same rich heritage of the Old Testament. They both believe in the fatherhood of one God, in the sanctity of the Ten Commandments, the wisdom of the prophets and the brotherhood of man." As for the question of dual loyalties: "The only loyalty of an American Jew is to the United States of America without any ifs, ands or buts. The state of Israel is the ancestral home of his forefathers, the birthplace of his faith. As a haven for over a million Jews after the agonies of the past 20 years it has special meaning for Jews all over the world. But spiritual bonds and emotional ties are quite different from political loyalty." As Kertzer put it, Jews were characterized by three principles: love of learning, worship of God, and good deeds. But these were not a source of a sense of either superiority or separation. On the contrary, the ancient rabbis taught that Jewish law stipulated: "We are *required* to feed the poor of the Gentiles as well as our Jewish brethren." [19] Even the matter of a taboo against intermarriage, which Jews in the 1950s seemed still willing to uphold, was not to be seen as a disqualifier for their being considered fully American since "practically all religions are opposed to marriage outside their faith." [20] Kertzer concluded with an explanation that made intermarriage sound practically un-American to readers who believed in the ideal of a stable, loving, middle-class family: "When husband and wife disagree on their religious creed, the prospect for a harmonious relationship may be harmed. Though divorce is permitted, the divorce rate among Jews is far below the community average." [21] No doubt about it; Jews were at home in America.

In spite of the large spurt of Jewish immigration by the DPs and as if to deny the negation of Diaspora Jewish existence which the Holocaust had tragically symbolized, during the same year of 1954 when the communists were being hunted by McCarthy and civil rights were being established by the Supreme Court, the more than five million Jews celebrated the tercentenary of Jewish life in America.[22] "Our participation in . . . American accomplishments is the American Jewish history we rejoice in celebrating tonight," announced Lee Friedman, honorary president of the American Jewish Historical Society, in typical remarks delivered at a Boston commemoration of the occasion.[23] (Of course, no one mentioned that in 1654, Peter Stuyvesant of New Amsterdam sent a letter to his superiors in the Dutch West India Company seeking permission to evict the Jews, whom he called a "very repugnant, deceitful race, hateful enemies and blasphemers of the name of Christ.")[24] American Jews were stressing, albeit subtly, that they were true Americans, here since the days of the *Mayflower*.

To be sure, as various observers realized, "in terms of *real*, effective history it [was] far from three hundred years old."[25] In fact, a majority of Jews came to the United States at the end of the nineteenth century, specifically between 1880 and World War I, trying almost from the start to become Americanized. Nevertheless, in the aftermath of the Holocaust and the tacit tolerance of it by America and the world, a year after the Rosenberg case, and in the atmosphere of McCarthyism, anxieties about anti-Semitism still reverberated, reminding American Jews of the limits of assimilation.[26] In the minds of many Jews, memories of the 1930s and figures like Father Coughlin or the German-American Bund were still strong. Some recalled the days of 1938, when surveys showed that "a majority of Americans believed that the persecution of German Jews was either wholly or partly their own fault," and 26 percent of Americans thought colleges should limit the number of Jews admitted.[27] But with the tercentenary celebrations, America's Jews wanted to forget or at least get past all that and celebrate and emphasize their feeling of being at home in America.

This seemed possible because, despite the postwar influx of immigrants, by the 1950s 95 percent of American Jewry had arrived and the demographic balance *had* shifted to the native-born, so-called second generation, who could make claims to being at home in America. Nowhere was this easier than on the suburban frontier, the place where America was remaking itself.

Jews in Suburbia

In suburbia "every American Jew, whatever his ideology, [was] an 'assimilationist,'" since "'assimilationism' in America was a rejection of the immigrant ghetto" and all it symbolized. Suburbanites knew that the Jewish ghetto in America "was entered into only to be abandoned."[28] This could neatly be accomplished in the Jewish movement to the suburbs. Here Jews might "create themselves anew, without the 'narrowness' . . . of spirit they associated with the parochial life of their parents."[29] Replanting themselves in a suburban environment that seemed to call for a homogenization of differences led them to diminish community and tribal ties while emphasizing continuing mobility and the individual pursuit of happiness above all else, and it encouraged a life-style that denied the importance of anything that happened before the move to the suburbs. This meant that ultimately tradition, a sense of Jewish uniqueness, tribalism, and ethnic separation would have to wither, while religion would become diluted into some sort of vague Judeo-Christian mix, a matter of personal choice and no longer an expression of collective destiny. American values and culture would increasingly supplant the Jewish ones in the suburban collective consciousness. But this was essentially what these postwar Jews wanted. Their reinvention of themselves as individuals pursuing happiness dovetailed neatly with the aspirations of all the new suburbanites.

For Jews, the move to the suburbs began at least partially also as an effort to escape the physical and cultural constrictions of the "old neighborhoods," both in style and in substance. It was also a reflection of their desire for mobility, both geographic and social. Here, in a new place, they could express their acculturative aspirations.

As Albert Gordon, rabbi on one such suburban frontier and writing at the end of the fifties, explained, "the new Jewish suburbanites believe . . . that since we are all Americans, it is not good for Jews—or any other ethnic or religious group—to live together, forming their own community. They *fear* segregation, in contrast to their parents, who in many cases sought it."[30] If once Jews had affirmed the psychological importance and value of their being different to ensure their survival, in this first postwar decade American Jews stressed the opposite. They too believed separate was not equal.

But while America was on the move to the suburbs, and Jews may have ideologically eschewed ghettoization, during the fifties they did not move quite as far from one another or as quickly as other Americans. American Jews were still an overwhelmingly urban people. A 1957 U.S. census report (the only census in which respondents were identified by religious affiliation and therefore a crucial and strikingly accurate indicator of Jewish American life) revealed that 96 percent of the approximately five million American Jews were still living in cities, 87 percent in urban areas of over a quarter of a million people. In contrast, 64 percent of the general American population was urbanized, only 37 percent of whom were in areas larger than a quarter of a million. Half of the fourteen cities where most of the Jews were located were on the eastern seaboard. In addition to the major centers in New York, Philadelphia, Boston, Baltimore, Newark, Miami, and the District of Columbia, there were Jewish population islands in Los Angeles, Chicago, Detroit, Cleveland, Pittsburgh, San Francisco, and St. Louis. Jews by and large remained residentially concentrated. No one yet spoke of a Sun Belt, but except for a high Jewish concentration in Miami and vicinity (where three-fourths of Florida's Jews live), only slightly less than 8 percent of American Jewry was in the South, and the next-smallest group, around 11 percent, was in the West, primarily in and around Los Angeles.[31]

Why did Jews not move more quickly? Although American individualism encouraged every person to pursue happiness freely wherever one could find it, Jews were a people for whom the group was always more important than the individual ("A Jew is a Jew when he is with other Jews," as philosopher Natan Rotenstreich has put it). This disposition is what Mark Zborowski and Elizabeth Herzog revealingly called the Jewish ethos of "life is with people" in their eponymous book.[32] To move away from the city, to be alone in the suburbs, was something Jews were not ready to do at first. They knew that one subordinated individual desires in order to ensure Jewish continuity through solidarity. They knew that a Jew alone was a Jew who got lost. And indeed the few who did move were quickly swallowed up by the world into which they relocated.

So although Jews moved, they did so slowly at first, and when they moved, they did not go far and migrated with other Jews into what would become *Jewish* suburbs. To be sure, in some measure this came about because for all the spirit of reconstruction after the war and the apparent inclusiveness of 1950s America, in practice Gentiles still did not want Jews in their neighborhoods. Many of these predominantly Jewish neighborhoods were "frequently the result [of] the withdrawal of non-Jews from the neighborhood" rather than an active embrace of Jewish ethnicity by the Jewish suburbanites.[33]

In those first waves of American Jewish movement during the 1950s and early 1960s, Jews tended to remain clustered with other Jews and to settle in suburban areas closest to dense urban Jewish communities. Nowhere is this as clear as in the New York metropolitan region, which at that time was without question at least numerically the primary locus of Jews in America: half of them lived there.[34] Thus, for example, there were 920,000 Jews in Brooklyn in 1950, many of whom had lived in Manhattan in the preceding decades; eight years later that number had declined to 854,000.[35] Similar declines were registered in the Bronx, another area of second settlement which had been a popular new home for Jews in the preceding decades. On the other hand, Queens, still a relatively rural, suburblike part of the city during the immediate postwar period, began steadily to increase its population of Jews, quadrupling its numbers between 1923 and 1950. The outlying suburbs of Nassau County on Long Island, just beyond the Queens border, and those in Westchester County, abutting the Bronx on the north, began to show a rise in the number of Jews living there. For example, in 1957, 218,000 Jews lived in the town of Hempstead in Nassau County, and 22,000 lived in New Rochelle in Westchester County.[36] By 1965, "about a third of all American Jews [had] left the big cities and established themselves in the suburbs."[37]

In following this modified residential drift, Jews were in some measure simultaneously reflecting the general American desire to start over after the war while also reflecting their lingering attachment to Jewish tribal ties. As Marshall Sklare has pointed out, the Jews had in the past tended "to resist the appeal of the one-family house and . . . marked *their* upward passage by moving from [walkups to elevator buildings and from] elevator buildings to so-called 'luxury apartments.' "[38] The move to the suburb and the dispersion of population were in a sense a removal of the Jews from an environment to which they had become particularly suited: the city, where they could remain in the close company of other Jews.

The row houses in suburban Philadelphia, the multifamily homes in suburban Boston, and the side-by-side tracts in the New York developments were simply Jewish tenements turned sideways. These Jewish suburbs were what Judith Kramer and Seymour Leventman have called "gilded ghettoes," areas of Jewish concentration and social mobility.[39] This clustering with other Jews in suburbia was the residential reflection of the aim to maintain a kind of controlled acculturation, "a process by which one culture accepts a practice from another culture but integrates the new practice into its own existing value system."[40]

To live in a suburb but to do so with other Jews who Americanized their Jewishness seemed a way of being like other Americans without having altogether to leave the Jewish orbit. It was a reflection of the widespread belief on the part of much of fifties American Jewry that their life choices facilitated cultural change but did not require a wholesale abandonment of their ethnic and religious identity. They believed they could be both genuine Jews and full-fledged citizens of the American suburb, and that they could pass on this dual heritage to their children. This "socialization of individuals into two or more cultures" defined a situation which anthropologist Steven Polgar has called "stabilized pluralism" and Horace Kallen has called "cultural dualism."[41] It aimed at what sociologist Erich Rosenthal has termed "acculturation without assimilation."[42]

Underlying this resistance to complete assimilation was an attitude of Jewish superiority that Jews could still assume in 1950s melting-pot America, a kind of ethnic antidote to the legacy of prejudice. This belief that it was better to be a Jew could be sustained only as long as one remained acutely conscious of being Jewish. Yet already by the fifties, Jews were redefining what being Jewish meant. "I have a friend who is not Jewish," a typical fifties Park Forest suburbanite is quoted as saying, "who told me how fortunate I was in being born Jewish. Otherwise I might be one of the sixteen or eighteen out of twenty Gentiles without a social conscience and liberal tendencies. . . . from the social and cultural standpoint a man is lucky to be born a Jew."[43] Being Jewish no longer had the traditional meaning of being chosen for a life dedicated to ritual observance and Torah study, but rather it now meant having a social conscience or a liberal political attitude.

These reverberations of superiority (however redefined) and the ethos of controlled acculturation made it possible in 1950 for sociologist Nathan Glazer writing in the pages of *Commentary* magazine to assert categorically: "Despite their prosperity, Jews show very little tendency to assimilate: they intermarry less than any other ethnic group. They do *acculturate*—that is they drop traditional habits and speech and become culturally indistinguishable from other Americans; yet the line that divides them from the others remains sharper than that separating any other white group of immigrants."[44] In a similar conclusion, Israeli sociologist Aryeh Tartakower suggested that American Jews at midcentury were "deeply rooted in the life of their country and becoming more culturally assimilated but, at the same time, not ready to give up their feelings of kinship with other parts of the Jewish people."[45] Yet in the suburb, attitudes of Jewish superiority and the felt need for ghetto-like, self-imposed segregation soon faded.

Why? As the great student of acculturation Ralph Linton explained in 1940, "everything indicates that the ultimate end of situations of close and continuous firsthand contact is the amalgamation of the societies and cultures involved, although this conclusion may be postponed almost indefinitely if there is opposition to it on both sides."[46] Although "it is possible to utilize the norms of one culture while participating in another," what is more likely is that a dominant culture overwhelms and absorbs all those who live within it and transforms them.[47] These imperatives were certainly part of the Jewish cultural condition in the 1950s and early 1960s and would become increasingly so in the years ahead.

To be sure, the Jews did not have to wait for the move to the suburbs, where there were fewer of them, to feel the culturally eroding impact of acculturation. The contact that occurred in the cities was already accomplishing this end. Moreover, even controlled acculturation can lead to assimilation, for "in time, the changes may accumulate to bring about a major shift in values which could destroy the group's existence as a separate ethnic identity."[48] Thus, the underlying dynamics of American Jewish existence and the movement to the new world of the suburbs, where America reinvented itself, were a combination of elements that together were ominous for Jewish survival from the beginning.

The pace of the Jewish residential shift may have been gradual during the fifties, but once the suburb had been reached, Jews were no less subject to its effects than other individuals on the suburban frontier. The very fact that the suburban American dream of a single-family home—which was an everyman's version of the English country house, a dream that put individual accomplishments at the apex of desire and separated individuals from a concentrated community —had become attractive to Jews was already a sign of their cultural transformation and a portent of things to come. Moreover, by exhibiting the American penchant for mobility, the Jews had embarked on a path that would ultimately lead them into residential patterns that would thin out the numbers of Jews among whom they lived.

The geography of suburbia would ultimately lead to residential dispersal. In its one- or two-family homes, population was far more spread out than in cities, where apartments were the rule. This meant that in any suburban neighborhood fewer Jews were available to support Jewish institutions. This made building and sustaining such institutions—everything from synagogues and Jewish schools to kosher butchers and Jewish bookstores—far more difficult in suburbia than in the cities. With fewer of these institutions and their fellow Jews around them in any given neighborhood, the Jews found far less at hand to bolster their Jewish identity. This of course undermined the possibility of controlled acculturation.

Hempstead (the municipal jurisdiction within which Levittown was built) in New York's Nassau County epitomized the ambiguities of the suburbanization process. In 1957, Jews made up almost a third of this suburban town's population. These were Jews who had moved away from the city but who still lived in an area where they would be surrounded by other Jews, as they had been while they were growing up. Nevertheless, because the entire town was relatively small, inevitably there was substantial contact between the Jews and the other two-thirds of the population. Indeed, while many Jewish suburbanites continued in some way to "identify themselves with the Jewish people," in their life decisions they demonstrated that they did not "feel compelled to live within a wholly Jewish environment."[49] Accordingly, life in Hempstead was not going to be like the relatively more insular experience of being one group in the large mosaic of New York City. To borrow a phrase from Herbert Gans, who described a similar Jewish experience in Park Forest, a Chicago suburb: "not only did Park Forest Jews live like other Park Foresters; they lived *with* them."[50] It should come as no surprise that these Jews of the fifties who moved to the suburbs would admit, as one housewife in Park Forest did: "My real close friends are Jewish, my after-dark friends in general are Jewish, but my daytime friends are Gentile."[51] "I think we should try to have friends that aren't Jewish. I don't like the fact that all my friends are Jewish," said another.[52] Slowly but surely, these suburban Jews were quietly loosening "old ties and community sentiments."[53]

Even the immigrants were finding their way into suburban American life with unprecedented speed, and Orthodox Jews, long the most visible holdouts against acculturation, became during the fifties "modern American" Orthodox Jews who displayed demographic and residential patterns not significantly different from those of other American Jews.[54] Their move from the cities to the suburbs barely took a generation.

The younger the suburbanites, the greater the significance of this suburban cultural contact and the swifter the loosening of tribal ties. In the fifties and a good part of the sixties, suburbia was an enclave of the young. A closer look at the Jews in 1957 Hempstead, for example, reveals this. Of 218,300 Jews there in 1957, 57 percent were thirty-four years old or younger. Even more significantly, a third were younger than fourteen, meaning that they would grow up in this suburb and absorb and be absorbed by its way of life.[55] They would know no other way to live.[56]

Indeed, as these figures indicate, the Jewish move to suburbia was not only a desire to be like other Americans, not only a reflection of acculturative or assimilative tendencies. It also had some Jewish meaning in that it was at least partially a product of the child-centered nature of the Jewish family. Whether they were moving to Hempstead, New York, or Newton, Massachusetts, Jews saw their decision as a means of ensuring their children's future: "I moved out here for the sake of the kids. I want them to have the best I can afford—the best schools, the nicest friends, the most beautiful clothes that my money can buy. Nothing is too good for my kids." [57]

In fact, as these children became increasingly indistinguishable from the other Americans around them, they would lead their parents away from the Jewish core culture. They were at home in that American culture that put so much emphasis on the young. They knew about it intimately, feeling greater kinship to King Elvis than King David, learning the words to rock and roll songs far more readily than the poetry of the Psalms. As for their parents, they in effect demonstrated that being solicitous and supportive of these Americanized and suburbanized youngsters—as difficult as that might be by the end of the decade and into the next one—was for many even more important than being a loyal Jew, with significant negative ramifications for Jewish continuity. The parents made it possible for their children to be at home in America, even if that meant they were no longer in touch with their Jewishness.

The movement into the suburbs symbolized movement away from the Jewish cultural core. By the next decade, the relocation into suburbia extended even further out, reaching towns where Jews were the smallest minorities. In Boston this meant moving from Brookline and Newton on to Wayland and Wellesley, where the Jews were few and far between. In Philadelphia, it meant going from Wynnefield and Bala Cynwyd to further out on the Main Line; and in New York, the eastern reaches of Nassau County and even Suffolk County on Long Island drew Jews away from the subway suburbs and the Hempstead/Levittown region. Ultimately, it would mean moving away from the eastern seaboard to areas of very low Jewish concentration. Of course, the young were the ones who moved farthest away. "Neighborhoods of major centers of Jewish concentration [became] heavily weighted toward the older segments of the age pyramid." [58]

What were the consequences of the geographic movement that occurred in the next three decades? The formula was: "The fewer the Jews relative to the Gentile population in the larger community, the higher will be the rate of Jewish intermarriage." [59] But intermarriage was only one result of this move. Calvin Goldscheider summed up the situation most succinctly:

Where Jews reside, and the Jewishness of those neighborhoods within the broader community, are major aspects of Jewish cohesion. In particular, the greater the density of Jewish settlement, the more likely it is that Jews will interact with other Jews in schools, as neighbors, and as friends. Moreover, residential concentration maintains the visibility of Jewish community for Jews as well as for society as a whole and, thus, may be viewed as a critical factor in fostering and strengthening ethnic bonds. The ethnic factor is likely to be most pronounced when ethnics are clustered residentially. In turn, residential clustering represents a core mechanism for the continuity of the community.[60]

Indeed, one might argue that throughout the last four decades one key index of Americanization has been the extent to which Jews have located themselves in Jewishly sparse suburbs and communities. It was as if geographic mobility and its reflection, social mobility, both combined to propel Jews away from their core culture. As they moved up and out, these suburban Jews were in a sense continuing what many of their forebears had done by leaving the Jewish cultural centers in Europe for America. While the distances traveled from Brooklyn to Far Rockaway in Queens and thence to Long Island's Nassau and Suffolk Counties, from the Bronx's Grand Concourse northward to Westchester, or from Boston's Roxbury to Brookline and then Wellesley were smaller, the cultural issues involved may have been no less critical. In these cases, the risk that faced the migrants was that by leaving the more densely populated Jewish localities, they were also forsaking the group that called that place home and joining another culture. More precisely, if the move from Europe seemed to threaten Jews with becoming Americanized, the move to suburbia, where they were not as clustered with other Jews, *sealed* this cultural change. Ongoing firsthand and close contact with their suburban neighbors, fewer of whom were Jews, would bring this about.

In a sense, during the fifties the brakes against assimilation increasingly failed to work. In the past deterrents had been (1) Jewish rejection by the dominant Gentile society, (2) a sense of the bankruptcy of non-Jewish culture, and (3) feelings of guilt for abandoning the Jewish community. In America in the postwar period, Jews no longer felt rejected. Moreover, Jews believed that American culture by the 1950s was far from bankrupt but rather quite attractive. As for feelings of guilt, they might be there, but because for the most part

Jews were moving into American society en masse with other Jews, these feelings seemed simply to be a natural condition of Jewish-American existence, part of the price for a ticket of admission to suburban living. The only exceptions to this process seemed to be the relatively few Orthodox Jews, but in the fifties the perception was that their days were numbered.[61] Besides, many of them seemed positioned to move to suburbia as well, and did so in the next decade.

Synagogues and the Turn to Religion

Americans were turning to religion in the postwar era.[62] In 1954, Gallup reported that 79 percent of American adults were members of a church. Thus, the easy and overwhelming approval of the addition of the words "under God" to the pledge of allegiance and of the phrase "In God We Trust" on all U.S. currency, both of which were initiated during this decade, was unsurprising. Like Rabbi Kertzer in his *Look* magazine explanation of Jews and Judaism, Americans assumed that everyone here shared the same basic religious outlook, if not the same God. Church attendance was encouraged. "There were no comparable figures applying specifically to American Jews but all evidence tended to show a movement of Jews into the synagogue parallel to that of other Americans into the church."[63] Jews were of a different religion, but did that matter? Certainly Rabbi Kertzer did not think so. As Will Herberg put it in his classic *Protestant Catholic Jew,* the commonplace was that the " 'three great faiths' were really 'saying the same thing' in affirming the 'spiritual ideals' and 'moral values' of the American Way of Life."[64] As if to endorse this view, President Dwight Eisenhower declared, "Our government makes no sense unless it is founded in a deeply felt religious faith—and I don't care what it is."[65]

In the atmosphere of religious affiliation during the fifties, synagogues in the suburbs played an important role. In building them, suburban Jews expressed what has sometimes been called their "Jewish edifice complex." That complex allowed both acculturation into America and a simultaneous self-conscious display of Jewish identity. The building of a synagogue could serve for the Jews who were moving into terra incognita as a kind of monument to their tribal identity. But it did not automatically exclude them from suburbia

or from America. In America being a "good Christian" and being a
"good citizen" were expected to mean by and large the same thing.
As good Christians went to church, so good Americans were expected to also. If the Christians had their churches, the Jews could
have their suburban temples to prove that they had arrived and that
they belonged in this new place. Between the end of the war and 1952,
"an estimated $50,000,000 to $60,000,000 was spent on synagogue
building." Herberg reported that "hundreds of synagogues and religious institutions are engaged in building-expansion programs; . . .
the figure [is] close to 1000. Synagogue membership is probably at a
record level." [66]

But these temples (and the organizations that often met inside
them) were not to be like the synagogues in the earlier eras and areas
of settlement. They would be sleek, modern buildings at home on the
suburban frontier. One, Beth Shalom in Elkins Park, Pennsylvania,
which was completed in 1954, was even designed by the quintessentially American (Gentile) architect Frank Lloyd Wright.[67] Although
these synagogues represented for suburban Jews the last outpost of
a purely Jewish existence, and inside them, the life-is-with-people
ethos still worked (although sometimes just barely), they were only
part-time ghettoes, what David de Sola Pool called a "subsidiary part
in the totality of Jewish life." [68] They were visited at most on a weekend or, more likely, on a few occasions per year.

While not everyone was sure that the weekend and therefore
weakened synagogues were going to guarantee acculturation without assimilation or even if such a condition was possible, synagogue membership nevertheless expanded for most of the decade.[69]
Although in the beginning of the fifties Will Herberg could report
that "with all its gains, the synagogue still represents only a minority
of American Jews," by the end of the decade and into the next one
synagogues increased their membership rolls. In the midsixties, affiliation was 60 percent, up from 20 percent only thirty years earlier.[70]

But affiliation was not the same as intense involvement. A 1958
poll of weekly attendance at synagogues showed that only 18 percent
of American Jews attended every week (versus 74 percent of Catholics and 40 percent of Protestants).[71] And even among so-called synagogue leaders, only one out of three admitted to attending services
with any frequency.[72] Suburban Jews might still be building syna-

gogues, but they were not filling them. This was perhaps illustrative of the dualistic attitude that many fifties Jews had toward their Jewish traditions and sectarianism: they were ready to both embrace and reject their separate Jewish identity. American Jews of the decade were, as David Reisman put it, "especially prey to the two extremes of a vindictive and aggressive and contemptuous attitude towards tradition and a honeyed and sentimental one." [73] The fact is that, as Will Herberg explained in 1950, "it [had] become 'normal' for Jews, and even for synagogue members, to believe in and observe nothing in particular." [74]

The suburban synagogue became a perfect reflection of the ambivalence of American Jews. It was built and joined as a sign of Jewish tribal consciousness and religious and ethnic identity, but participation in its activities (and especially those that were particularly religious) was part-time at best, which served to signal that its members were busy doing other things and did not want to be completely identified with what went on inside or even to acknowledge that the synagogue played a large part in their lives. Unlike Jews of an earlier generation whose community life was focused on the house of worship, where they could still celebrate their differences, these suburban Jews no longer wanted a synagogue that was an insular environment, a ghetto. Unlike their immigrant forebears, they no longer felt they were being their truest selves inside the confines of an exclusively Jewish institution like the synagogue. Instead, they were following the American version of the famous dictum "They were Jews in the synagogue and people everywhere else."

Thus the synagogues in suburbia were not as salient in the Jewish experience as they might once have been. It was possible to note that already in the fifties, "the synagogue in America no longer represents a country of believers. Nothing in the way of belief or practice— not even the belief in God or the practice of the most elementary *Mitzvot* [religious observances]—may be taken for granted among synagogue members." [75] To attract suburban Jews, their synagogues would ultimately have to become institutions that mirrored successful acculturation to the American suburb. The shul got a pool and a well-appointed social hall, all run by an executive director. Sunday brotherhood breakfasts got a bigger attendance than the daily minyan. There was a religious school that demanded less and less involvement by members and their children, a library for the Jewish books no one read or studied, a gift shop, and sometimes even a little Jewish museum, a kind of diorama of what Jewish life once had been. The days of their members were spent elsewhere and with others than those they might meet at the synagogue.

Looked at analytically, the synagogue could be either a propaedeutic to assimilation (if it was like a church) or else a brake against it as an ethnic and religious enclave in which a separate cultural life was nurtured under the protective cover of religious freedom (if the synagogue was like the ghetto). Some synagogues—"shuls"— tried to serve as cultural enclaves, in effect suburban Jewry's private ghettoes. Others—the suburban "temples," the Jewish "churches"— were exactly the opposite. Some new synagogues oscillated between the two extremes.

Suburban synagogues thus reflected American Jewish ambivalence in two ways: first in the two opposite kinds of institutions they represented, and second in the fact that although Jews built and joined these synagogues, they seldom came to them and even more seldom identified with what was going on inside.

Thus the suburban synagogue of the fifties was an institution that exemplified how the Jews of the fifties were still caught (as they had been in the years before the war) "in the competing but assimilating relationship between two or more . . . cultures."[76] They were "torn between two sets of values—those of integration and acceptance into American society and those of Jewish group survival."[77] In another time, this was called *Judenschmerz*, the pain of being Jewish. The pain had begun in the America of the 1940s, as the so-called second generation had tried to loose the bonds of immigrant experience and ghetto life. It continued into the fifties even in the new culture that was emerging in suburbia. On the one hand was their Jewish heritage of the immigrant experience and of the ghettoes in which many of these new suburbanites had grown up and which they still recalled, often most vividly when they went to visit their parents still living in the city, as well as their undigested memories of anti-Semitism before the war and of the Holocaust, which no one seemed to want to discuss or recall, but everyone knew about. On the other hand, now Jews were facing a new future, with a new identity as American suburbanites. For many, this transition intensified old feelings of "insecurity, ambivalence, [and] excessive self-consciousness."[78]

Yet if this ambivalence was painful for the individual, the Jewish self-consciousness it fostered was at least in the short term useful for the Jewish people as a whole, for it acted as a drag against the wholesale abandonment of Jewish identity. By the 1950s, however, *Judenschmerz* became increasingly a condition that parents hoped and believed would soon pass and that their children had no tolerance for whatsoever.

Jewish Education

Even more than the synagogues or the move to the suburbs, the decisions American Jews made during this decade about the education of their young exhibited this ambivalence. On the one hand, Jewish education implied a concern with Jewish survival by stressing and presumably enhancing the knowledge of what was uniquely Jewish. On the other, secular education, which Jews pursued in a very big way, facilitated integration into American society and culture. Both underwent important changes during this decade.

In America today, when we speak of Jewish education, we think of its four major settings: (1) the supplementary, afternoon, religious (often called "Hebrew") synagogue school; (2) the independent (all-) day school; (3) the yeshiva; and (4) university-based Jewish studies. But during the decade of the fifties and into the early years of the sixties, the Jewish educational panorama was significantly narrower.

Yeshivas were created by European Jewry and were perhaps the premier institutions of Jewish learning, but they did not loom large in the Jewish educational scene of the fifties. Although places such as the Lower East Side of Manhattan had yeshivas—many of which, like the famous Torah Vodaath, Chofetz Chaim, and Mesivta Tifereth Jerusalem, were founded just prior to and after the Second World War—and there were important institutions like Ner Israel in Baltimore, the Hebrew Theological College of Chicago, Telshe in Cleveland, Etz Chayim in Brooklyn, and of course New York's Yeshiva College with its Isaac Elchanan Seminary and its predecessor institutions, these schools served a relatively small number of American

Jews.[79] Moreover, it was not until after the war that many others were founded, and not until the decades of the sixties and early seventies that they began to attract more students, although never more than a small fraction of American young Jews.

As for day schools, although steadily increasing their number and enrollments, they were comparatively rare in the fifties. During that decade, even Orthodox Jews did not always send their children to study in them. While the day school has grown in importance and many today would argue persuasively that day schools represent a key tool for successful Jewish education, the National Jewish Population Survey revealed that even by the 1970s, they reached no "more than about one in five or six Jewish males, and much smaller proportions of Jewish females."[80]

In 1950, *The American Jewish Yearbook* thus reported that "the majority of Jewish children in communities receive their Jewish education through weekday and Sunday schooling and not through all-day parochial schools."[81] Whereas the number of day school students was somewhere around 20,000 at the beginning of the decade, over sixteen times that number were enrolled in supplementary, afternoon synagogue schools.[82] Neither yeshivas nor day schools—with their aim of isolating Jewish children from their non-Jewish American peers—reflected the prevalent acculturative attitude of the times. Even by 1958, *The American Jewish Yearbook* reported that the synagogue school was still the Jewish education of choice for most of those who received one: 47 percent of Jewish students were in weekday-afternoon schools, 45 percent were in one-day-a-week schools, and only 8 percent were in day schools.[83] In addition, and perhaps more ominously for those who saw Jewish education as crucial to Jewish survival, the 1950 *Yearbook* reported that "perhaps one fifth to one third of American Jews receive no instruction in things Jewish."[84]

Thus, the primary setting for Jewish education throughout the fifties and into the next decade remained the part-time synagogue school, or Hebrew school. During the fifties, the young Jew would go to his good (often suburban) public school in the morning, pledge allegiance to the flag and to the Republic for which it stands under God, and blend in with his fellow students. Then this same young American would be reminded (often uncomfortably) of his Jewish

connections and spend three to five afternoons a week and usually a
Sunday morning in Hebrew school. Sometimes this went along with
"junior congregation" in the synagogue on Saturday mornings; this
was the prayer service for children (parents were otherwise engaged).
The whole process commonly ended with a lavish bar mitzvah or
some sort of confirmation (a uniquely American invention meant to
parallel Christian experiences in church) and led to the entry into
high school and an abandonment of Jewish education.

Moreover, attendance at Hebrew school often meant missing
extracurricular activities at "real" school, something the students
frequently resented, and which, when they got the chance, they tried
to avoid. Cutting Hebrew school because of other obligations or
school demands became almost as frequent as attending it. The same
parents who sent their children to Hebrew school often abetted this
truancy. Baseball practice, band practice, or other extracurricular activities often took precedence over Hebrew school attendance. And
of course, a hard test in public school that required cramming was as
good an excuse as any for skipping Hebrew school. Those who did
not do well in public school were sometimes (as the current head of
the Boston Board of Jewish Education reported to me he was) *threat-
ened* with being sent to a yeshiva if they did not improve their public
school grades. Yet the parents nevertheless still formally encouraged
their children to go to the Jewish educational institutions. Why?

In a sense, there was (and is) always a cultural lag between what
Jewish education in America offered and what Jewish life in America
required at the time. Each generation of parents looked for an education in tune with their sense of what it meant to be Jewish in
America—but theirs was commonly a vision of the past. What the
parents of the fifties thought would have worked just fine for them,
had they been children at the time—in this case, a limited sojourn in
Hebrew school (which for the parents' generation would have been
buttressed by life in an ethnic enclave)—more often than not was
out of harmony with the needs and desires of their offspring, who,
living in a far more acculturated milieu, could not see the point of
this limited exposure so at odds with the rest of their lives. Thus,
what fifties parents wanted and expected from a Jewish education
was by no means what their offspring wanted or received. The same
would turn out to be true in subsequent decades.

As implied by the educational process they created—predomi-nantly the part-time synagogue religious school—the parents seemed to want to offer their children some link with Jewish life, but they remained unprepared for it to be more than part-time. To their chil-dren, these parents seemed at best more concerned about the Judaism of their children than with their own Jewish involvement. At worst, they seemed to be hypocritically forcing something on their children that they themselves had already abandoned. How exquisite was the ambivalence in all this: here was the synagogue that the parents had built but did not usually attend yet to which they nevertheless sent their children for a Jewish education that everyone could see was really just "kid stuff" and that did not require full-time involvement.

As if to underscore the fact that what went on in the synagogue school belonged to another era and world, the parents often hired immigrants or aging scholars as teachers, people who were far more closely identified with parochial life and another place. It was not un-usual to find that the schoolteacher was not only more informed Jew-ishly than either the students or their parents but also more visibly ethnic and religiously observant. The teacher commonly perceived Jewish identity as a more salient element of his or her life. Many of these teachers were the last full-time Jews to which these young people were exposed. Thus, cultural dissonance existed between the teachers and their students. Moreover, insofar as the subjects taught by these "different" people were traditional sacred texts, in Hebrew or in another "Jewish" language, or a self-consciously Jewish history, the school was "foreign" to America, an enclave of Jewish cultural life rather than a medium of acculturation. Going from their new math to studying the old Torah, students who came to the Hebrew school at midcentury were stepping into an environment different from the rest of their world. From the point of view of the students, attendance at Hebrew school often seemed to act like a drag on their efforts to be like everyone else in public school and the suburban community.

Nevertheless, young people continued to attend these religious schools in increasing numbers—even if they disliked going. They did so at the insistence of their parents, who often sent them more out of an inertial or sentimental attachment to Judaism rather than a genu-ine desire to have them absorb what the school taught (and if the children asked their parents why they had to go, more often than not, the parents could not give a very persuasive reply). In fact, the motivation behind sending their youngsters to Hebrew school was probably not that different from what made them build the synagogues they joined but did not attend.

Whatever its inherent contradictions, this motivation was a powerful force for getting the young into the schools: between 1950 and 1960 enrollment in Jewish education increased by over 131 percent.[85] By 1970, over 80 percent of American Jewish males and 70 percent of the females were reported to have received some formal Jewish education in their lives (although a closer look at the actual data reveals a weakening of the intensity of that education among the youngest segment of the population—about which more later).[86]

But the schools changed. Like the synagogue that was meant to reflect the America in which it found itself, so too the synagogue school became a place that grew less parochial and involving over time. Not only were fewer days and hours spent at the school, as the norm dropped from five to three or fewer days a week, but the content of the education changed. A Jewish text was often taught in English translation or through summaries; Hebrew language learning devolved into learning a few catchphrases at best; and the central subjects of study became far more culturally neutral. Where children of the early fifties struggled with the Hebrew Bible and Prophets as well as grammar and vocabulary, those in the synagogue school in the middle of the next decade were more likely learning about general Judaic values, history, folkways, and holidays. These are still parochial subjects but when handled in often freewheeling discussions seemed far less exclusively so than in the past. As American Jewry became more American, so too did its Hebrew schools.[87]

Furthermore, as a generation of teachers either died out or found other work, their replacements were closer in character to (though seldom identical with) those they served. Some teachers were suburban mothers who found the part-time work in the Hebrew school fit their schedule and life-style. Others were college or rabbinical students who needed to make some extra money. Notwithstanding these new sources of personnel, finding appropriate teachers for synagogue schools became increasingly difficult during the decade and those succeeding it. "Able young Jews abandoned Jewish concerns in search of careers in the larger society and in the service of universal causes."[88] This movement would be most acutely felt in the domains of Jewish education. Within twenty years, George Lebovitz would discover that even among Jewish day school teachers, supposedly the most dedicated to the programs and promise of Jewish education, fewer than half those surveyed planned still to be teaching in five years, nearly all those planning to leave were under forty years old, and 30 percent of the teachers planned to leave at the first opportunity.[89]

Lastly, by the end of the fifties, with the decline of young people's concern about anti-Semitism and with a turning away from a belief in Jewish superiority, the Jewish school was no longer perceived as a haven from a storm of anti-Jewish prejudice raging outside. It no longer offered a psychological antidote of cultural self-esteem to offset the pain of rejection and hostility outside. Nor did it seem to be a place that enhanced the students' commitment to Jewish survival. Instead, it seemed a prison which confined Jews in the tribal cage of parochialism and kept them from entering a world that they were certain stood ready to accept them fully. As Jews sought to be "like everybody else—only more so," the religious school seemed hopelessly at odds with their aspirations and style of life.[90]

In the domain of Jewish education, much is these days made of college Jewish studies. Leaving aside, for the moment, the question of how large a role these university-based courses play in providing Jews with a Jewish education, in the fifties Jewish studies at the university level were weak, and in most cases nonexistent. While Hebrew may have been taught, often within the context of a classical languages department, and there were Bible courses within divinity schools, these were not considered to be part of an expressly *Jewish* studies curriculum. With the exception of single faculty positions in places like Columbia, Harvard, and Johns Hopkins, the Hebrew language component of the education school at New York University, and the new Near Eastern and Judaic studies department at Brandeis University (founded in 1948), the higher-educational institutions were generally not places to pursue Jewish studies. Only ten universities even accepted Jewish studies as a discipline.[91]

Perhaps nothing more dramatically demonstrates this dearth of Jewish studies at the university level during this first postwar decade than the tragic case of Dr. Joshua Starr. Associate editor of historian Salo Baron's respected journal *Jewish Social Studies,* Starr had degrees from Chicago and Columbia Universities. He had published two books and many articles; had been involved in Jewish population studies; was proficient in Hebrew, Yiddish, Latin, Greek, Italian, French, German, and Rumanian; had served as an editor at the Schocken publishing house and as a researcher for the American Jewish Congress; was executive secretary and a member of the board of directors of the Conference on Jewish Relations; and was a scholar in Byzantine Jewish history. After the war, he was sent to Germany, where he was put in charge of the especially sensitive task of restoring Jewish books and cultural objects stolen and mutilated by the Nazis. Although for a time he taught at a synagogue school, his primary ambition was to teach Jewish studies at the university level. Yet he simply could not find such a job; and on 6 December 1949, a disheartened Joshua Starr committed suicide. The fact was, as A.G. Duker, one of Starr's eulogists noted, at the dawn of the fifties, "the American Jewish community with its manifold institutions and tremendous expenditures for all types of functions has been most delinquent in providing research and teaching opportunities even for men of Joshua Starr's outstanding scholarly calibre, equipment and devotion." [92] And if there were few positions for teachers, there were even fewer opportunities for students.

Secular Education

If Jews of the fifties seemed to display a reduced interest in Jewish education, albeit not as marked as in subsequent decades, they by no means lacked a concern for learning. On the contrary, American Jews had always taken maximum advantage of the educational opportunities that America offered. They embraced public education both as teachers and as students, seeing it as inherently valuable in its own right as well as a ticket to a better life. As already noted, the move to the suburbs was at least in part stimulated by a desire to get children into good public schools, into which Jews had been streaming for generations.

It was at the level of higher education that the real quest for learning expanded in the fifties. Not that Jews were uninterested in college in previous decades: between 1906 and 1916, the last great year of Jewish immigration, the number of Jewish college students quadrupled, many of them attending the City College of New York, which opened the doors of opportunity more than any other American institution of the time (already by 1906 more than 75 percent of the students there were Jewish).[93] Jews saw a college education as a way to escape the poverty and second-class citizenship which their immigrant status and identity had imposed upon them. Through it, they would gain "prestige, respect, authority and status," something they had always believed learning could provide.[94] As Barry Chiswick has put it: "Jews value education not only for its monetary benefits, but also because it fulfills cultural and peer-group expectations"; it propels them into a new social order.[95]

However, because of the economic depression and the world wars, it was not until the fifties that they could really begin a mass program of college education. Until the war years, high school diplomas had been the best most Jews could hope to achieve. The fifties, however, saw an explosion of openings in college and the decline of most Jewish quotas and barriers (although some, like the one at Yale, lasted into the sixties). In the growing prosperity which America enjoyed and in which Jews shared, high school diplomas were no longer enough; college education for every Jew who wanted it became an achievable goal. All that was necessary as a ticket of admission was demonstrated merit and the price of tuition (and the government GI bill was helpful in this last regard). By 1955, 62 percent of American Jews were attending college; although they were only about 3 percent of the American population, Jews made up about 7.5 percent of the college population.[96] By 1990 about 75 percent of American Jews between the ages of twenty-five and forty-four reported having a college degree (an additional 15.6 percent reported having at least some college), significantly above the rate of just under 25 percent for the U.S. white population as a whole.[97]

Jews were also playing a growing role in college teaching. In the twenties slightly less than 4 percent of all colleges had Jewish professors; fifty years later the proportion was 12 percent—and the number of colleges had grown as well. A look only at the elite colleges pro-

vides even more impressive numbers: nearly 21 percent of the faculty
were Jews. To summarize, in postwar America, a Jew was more likely
to get an extensive and intensive secular education than a Jewish one.

There were professional consequences of this. Jews had begun the
century as a working class of light-industry workers, petty traders,
and merchants. "In general during the period before World War
Two Jews occupied a marginal position in the professions."[98] But by
the end of the war, this changed markedly. "In 1950 there was no
longer a single national trade union in which the Jews were a majority of the membership"; even the International Ladies' Garment
Workers' Union, long identified with Jews, had only 30 percent of its
four hundred thousand members that year who were Jewish.[99] Now
Jews were overwhelmingly middle class and moving toward professionalization. This was an astonishing change from the turn of the
century, when union "wage-workers were the largest single class."[100]
Working-class Jews had wanted their children to be spared their kind
of life. To do that they sent them to college and on to the professions.
In a true death of the salesman, even the merchants and traders saw
college as a necessary step for their children and wanted them to
enter professions.

Their children's professional objectives were more varied than
those of their parents as well. Between 1948 and 1953 "the proportion
of Jews in the non-manual occupations (that is, of those working in
the professions, as proprietors, managers, and officials, and as clerks
and salesmen) ranged from 75 to 96%."[101] At the same time, only
38 percent of the American general population was so employed. In
1957, 58 percent of Jewish college graduates were in professional,
technical, and kindred occupations, and 22 percent were employed
as managers, proprietors, and officials. Salaried professionals were
39 percent of all employed Jewish college graduates, while self-
employed professionals were 19 percent.[102] By the latter half of the
fifties, over 55 percent of the Jews employed in the United States were
in nonmanual professions. By the sixties this figure would approach
80 percent, compared with only 23 percent of Americans as a whole.
Already in 1950, Seligman reported that "the most popular [Jewish]
professions are medicine, law, dentistry, and teaching"; and in Los
Angeles, for example, the number of professionals who headed Jew-

ish households increased from 11 to 25 percent between 1941 and 1959.[103] This was a radical change from an American Jewry which before the Second World War "occupied a marginal position in the professions."

If long hours immersed in Judaic studies would have kept young Jews somewhat attached to Jewish identity, increased secular education from the public school through the university and professionalization acted as a powerful counterforce. Moreover, when the professions Jews entered demanded even more than an undergraduate degree, their training lasted even longer, with significant consequences for every domain connected to their Jewish life. The longer they spent in establishing a professional career and identity, the less time and concern they seemed to have for exploring their Jewish identity. Getting ahead had many consequences. We have already considered geographic mobility and the related aspirations for extensive secular education and professionalization. We know too that to such upwardly mobile Jews, Jewish education became increasingly marginal to their life choices. But perhaps the most important consequence was in the matter of Jewish fertility.

Marriage and Fertility

The decade of the fifties was a time when "making it," achieving financial security and stability, was as important as making it into America. Indeed the two were conflated in the minds of many Jews of that generation: moving up meant moving out, out of the ghetto and out of the constraints of Jewish tribal identity. This led to changes in what sociologist Everett C. Hughes has called "life organization," the impact of which would become far more apparent in the following decade.[104]

Perhaps one of the most important changes in life organization for the Jews in 1950s America and directly related to this pattern of secular education was in the timing of their marriages. By spending more years in school than either their forebears or many of their non-Jewish peers, Jews were marrying later than them. In 1957, whereas slightly more than 3 percent of Jewish females between the ages of fourteen and nineteen were married, nearly 13 percent of all other

religious groups in this age bracket were married.[105] Later marriage
would lead to birthrates lower for Jews than for the rest of the American white population.

But late marriage was not the only consequence of making it; an
even more portentous one had to do with fertility. In spite of the
fact that Jews had lost over six million of their people in the seven
years between 1938 and 1945, there was no organized Jewish plan
to try to enhance their numbers through a program of community-
encouraged fertility. Although the general American baby boom
made some assume that the Jewish birthrate would steadily increase,
and one sociological observer as late as 1961 even suggested that the
move by the most fertile age groups of Jews to the suburbs and the
transition from crowded tenements to more-spacious homes might
enhance Jewish fertility, the demographic evidence did not seem to
support this.[106] To be sure, when compared with the fewer than two
Jewish children born per family on average in America between the
late twenties and the end of the Second World War (probably reflecting the harsh economic and political realities of the era), the rise in
the Jewish birthrate after 1946 appeared to be a boom. However, the
1957 census report made undeniably clear that "Jews in the United
States did not participate in the post war baby boom as much as
Roman Catholics and Protestants." [107] For both those of childbearing
age (fifteen to forty-four years) and those past it (forty-five and over),
"the fertility of Jewish women was lower than Protestants, Catholics, or those not included under these classifications. The Jewish
fertility rate in both major age groups remained constant at slightly
over three-quarters of the rates for the total population." [108] Indeed,
regardless of the temporary fluctuation of the postwar baby boom
(when the rate was around 2.3 to 2.5 children per family on average), the trends among American Jews have generally evidenced a
fairly steady "decline of fertility and the transition from the large to
the small family." [109] By 1959, it was clear at least to demographer
Alvin Chenkin that "the Jewish population is not keeping pace with
the general population," and that in "each of the younger groups the
Jewish population is smaller than in the older age groups." [110]

The reasons for this low birthrate were not really a surprise to
anyone who looked closely at the situation of American Jewry since
the 1950s. For all of their child-centeredness as a people, American

Jews realized that to make it, they could not afford to have large families. Moreover, the route they chose for making it in America was one that discouraged high fertility. Extensive education and professional careers, life on the suburban edge of large cities, and an emphasis on both social and geographic mobility all lead to having small families. Children make emotional and economic demands, to say nothing of the investment of time and energy they require. Many studies have demonstrated that the higher one's education level, the lower one's fertility.[111] Professionals tend to have fewer children than those in the working class or even those in the trades.

The life choices that moved Jews away from these latter social situations were first made in the fifties. As Chenkin noted, the lowest birthrates were in categories where Jews were heavily represented. These included "higher school-leaving age, and certain occupational groups, particularly professional, technical, and kindred workers." He concluded therefore: "As long as this situation continues Jews will have a lower fertility rate than the general population."[112]

In fact, throughout the decades that followed, Jews experienced "the most sustained decline without direct government intervention recorded for any group in recent history."[113] Indeed, except for a boomlet in the 1980s that coincided with the baby boomers' generation approaching the end of their age of fertility and choosing to have the children they had put off having during the previous decade (during which Jewish fertility was particularly low), the Jewish birthrate has hovered at or slightly below replacement level through most of the years of the second half of this century. The fact is, as demographer Calvin Goldscheider has irrefutably insisted: "The traditional variables associated with higher fertility in America—rural residence, poverty, contraceptive ignorance, low education, farm and blue collar occupations—are virtually nonexistent among Jewish men and women during the childbearing years."[114] This was true in the fifties, has remained true throughout the subsequent years, and is not likely to change in the foreseeable future.

The desire to make it in America would, however, negatively affect not only fertility. It also had an ominous impact on another element connected to Jewish survival: intermarriage. In America from the fifties onward—and especially the America of the meritocracy—social and ethnic barriers were expected to disappear. Both the university experience and the quest for a career in the professions would move American Jews into social orbits where they would come into close and often intimate contact with non-Jews, the very same people who had been their neighbors in the suburbs and their chums in the public schools. These would be people they would date and during the following decades marry. As social integration became the ideal, love could know no bounds.

The late Robert Gordis once argued that "intermarriage is part of the price that modern Jewry must pay for freedom and equality in an open society."[115] During the fifties, that price was still relatively small. While, for example, 50 percent of the Lutherans marrying between 1946 and 1950 married non-Lutherans, nine out of ten Jews during that period still married other Jews.[116] In the 1957 census figures the proportion of the U.S. population married to a member of the same religion was 88 percent among Catholics, on average between 81 and 83 percent for various types of Protestants, and still a whopping 94 percent for Jews.[117] In Washington, D.C., for example, only 13 percent of Jewish households were intermarried in 1956. "[In 1957] of all married couples with at least one Jewish partner, 7.2% included a non-Jewish partner."[118] While this number may have been higher than in the past, it was not yet a cause for alarm. Yet the cultural and social conditions that would gradually lead the next generation to see the taboos against intermarriage as passé and obsolete were set into place by the priorities and life patterns of the fifties.

The generation that dominated life in the fifties still viewed intermarriage as ethnic suicide, and therefore it was to be avoided. In 1959, Erich Rosenthal, looking at the data on those who did marry non-Jews, concluded that "intermarriage usually spells the end of belonging to the Jewish group," pointing out that "in at least 70 of the mixed families in Greater Washington the children were not identified with the Jewish group."[119]

In the fifties few imagined either that intermarriage might become an unstoppable trend reaching over 52 percent of all marriages by 1990 or that, contrary to the given wisdom of the decade, Jews could intermarry without necessarily abandoning their ties to the Jewish community or even to some Jewish traditions. That discovery would not come until the seventies and beyond.

Conclusion

At the end of the fifties, while American Jews focused on their accomplishments in educational and professional advancement, on their entry into the mainstream of American life, on making it into the meritocracy and the upper reaches of the middle class, on the decline of anti-Semitism, on the miraculous successes of the fledgling State of Israel, and even on their accomplishments in Jewish institution building during this decade, at the same time they ignored the falling birthrate and they remained blind to what the long-term costs of their decisions would be in the years ahead. By the end of this first postwar decade, Judaism (the religion) and Jewishness (ethnic self-consciousness), although far from having totally evaporated, no longer completely filled the cognitive and behavioral universe American Jews inhabited. Although those who were parents during these years still felt some attachments to Jewish identity, they were ambivalent at best and empty of much content at worst. To their children, these attachments were often incomprehensible and not very important—residues of another kind of life. Often it was an aging grandparent who had stayed behind in the city and in the world of tradition who was the youngsters' only genuine—although residual—connection to Jewish ethnicity and religion. But for the most part, attention was concentrated elsewhere, both by the parents and by the children of the fifties.

Jewry of the fifties had little if any awareness of all this. Indeed, they did not bother to look very carefully at themselves. The truth was, as Seymour Martin Lipset asserted in 1954 (as part of the tercentenary celebrations), "while it is easy to reel off the names of dozens of important Jewish sociologists, it would be difficult, if not impossible, to list a dozen important sociological studies of the Jews."[120]

But not only an understanding of the present was missing; few if any had long-term plans for their Jewish future. They assumed it would take care of itself. Life was going too well to worry. This lack of preparation and understanding was tragic, for it meant that American Jewry was not fully prepared for the upheavals and threats to its survival which would become vividly apparent in the years ahead. By the end of the next decade, they would begin to feel the anxieties about Jewish life in America that would color much of the rest of the century for those who cared about the future of Jewish life here. In the fifties, those Jews who were pleased with themselves and the Jewish condition in America we now know were living in a fool's paradise.

2

The Emergence of Two Types of Jews: *Choices Made in the 1960s and 1970s*

Succeeding at Assimilation

AT THE OUTSET OF THE 1960S, LITTLE SEEMED TO HAVE changed from the previous decade. Yet there were changes. By 1960, Jewish immigration to America had virtually ended. Jews, including many, if not most, of the few hundred thousand postwar immigrants, now defined themselves as belonging fully to America and identified with its cultural patterns and values while consolidating the economic and social gains of the 1950s. Articles like Israel Knox's "Is America Exile or Home?" in *Commentary* magazine in November 1946, which betrayed (even as it explicitly denied) lingering doubts about Jewish integration in this country, were by now unthinkable. Rather, this was the period of what Milton Gordon called "assimilation in American life" in his book of that title published during the decade.[1] At the beginning of the sixties, Rabbi William Rosenblum spoke for many Jews when he declared: "What we Jews want is what others desire, just to be let alone to enjoy life, liberty, and happiness along with our neighbors."[2] Significantly, this Jewish request was not very different from what all Americans wanted; even in their aspirations, Jews were assimilating.

The evidence was that Rabbi Rosenblum's wish would be granted. The mobility that had become the hallmark of American life in the immediate postwar period seemed no less vigorous at the start of the new decade. Jews would share in the economic prosperity—a 45 percent increase in gross national product, the largest since the war—that would mark the decade.[3] If they stood out in any respect it was through their increasing affluence and social success. Already by the late fifties, the median income in Jewish America was 30 percent above that of the total population; in places like New York, the gap was even greater. This advantage continued into the six-

ties and seventies. In 1970, for example, the median income of Jews
was $16,176, which was 55 percent greater than the $10,431 their
non-Jewish counterparts earned.[4] Moreover, social success was also
reflected in their increased education (fourteen years on average for
Jews by 1970 versus a bit under twelve for non-Jews), university attendance, and rapid career advancement, which put them ahead of
the average white American.[5] As economist Barry Chiswick noted,
from 1957 to the 1970s, "at the median schooling level, Jews earn
more than other white men."[6] Indeed, he concluded, comparing data
collected between 1909 and 1970, "the relative earnings of Jewish
men has improved dramatically over the period."[7]

American Jews saw the sixties open with a promise of steadily
improving life in America. At first, much of this seemed articulated in political terms as the transition from the Eisenhower to the
Kennedy administration occurred in Washington. This was a generational change; Kennedy was the first president born in the twentieth
century and the youngest ever elected, and he exuded all the promise
of youth. For American Jews, however, it was not his age that mattered most but rather his religion. If a Catholic could make it to the
highest office in the land, perhaps this meant that religion was no
longer an obstacle to advancement to the pinnacles of power and influence in American society. Kennedy's election was a confirmation
of the aspirations that had so characterized the previous decade and
seemed to promise that Jews too could make it to the top.

Indeed, Jews were reaching new heights on their road to the top.
"Beginning in the 1960s, Jews headed some of the most important
branches of the federal government, including the Federal Reserve
System and the labor, commerce, state, and treasury departments,"
positions of political power unprecedented in their American history.[8] By 1964, the Republicans had nominated a man for president
whose father was a Jew and who, although raised as an Episcopalian,
still carried his father's recognizably Jewish name: "Goldwater."[9]
And while the Jewish ascension to the zenith of corporate power and
college presidencies would come more impressively in the following
decade, the first important steps in that ascent took place during the
sixties. They included the entry of large numbers of Jews into some
of the most elite colleges, into higher management positions in major
corporations, and into the life-styles and social classes from which

the meritocratic new leadership would emerge in the following decades. It was no longer questionable whether Jews had found their place in America. Indeed, the postwar years right into the early sixties seemed very much a golden age for Jewish life here.[10] By the end of the decade, it was possible to say without exaggeration that "Jews on the whole are probably America's most successful minority." [11]

The success, moreover, was not going to be for men alone. Perhaps the most remarkable development beginning already in the early sixties was a subtle (later to become far more dramatic) shift in the situation of women, particularly the younger ones. Although Jewish women had a lower labor force participation rate than did other women with children, particularly small children, at home, more and more of them chose to explore careers outside the home.[12] Daughters, who were offered as much education as their brothers and were no longer forced to choose a life career as homemaker and mother, had many new opportunities to explore. These opportunities changed their perceptions of who and what they were. By the end of the sixties these feelings would be fired by the increased educational achievements of women, economic opportunity, and a changing social climate augmented by a rising feminist consciousness that was growing more popular especially among women who were coming of age during the decade.[13] Many Jewish women—especially the most educated among them—were in the forefront in embracing and expressing this new consciousness. After all, it was a Jewish mother, Betty Friedan, who with the 1963 publication of her landmark *The Feminine Mystique* would alert all American women to the new possibilities.

Much of the Jewish success in making it in America was experienced in the suburbs, where Jews continued to gravitate in growing numbers. By the 1960s, Jewish suburbanites (like their white, middle-class, and upwardly mobile neighbors, whose roots seemed to have miraculously disappeared) could imagine they had melted into the American pot. To an exceptional extent, they had. As Nathan Glazer would note, reflecting on the patterns of Jewish life emerging in the sixties: "Less and less of the life of American Jews is derived from Jewish history, experience, culture, and religion. More and more of it is derived from the current and existing realities of American culture, American politics, and the general American religion." [14] All this was seasoned with doses of middle-class, white liberalism that

implied that suburbanites could be anything they wished as long as
they remained open to outside influence and relatively undifferentiated. Life in suburbia represented, as Milton Gordon observed, "the
real melting pot in American life." [15]

As if to illustrate the willingness of Jews of the period to melt,
to present themselves as open and undifferentiated, the following
story appeared in the *New York Times* in January 1960. It reported
that in affluent Stamford, Connecticut, a community then on the far-
thest reaches of the metropolitan New York suburban frontier, the
congregation of Temple Sinai had, in response to a request from
the First Presbyterian Church's Couples Club to witness Jewish religious worship, "agreed to hold their regular Friday evening service
in the assembly hall of the Church. This move came about because
nearby Temple Sinai was too small to accommodate the Presbyterians." [16] These suburban Jewish neighbors were ready to open this
last purely Jewish preserve up for examination in order to demonstrate to the Presbyterians and through the newspaper accounts to
everyone who was interested that, in Arthur Hertzberg's felicitous
phrasing, "in their very Jewishness, they were behaving like all other
Americans." [17]

From Generation to Generation

In this galloping assimilation that the sixties marked, generational
differences began to become especially apparent for Jews. Whereas
the transitional generation of Jews who moved to the suburbs might
have been driven to display their assimilation to America in places
like Stamford by their memories of having been outsiders or the children of outsiders and whereas they concentrated on financial and
social success (part of which required sending their children to the
best schools and encouraging them to do whatever they felt suited to
do regardless of the social consequences), their children—the baby
boomers who grew up in these places in the fifties and sixties—found
themselves lacking those memories and drives that so propelled their
parents. They took their Americanism for granted.

If at least some of the parents (commonly the older ones, who
came of age in the forties) believed that the secret of the Jew living
happily in America is "to assimilate as soon as possible—but, always

to remember he's a Jew" (in fact to be unable to forget it or to be obsessed with forgetting it), their children often did not even have to try in order to forget they were Jews.[18] For this younger suburban generation, interaction across ethnic lines was occurring naturally. It was breaking down the physical and mental barriers separating Jews from other white Americans. (The connections with black America were far more complex and would crystallize later in the decade and in the next one—but more about this later.) Increasingly, young Jews in the suburban gilded ghettoes did not act in ways that were noticeably different from non-Jewish suburbanites. To them, school ties and friendships were becoming more important than primordial tribal ties, religious identities, or even neighborhood relations. When Will Herberg suggested that "the authentic Jew lives on two levels . . . *in* this world [of America] but never quite *of* it, never fully conformed or adjusted to the [American] world in which he lives," although he was writing in 1961, he was talking more about his generation rather than the generation of Americans who would come of age during this decade and the next, who were born and bred in suburbia.[19]

Herberg's assertion of what constituted the "authentic Jew" notwithstanding, being distinctively Jewish was gradually becoming less important in the homogenized suburban world of the late fifties and early sixties (to which young Jews especially seemed to adjust quite well indeed). In fact, these younger suburban American Jews felt particularly uncomfortable with anything that made them stand out as Jews and would have found Herberg's definition of Jewish authenticity hard to accept. For all of their parents' temple building and joining, and even though they themselves attended the synagogue schools and had bar or bat mitzvahs, they grew increasingly discomfited by or, more likely, oblivious to their Jewish identity the older they got. Bar or bat mitzvah was increasingly a celebration marking the end of one's active involvement with Judaism rather than a time when it would begin in earnest, as the tradition had intended. Many Jewish adolescents during the early sixties spent most of their time outside the synagogue and the Jewish parochial universe. Moreover, unlike their parents, they did not have memories of an ethnic past (even though their parents had tried to escape that past), and so they found it hard to appreciate, articulate, or even remember the essential uniqueness of their Jewish identity. And what little of that

identity they did sense—ever more faintly recalled from the quickly
receding childhood experiences (which were never that powerful) in
the temple Hebrew school—was not something they embraced with
enthusiasm or something they believed accurately reflected who or
what they were. They all too often took for granted that they were
indistinguishable from their non-Jewish peers and were involved in
interfaith friendship, dating, and marriage far more frequently than
their parents could have imagined. Some of these young Jewish products of suburbia were downright embarrassed by their Jewishness
and were put off by anything even slightly parochial or sectarian.
Likewise, the age-old sense of Jewish superiority that, as we have
seen, sustained some of their parents in the city and in those first years
of their suburban existence seemed preposterous and thoroughly un-
American to these Jewish young of the sixties.

Reflecting this attitude, Judith Kerman, in 1966 a junior at the
University of Rochester, probably articulated the feelings of many
of her generation when she described herself in print as "an embarrassed Jew." "Jewish organizations," she explained, so patently
sectarian, "make me nervous." Moreover, because of this embarrassment and discomfort, she raised the old Jewish anxiety about dual
loyalties and wondered: "Am I a Jew before I am an American, or an
American before I am a Jew?" Although she had no answer to this
question, she admitted that eighteen years after the founding of the
Jewish state, she could not call herself a "Zionist" because "when
I am categorized as a Jew by strangers, even (especially?) by other
Jews, I become uncomfortable." At best, she was able to conclude,
"all that I can lay claim to so far is a sense of Jewish history as my
own, a feeling of esthetic comfort with the few religious ceremonies
I do know and a basic humanism." This, however, she admitted was
"a very vague definition, more an emotional presentiment than a
creed." To be sure, she was not antipathetic toward Jewry and even
acknowledged, "I envy [the sectarian Jew] because he, at least, knows
who he is." But such an envy did not lead her to try to be like him,
for her envy was accompanied by the realization that she was also
"embarrassed by the sectarian Jew." [20]

Judith Kerman and others like her, so much a product of the fifties
and coming of age in the sixties, were the forerunners of people who

would in the years ahead become unaffiliated Jews or—if they really became alienated from and not just embarrassed by obviously Jewish people—those who in the 1990 National Jewish Population Survey (NJPS) would identify themselves as Jewish but report "none" as their current religion. If Kerman did remain affiliated with the Jewish community, from her testimony in 1966 one might conclude that the kind of Jewishness she would be most comfortable with would be an Americanized version that did away with all vestiges of sectarianism. She might join a local YMHA or YWHA but would use it for its health club and swimming pool or for theater parties, ignoring its programs with specifically Jewish content. The synagogue she joined and which she would attend only rarely would likely be a Reform one where the prayers were in English and the style and content all emphasized the American experience. The charity she would give would probably go overwhelmingly to general causes like the United Fund rather than to the UJA. Like most of her coreligionists, she would never have visited Israel (although she might claim a vague yearning to "visit someday"). Her home would probably lack Jewish symbols, although she might have a small mezuzah on her door. At Christmastime, although she probably would not have a tree, someone in her family might. In a nod to Jewish heritage, she would have a Hanukkah menorah; she might even light its candles, but not punctiliously. At Passover time, she might attend a seder in which both Jews and non-Jews participated. Indeed, some of those non-Jews would probably be relatives. And so that she would not be too embarrassed or uncomfortable at the seder or because of her inability to use the Hebrew she once learned but long ago forgot, her seder (more a family dinner than a Jewish ritual meal) would not include a reading of the Haggadah. She might occasionally wonder about the Orthodox Jews, especially the bearded and earlocked ones she now and then heard about who seemed so committed to their tradition; maybe she would envy their "naive" faith. Yet she would not really know much about them or think about them very often. But all this would come later. In 1966, Judith Kerman was simply an embarrassed Jew, albeit one who still admitted to her Jewishness.

The Decline of Anti-Semitism

Ironically, in 1966 Kerman should not have worried about standing out as a Jew. America did not have Jews on its mind very much anymore. As a major study of Jews in the mind of America commissioned by the American Jewish Committee in the first half of the decade demonstrated, the Jews had melted so well into America that the American public's awareness of them, quite sharp even fifteen years earlier, had declined markedly. Already by 1962, "no less than 43 percent of the respondents [to the American Jewish Committee survey] believe[d] that Jews have no distinctive group traits at all." [21] Morton Keller called this attitude "asemitism," an indifference to or unawareness of Jewish identity.

Some of the slightly more than five and a half million American Jews (3 percent of the nation's population at the dawn of the sixties), however, who had been working so hard to emphasize their attachment to America throughout the fifties, could not fully absorb the fact that their Americanism was by now very much taken for granted. "The American Jew," wrote Lothar Kahn in 1961, "is not fully accustomed to his new security and alternatively revels in it and doubts it." [22] The Jews who held lingering doubts and anxieties about Jewish acceptance in America were generally of the generation who had come of age in the thirties and forties, the parents of the Judith Kermans. They were haunted by the economic hardships of the Depression, by memories of war, Holocaust, and anti-Semitism, or by their escape from the city. The anxiety of the parents about their Jewishness helped give birth to their children's embarrassment or ignorance.

To be sure, these parental anxieties were not without occasional substance. Even at the beginning of the decade there continued to be signs that not everyone necessarily perceived Jews to be fully acceptable Americans and that anti-Jewish feelings still existed. The front page of the *New York Times* on 11 January 1960, for example, reported "the swift spread of anti-Semitic incidents in many parts of the world"; and lest one believe that America was an exception, one needed only to turn to page 15 in that same paper to learn that "five incidents of swastika-daubing and vandalism occurred over the weekend in Brooklyn and Queens." While the report went on to explain that Jewish leaders were of "the opinion that the wave of desecration was imitative and not an organized plot," citing "a sharp decrease in the organized activities of hatemongers and bigots since the end of World War II," others were not as sure. In Philadelphia, the *Times* reporter noted that a group of Protestant clergymen, one of whom was Billy Graham, saw the vandalism as indicating a "central organizing force of the same vicious type that existed in Nazi Germany."

But such reverberations of Jewish hatred notwithstanding, the real news seemed to be that by the first half of the 1960s polls measured "the steepest drop in anti-Semitic sentiment since the Second World War."[23] Neither the Rosenberg case nor the era of McCarthyism led to any dramatic increase in overt anti-Semitism such as that which had been part of the interwar period. This was a change from even the immediate postwar period: in 1946, 55 percent of Americans polled believed that "Jews have too much power in the United States," and less than a third said that if a candidate for Congress should declare himself as being against the Jews, this would influence them to vote against him.[24] Even as late as 1948, after the world knew about the horrors of the Holocaust and after the Displaced Persons Act had been passed and was being implemented, while 53 percent of Americans polled said they would limit the number of German immigrants allowed into this country, 60 percent said they would limit the number of Jews allowed to immigrate.[25] By 1962, many of these anti-Jewish attitudes had changed. Polls that year discovered that only about 1 percent of American Gentiles considered Jews to be a national menace nor did they see reasons for anti-Jewish discrimination in employment.[26] Only 4 percent thought colleges should limit the number of Jews they admitted (fully 88 percent were in favor of unlimited admission of Jews). In June 1962, only 17 percent thought that Jews had too much power in America—a drop of 70 percent in sixteen years. And fully 60 percent of Americans polled that year said they would be influenced to vote against a candidate for Congress who declared himself as being against Jews (nearly double the number that had expressed this opposition in 1946). By now, "almost all restrictions against Jews . . . began to decline or disappear."[27]

As the sixties dawned, then, anti-Semitism appeared no longer to be a significant part of the American Jewish story. Although the Holocaust would continue to haunt those who grew up before the war, in this post-Holocaust world it was possible for Charles H. Stember, who directed the American Jewish Committee survey of anti-Semitism, to conclude: "For most Jews today, bigotry and discrimination are felt to exist, if at all, at a far remove from the actual course of their lives."[28] Indeed, by the start of the sixties, some Jews even went so far as to suggest that anti-Semitism should not be a singularly Jewish concern.[29] If it existed here, it was an *American,* not simply a *Jewish,* problem.

As for the relationship with Israel, although in the first years of the decade it continued to deepen in the American Jewish consciousness, beginning to fill the vacuum left by the disappearance of ethnic *landsmanschaftn* (associations of immigrants sharing common origins), immigrant neighborhoods, and Jewish urban community life and by the diminishing role of religious practices and distinctiveness, it still remained limited. In this era of assimilation and before 1967, when everything would change, Jews still wanted to remind Americans not to worry about or distrust them because of dual loyalties. "Zionists hailed as loyal to U.S. Convention in Atlantic City told link to Israel is only cultural and religious," a January 1960 headline declared.[30] Even the Orthodox Jews, who by their unyielding attachments to religious traditions and observances seemed more separatist and ethnic than their coreligionists, now emphasized their American allegiances: Dr. H. Raphael Gold, a New York psychiatrist who was chair of the National Council of Torah Education of the Religious Zionists of America, declared in that same January that American Zionists were "intensely American, patriotic citizens who have only one loyalty and citizenship—that for the United States."[31] On the Israeli side, Ben Gurion and others largely supported that stance, arguing that only those Jews who settled in Israel would have a voice in what happened there; all the others, who were in and of America, could at best be boosters and supporters.[32] Indeed, this relatively passive role remained the ideal one for American Jews vis-à-vis Israel for many years. Finally, because it was clear by the first half of the sixties that aliyah (emigration to Israel) was not going to become a reality for most American Jews in the foreseeable future, and even visits there were something only a minority did, American Jews were in effect firmly defined as belonging to America. Israel might continue to play a role in American Jewish identity, but—as historian Edward

Shapiro has felicitously put it—"the American Jewish theme song was not 'Hatikvah' but 'God Bless America,' a song written by Irving Berlin, a first generation product of New York's Lower East Side."[33]

To recap, here was the Jewish situation at the dawn of the sixties: diminished anti-Semitism, growing Jewish affluence and influence, and a real feeling of being in and of America, especially by the young Jews coming of age during the decade, many of whom had grown up in suburbia. For the older members of the parents' generation this was all accompanied by a lingering anxiety or at least disbelief that it was all so easy, along with a conviction that even in their successful amalgamation into America they should remember that they were Jews, although exactly what the substance of this memory was to be remained vague and at best sentimental. On the other hand, for their children, who took their Americanism for granted and whose Jewish identity was either tinged with embarrassment or more commonly lacked even the little substance or residual ethnicity their parents' had, the obvious question became: "If we are not different, why do we stand apart?"[34] This question was not just a child's inquiry. On the contrary, although children of the postwar era might be more prone to ask it, many of their parents (especially the younger ones, those who had started families during the later years of the fifties), when they recognized their success in becoming part of the American tapestry and lost their anxiety about being Jewish, also were beginning to harbor these same questions, although they may not have always expressed them as unreservedly. By the middle of the decade, they too faced a situation where they could ask, "Why should I be Jewish?"

The Vanishing American Jews: Signs and Countersigns

The European Jews before the war who had also asked this question found that if they chose not to stand apart as Jews, they would be expected to convert to Christianity or else give up all religion (this, of course, was before the rise to power of the Nazis, whose doctrine asserted there was no way for Jews to stop being Jews). The American postwar assimilating Jews, however, found America was different. The United States called itself a "nation under God" that allowed for the free expression of religion, even encouraged it. Indeed, rather than demanding conversion, America had allowed the "channel for Jewish identity . . . from the start [to be] that of a religious faith."[35] But by the beginning of the sixties, American Judaism was vague, undifferentiated, and totally voluntary. So when American Jews asked, "Why be Jewish?" some could answer, "Why not?" "No act of conversion was demanded, no pledge of disallegiance."[36] Nor was much in the way of content particularly required for calling oneself a Jew.

Whereas European Jews in the past had faced a situation in which they could either be Jews or be something else, American Jews by the sixties discovered they could continue to call themselves Jewish even though they also became something else. All that was necessary was to reform the meaning of being Jewish so that it could be demonstrated to non-Jewish America (as the Jews of Stamford, Connecticut, did) that "we are . . . no different from you in the things that matter."[37] As long as being a Jew did not make them stand distinctively apart from America, "American Jews, too, defined themselves by religion, even if they were not always religious."[38]

Indeed, their American Judaism was rather increasingly sustained by its association with the dominant values and life-styles of America, which were inherently non-Jewish. In time, even some of the Orthodox would fall under the influence of America and make many of their Jewish observances practically invisible while they adopted an American demeanor. Without converting, as a group American Jews seemed to be increasingly indistinct to Americans and even to many among themselves. To anyone who closely observed this emerging reality, *Look* magazine's 1964 proclamation to its more than seven and a half million readers that we had reached the era of "the vanishing American Jew" should have come as no surprise.[39]

To be sure, this was not simply a matter of consciousness or perception. A diminished Jewish presence was a demographic matter as well. We have already seen that the Jews did not participate in the postwar baby boom as much as other Americans. The sixties simply continued these trends of low growth. Estimates of the number of American Jews hovered between 5.5 million at the beginning of the decade and about 5.8 million at the end, for a growth rate of 1.15 percent a year, compared with 1.425 percent annually for the rest of white America.[40] This was certainly not booming growth. Although "very little relevant data on Jewish fertility existed before the 1957

Census study," to demographers who documented these trends it would be clear that the American Jewish population was slowly but surely shrinking, both in absolute terms and even more so relative to the American one.[41] While Jews still claimed to want on average about three children per family, in fact those with completed families had fewer than 2.5 in the late fifties, a rate that decreased to about 2.3 in the sixties, dangerously close to the minimum replacement level.[42] In the seventies, it would drop even further to below replacement.[43] Even household size was remarkably small. Thus, for example, in Greater New York (still the area of greatest Jewish concentration in America), the largest average household was 3.64 persons in the Long Island suburbs, next came Westchester County and the northern suburbs with 3.28 and Queens County with 2.85, while Manhattan weighed in with a strikingly low 1.7, and even Brooklyn (perhaps symbolically synonymous with Jewish life in America) reported a 2.62 average household size in the 1970–71 NJPS.[44]

Jewish population growth in America had been "largely the result of net immigration rather than natural increase."[45] By the sixties, as already noted, this immigration was largely over. During the decade, "both families of orientation and procreation were small in size."[46] Not surprisingly, therefore, within twenty years, Jews in America would be down from their peak of 3.7 percent of America (reached in 1937 on the eve of the Holocaust) to about 2.5 percent.[47]

The *Look* magazine declaration was also not a surprise to sociologists who had been looking at and reporting on the rising rate of intermarriage of American Jews (particularly in areas of sparse Jewish population, beyond the Northeast). The 13 percent rate of intermarriage in Washington, D.C., in 1953 and the 54 percent rate in Iowa in 1959 were illustrative of a trend that the 1971 NJPS, which reported on the developments of the sixties, confirmed.[48] What was once relatively rare was with each passing generation becoming more common. Whereas between 1955 and 1960 about 7 percent of Jews were married to non-Jewish partners, the second half of the decade saw the figure jump precipitously.[49] The figures for those marrying between 1965 and 1971 were as follows: "41 percent of Jewish males marrying wives not born Jews and 10.3 percent of Jewish females marrying husbands not born Jews, for a combined rate of 29.2 percent."[50] Looking at the data from a different angle, we discover that while inmarriage (two Jews marrying each other) was about 94 percent prior to 1960, it dropped to 84 percent overall during the sixties.[51]

Sociologists, who had now started systematically to study the Jews, argued that this trend was a direct result of American nativity and assimilation, secular education, growing professionalization, and increasing income among the Jews—trends that like the intermarriage rate would multiply exponentially in the new decade. The notion of a disappearing American Jewry was thus not some imagined threat thought up by a *Look* reporter; it was rather a dramatic public statement of the emerging data that sociologists and demographers had begun to discover. For those who were concerned with the matter of Jewish survival in America, *Look* showed, in bold headlines, the high price of successful acculturation for Jews of the fifties and sixties. It was a price that would continue to escalate in the years ahead.

The news was thus not the data but that this magazine considered the development of interest to millions of its readers. All America would see what was happening to the Jews, who less than two decades earlier had been ravaged by the loss of six million in what had once been the largest Diaspora community. Now the Jews seemed about to be wiped out in their new home, not by a society that sought to spit them out, but rather by one that ate them up.

Yet if the 1964 article heralded the "vanishing American Jew," this decade, especially after 1967, would also reveal an alternative, more expressive and culturally assertive, American Jewish identity, a reappearing American Jew. Until the beginning of the sixties, to be both American and Jewish might have required a gradual diminution of the distinctively Jewish, but in the years that followed some Jews discovered that the both/and option also allowed for a vital and active American Jewish identity. In fact, as the sixties progressed and even more in the seventies, there was "enormous growth in Jewish activities, and new forms of Jewish identity . . . emerged."[52]

Significantly as well, these invigorated Jewish activities did not occur among older Jews, a kind of residual element of a dying faith, but rather, they were "particularly concentrated among those age segments in the Jewish community that in the past [had] been the least Jewish-committed—the teenage, college, and young adult populations. The impressive growth of Habad houses, Jewish consciousness among college students, kosher facilities, Jewish studies, the wearing of the skullcap, and Israel-Zionism-Soviet Jewry activities, among others, [were] revolutionary forces in American Jewish life that few if any social scientists imagined or predicted." [53] As the sixties gave way to the seventies, it became increasingly clear that here in America, where religious or ethnic identity and activity were essentially a matter of one's choosing, total assimilation or even a washed-out acculturation were not the only options; there was more than one way to choose to be a Jew. Committed Jews were increasingly being public about their Jewish identity. Whereas in the past they were hidden in pockets or left at home, yarmulkes appeared on campus; once missing altogether, Jewish studies demonstrated a growing presence in the academic pantheon; Jewish tradition and observance, once considered passé, were celebrated; and, especially after 1967, support for Israel, trips there, and even aliyah became public American Jewish preoccupations even greater than they had been in the days leading up to independence. After the public silence of the fifties, when being Jewish seemed submerged in the efforts to establish an American identity and prove loyalty, many Jews of the 1960s and the 1970s seemed to revel in "being 'noisy' about Jewishness," as sociologist Calvin Goldscheider put it. For them this Jewish coming out became "the norm." [54]

Although a minority of a minority, much of what they did exuded and reflected the fact that they were Jews. They continued to emphasize *actively* the distinctive Jewish component of their lives, making Jewish identity a large part of their consciousness and the most public of their faces. They made Jewish heritage a living element rather than a half-forgotten background of their contemporary existence. They focused their concerns and oriented both their demeanor and their involvement on Jewish survival, growth, education, and development. While recognizing they were in America, they looked upon that existence through the prism of their being Jews.

The most extreme among them were the Orthodox, who by the latter half of the sixties had begun to make their presence felt in America and who in emphasizing their uniquely Jewish customs and practices seemed in much that they did to be purposefully contra-acculturative, choosing to swim against the tide of Americanization. Perhaps the most visibly different among them were the black-frocked and bearded Hasidim and their families as well as those whose lives orbited around the yeshivas. These people might be said to be Jews who happened to be in America but tried very much to demonstrate that they were not caught up by it. The only valuable aspect of America was the liberty it gave them to practice their tradition unhindered; the danger of it was that it could corrupt their young with its libertarian permissiveness and anomie. That these kinds of Jews, who seemed a portrait of the past, were still around and apparently thriving institutionally and spiritually was a surprise to those who believed that all orthodoxies were fated to fade away in the bright light of American acculturation.

But, these were not the only observant Jews who were a visible part of America after the late sixties. On the contrary, the so-called modern Orthodox, the larger and at the time more influential segment of this movement, those who were ready to be part of mainstream America, were also publicly exhibiting their active Judaism in more and more ways. They were in a sense demonstrating that the new Orthodoxy was no longer simply the result of having been born into and remaining locked in an insular ethnic community of the observant but was now a matter of informed religious choice.[55] While their coreligionists were choosing to be Reform or perhaps Conservative Jews, or (in growing numbers) nondenominational people of Jewish heritage, they (approximately 12 percent of American Jews at the time) were choosing to ally themselves with Jewish law and traditional practice in relatively uncompromising ways, all the while claiming and demonstrating that this would not exclude them from professional and educational advancement and participation in the emergent meritocracy.

Orthodox Jews, most of whom had come to America only under duress as refugees just before or after the Nazi firestorm had destroyed their world in Europe, were by no means the only, the most numerous, and surely not the most important of the emerging actively Jewish Jews. Some Jews from *all* the denominations conceived of themselves in terms of their Jewish involvement. These were people who saw their Jewish being as a salient, essential, engaging, and distinctive aspect of their lives, although they varied widely in the ways they sought to express this. These were people who (in the words on the program of the first Jewish Assembly of World Jewish Studies, convened in Jerusalem in August 1962) searched for "a program to counteract 'assimilation'" and to focus on specifically Jewish concerns. This included at times displaying characteristics that might appear to set them apart from America, such as celebrating distinctively Jewish religious observances or emphasizing the knowledge (and use) of Hebrew or Yiddish, pursuing Jewish education with greater intensity, and living with and maintaining special relationships with (and marrying only) other Jews. These were people who did more than care about Israel; they actually visited or at least involved themselves in activities on behalf of Zionist causes. They gave money to Jewish charities or programs and made support of the Jewish community and its needs a crucial concern in their lives. They engaged in political activity that emphasized their Jewishness and furthered its concerns. These were the Jews who were active in their synagogues or in the implementation of Jewish education, and who saw to it that their young got the most intensive exposure to such education as was possible, including if necessary creating new model Jewish schools.

To be sure, even among this group, most argued that being actively and openly Jewish did not necessarily make them un-American. And not all of them expressed their Jewish identity identically. Many of these Jews affirmed that "one could choose to be Jewish, after whatever fashion, without thereby separating oneself from the rest of society."[56] They asserted (although more so at the end of the decade than at the beginning) that America was a pluralist, multicultural immigrant society that allowed for a variety of legitimate life patterns and encouraged free religious expression, among which was the distinctively Jewish one. Therefore, this argument ran, being actively and hence distinctively Jewish was to be quintessentially American.

Ironically, the confidence to make this argument was inspired at least in part by African-Americans, who by the late sixties defiantly declared to white America that "black is beautiful." It was given an even greater boost by the unmeltable ethnics, who during the following decade expressed open pride in their cultural difference, thereby asserting the possibility of an American life that existed beyond the melting pot. Together, actively Jewish Jews, proud blacks, and other ethnics would remind Americans that cultural and ethnic diversity was American and that heritage needed to be celebrated and expressed in every generation. This celebration of ethnicity would have been unthinkable even a few years before when ethnic difference was not yet celebrated and actively Jewish Jews ran the risk of seeming to be foreigners running against the grain of American trends. But by the seventies, cultural pluralism was acceptable, marked by the congressional passage of the "Ethnic Heritage" act, which violated the once dominant theory of the melting pot.[57] For many actively Jewish Jews, "ethnic pride" replaced the "Judith-Kermanism," "the semi-embarrassment, associated with the retention of Jewish culture and consciousness."[58]

Salient and active Jewishness was however not simply the Jewish version of African-American and other ethnic trends; there were Jewish root causes as well. One was a counterreaction to the demographic trends that *Look* magazine and the discussions around it had highlighted in so public a fashion. Another might have been the capture of Adolf Eichmann in 1960, his trial in 1961, and his execution in 1962, all of which reawakened in many Jews the anxieties and lessons of the Holocaust—thoughts that served for some Jews as a stimulus not only to engage in memorialization (a process that would become for many American Jews a growing part of their Jewish consciousness) but also to revitalize Jewish life and prevent another wholesale Jewish disappearance. Still another stimulus for active Jewish identity and engagement was the undeniable presence of an openly triumphalist modern Orthodoxy that in the sixties was still in the rebuilding stage but was becoming ever more visible and would by the seventies demonstrate that one could be publicly Jewish and not sacrifice American belongingness.

Yet perhaps above all other Jewish root causes was the perceived threat to Israel's existence in those anxious days leading up to the 1967 war and later again during the Yom Kippur War of 1973, which would vitalize and galvanize those who embraced an active Jewish identity. Israel, so seemingly far away, leapt into the heart of American Jewry and began to give a national substance to that emerging ethnic identity. Moreover, Israel's refusal to be wiped out presented a symbolic model and challenge to those Jews in the Diaspora who likewise refused to disappear. This was reaffirmed in the reactions to the subsequent anti-Israel resolutions by the New Left and the United Nations that marked the early seventies.

In addition, the "maturation of a Jewish educational system that established institutions for intensive Jewish education" throughout the preceding twenty-odd years and of its students, who came of age by the late sixties and early seventies and carried its lessons close to heart, also played a part in this Jewish renaissance.[59] Not everyone had been untouched by their Jewish education in America.

As the decade ripened and as the new one began, a polarization took place; but the choice was not simply between total assimilation and "complete inclusion in the American system" on the one hand versus insularity or ghettoization and "a desire for some inviolable separateness" on the other, which a tiny fraction pursued.[60] Rather, the choice became how to personify, typify, and express American Jewish identity and behavior. The result was the emergence in the late sixties and the seventies of *two distinct types of American Jews.* One type, by far the more numerous and dominant, whose pattern of life had been firmly established in the fifties and the early sixties, was the Jews for whom being both American and Jewish meant making their Jewish identity and involvement subordinate to their being American. These people, whose Jewish attachments were relatively minimal, were simply "Jewish-Americans," no different from other hyphenated Americans, such as the "Irish-Americans" or the "Italian-Americans." These Jewish-Americans were taking advantage of the opportunities for individual mobility that the meritocratic society allowed, absorbing American values as well as culture patterns and leaving behind those elements of Jewish life that set them firmly apart. As a result, the "Jewish" aspect of their status became weakened while the primary emphasis in their identity was on the "American." As Arthur A. Cohen described them in 1963, they were Jews who "divested themselves of that which they considered most noticeable, provocative, and embarrassing," which meant relinquishing their distinctive Jewish beliefs and, even more so, reforming their behavior patterns (many of which were associated with other places —the city, the old country—and other times).[61] A Passover seder of some sort, Hanukkah candles on at least some nights, maybe a stop into the synagogue a few times a year, or a bar or bat mitzvah might be enough. For other such Jews, it might be a general reverence for intellect, explained as deriving from a Jewish heritage of learning. For still others, to be a Jewish-American was to be a liberal, a re-

sponse to a collective awareness of a national history of Jewish op-
pression. (In the 1980s this association would be substantiated by
a nationwide *Los Angeles Times* survey of American Jews in which
half those questioned asserted that a commitment to social equality
was "most important" to their Jewish identity.) There were probably
even some Jewish-Americans who considered a Sunday brunch of lox
and bagels or a piece of herring at a gathering with other Jews sufficient to signal their Jewish heritage. In short, this sort of connection
to being a Jew was relatively minimal, a commitment without much
content, making few practical demands upon those who embraced it
and separating them only very subtly if at all from the America in
which they found themselves from the sixties onward.

To be sure, these Jews were not aiming for total assimilation and
remained *proud* of their heritage, but after the sixties that pride became more symbolic than substantive and did not lead to much Jewish activity; the self, or at most also the nuclear family—and not the
tribe or the People—was at the center of their concern. And in response to those who argued that more was necessary, they allowed
themselves to assume that someone somewhere—a Jew back in the
ghetto, the Orthodox, those still in the synagogue, the rabbi—could
be counted on to keep the flame burning. Reflecting an attitude that
gave diminished attention to group belongingness and greater importance to individualization, these Jews still identified with their
religious and ethnic group but it was an identification that was "voluntary, contingent, fluid, not 'given,' fixed and rigid." [62] They cared
about being identified as Jewish, but this concern about identity
could be expressed simply by stressing that they were *not* Christian.[63] ("I was born Jewish" or "I grew up as a Jew" were the key
phrases here.) This sort of a Jewish identity did not have to be raised
"constantly to the level of conscious awareness." [64] It was enough to
remember and stress it at certain moments of Jewish life—family
passages, weddings, and funerals—or in situations when the community was under perceived attack—occasions of anti-Semitic as-
saults or when Israel or some other Jewish population was in distress
and required displays of support. These Jews were not ready to dis-
avow their past and Jewish religious identity—conversions were not
called for by America—but they were also not prepared to make too
much of it. For them, neither Judaism as a religion nor Jewish ethnic

self-consciousness completely filled their cognitive and behavioral universe. Being Jewish no longer determined the way they looked at and understood the cosmos and reality, no longer very much affected the way they felt about the world, themselves, and others or what they did.

To these Jewish-Americans so comfortable in America, moreover, the anxieties about the potential disappearance of the Jews, as reported by *Look* and the demographers, had no meaning, at least not in 1964. They did not really believe Jews in America were going to disappear. They were not then upset about the quality of American Jewish life, nor did they consider themselves personally responsible for it. To them Jewish heritage did not require more in terms of action and commitment than they were giving it. In fact, their lives tended to shun exclusively Jewish ties and above all else "reflected the general trends of contemporary society" in America (or at least the white, middle-class, often suburban and liberal, version of that society).[65] In their study of American Jewish suburbia, Marshall Sklare and Joseph Greenblum summed up the implicit criteria delineating what these sorts of Jews were willing to practice. For them, the acceptable included that which (1) could be redefined in modern terms, (2) did not demand social isolation, (3) was responsive to and in harmony with the circumambient American religious culture, (4) was child centered, and (5) demanded only infrequent performance.[66] A vague attachment to Jewish heritage perfectly fit the bill.

On the other hand, the active and distinctive Jews who did regularly attend the synagogue or the day school and maintained Jewish organizations and charities *were* worried about the idea of Jews vanishing in America. Predictions of a precipitous demographic decline and rampant assimilation made these Jews wonder whether they would indeed soon be swallowed up by America and history. To them, the openness of American life and society which had made Judaism totally voluntary was "the key challenge and dilemma," which they were not at all certain they could survive.[67] To see these doubts trumpeted to the general non-Jewish public ("the goyim") in the 1964 *Look*, then still a mass-market publication, jolted them deeply.

The magazine article "The Vanishing American Jew" as well as the data on which it was based was much discussed by these active

Jews, who believed that without a strategy for greater Jewish engagement, "American Jewish history will soon end and become a part of American memory as a whole."[68] That was the paradox: those who were contributing most to the process of Jewish assimilation, fertility decline, and cultural disappearance, whose Jewish identity was a matter of little more than symbolic heritage, tended to believe that there was no real threat to the Jewish future, while those who were most active Jewishly and whose style of life and concerns were the best defense against such wholesale disappearance worried about it a great deal.

The Shrinking Middle

This polarization of Jewish life in America was not always the dominant model. On the contrary, in every decade since the great Jewish immigrations of 1880, a continuing flow of people who came from a Europe where being Jewish was inseparable from their existential condition as a minority and who lived in (or were just escaping from) the American ghetto reflection of this kept up the supply of those who, in spite of their desire to Americanize, always remembered (could never forget) that, as Herberg put it, "they were Jews." These first- and second-generation memories nourished a sort of middle-level kind of Judaism.

The content of this middle level might vary from individual to individual, but generally it included in the ritual domain an obligatory attendance at the synagogue and maybe even a soul-searching prayer on the High Holy Days, observance of a Passover seder that was more than simply a family meal and at which at least some of the religious rituals were enacted, a consistent but not always strictly traditional celebration of major Jewish rites of passage, and the lighting of and blessing over Hanukkah candles (often as a means of publicly distinguishing these people from those who celebrated Christmas in America). In the institutional domain, it included a lifelong synagogue affiliation or at the very least from the moment that their children reached school age, at which point these Jews commonly sent their offspring to some part-time Hebrew school. It also included some support of a Jewish federation or the UJA, usually in the form of a regular philanthropic donation. Finally, in the domain of civil

Judaism, it came increasingly to embrace a concern with commemorating the Holocaust, along with the warning that it must never happen again, support for (although not necessarily much in the way of active involvement in) political efforts to ensure the security of Israel, occasional participation in a gathering on behalf of Soviet or other oppressed Jewries, and some basic level of interest in developments in American Jewish life (commonly expressed by reading, however cursorily or irregularly, some Jewish-based publication—a newspaper, magazine, or bulletin). These partial but consistent attachments to Judaism and Jewish life were from people who could not conceive themselves to be anything but Jewish, no matter what else they became or how limited their Jewish activity. These were the people who, although not likely to be scrupulous about observing the Jewish dietary laws, would find it hard to swallow a ham-and-swiss sandwich or to have a Passover seder that included bread or even a Thanksgiving dinner that included lobster. In a sense, this kind of middle-level Judaism was captured in the uniquely American Jewish notion of "kosher-style."

The continuing existence of this sort of middle-level, ethnic Judaism suggested that there was in America a Jewish identity that allowed for something less than intense activity but assumed something more than an undemanding attachment to and pride in Jewish heritage. For these people of the middle, Jewish identity remained salient but not overbearing, demanding some level of activity and obligation but not too much. They might celebrate Yom Kippur and Thanksgiving with the same degree of enthusiasm and care. For them, being Jewish was a living heritage but not a contra-acculturative one.

Although they had grown up overwhelmingly among other Jews, many of these sorts of Jews were people who by the sixties admitted that probably no more than a quarter of their children's closest friends were Jewish. And they themselves also had significant numbers of non-Jewish friends who had attended school with them, came from the workplace, or from their new suburban neighborhoods. They would never encourage the possibility of outmarriage among their children, although they recognized that it might occur. If it did happen, "God forbid," they would not allow it to sever their children from their families or Jewish connections. They would find some way to integrate the Gentile (and certainly their grandchildren) into their kosher-style, or ethnic, heritage, hopefully through some sort of conversion—if not formal at the very least de facto. (While the rabbis of all movements looked for subtle but serious means of effecting these conversions, the laity, about whom I speak, were not interested in these ritual details. The key was to get the Gentile to call himself or herself a Jew or to at least act like a Jew—let the rabbis work out the particulars.)

Those who made up the middle level could in theory come from any of the denominations and did. They included the nominally Orthodox, who were in practice rather lax in their actual Jewish observances and commitments though still chose to call themselves "Orthodox."[69] They consisted as well of those newly Reform Jews who remained attached to old Jewish traditions and many ethnic practices. They even included people without a denominational affiliation who, through either their connections to immigrant culture or their use of and attachment to Yiddish or Hebrew, were clearly placing themselves somewhere at a middle level of Jewish involvement.

Yet perhaps most of the people of the middle level were at home within the nominal domain of Conservative Judaism, which had staked out its territory between the ideological and denominational extremes. But as the century moved into its second half, the Conservative middle was not holding. While its numbers might have grown in the first half of the century, the second half would see the character of its content become progressively more hollow.

Since at least the fifties, Conservative Judaism had been faced by the fact that its laity, while ostensibly loyal to halacha, or Jewish religious law (albeit a halacha subject to change by a Committee on Law and Standards whose members included nonhalachists and laypeople as well as rabbis and talmudists), were less and less likely to abide by it in practice. Already in 1950, the Conservatives' Rabbinical Assembly Committee on Jewish Law and Standards "devoted serious attention during the year to the possibility of liberalizing some phases of traditional Jewish law, as part of a campaign for increased observance of the fundamental *Mitzvot* of Conservative Jews."[70] This was an effort not only to reduce the restrictive demands of Judaism but also to redefine the middle in light of the religious erosion the movement was experiencing. It was a bid to create new standards for being Jewish among those who were increasingly unwilling (or unable) to remain anchored to a demanding Judaism that they felt was not adaptable to changing American realities.

Along with the changing character of what people meant when they affiliated themselves with Conservative Judaism were the changing numbers of those who actually called themselves Conservative. For example, in Boston in 1965, 44 percent of those surveyed thought of themselves as Conservative; 27 percent as Reform; and 14 percent as Orthodox. But by 1975 a similar survey in Boston found "only five percent identified as Orthodox, and the rest were about equally distributed between Conservative and Reform." [71] Movement was away from the commitments of the religious right, and the big winner here was obviously the Reform movement. Indeed, by 3 to 1, throughout the last forty years Jews have been moving religiously leftward.[72] Nationally, in 1970, Conservative Jews were still the largest denomination among American Jews—42 percent as opposed to 33 percent for Reform and 11 percent for the Orthodox. But throughout the seventies and even more so in subsequent decades, Reform Judaism has grown at the expense of Conservative Judaism, which, as Charles Liebman has concluded, "suggests a decline in commitment among American Jews . . . [while] lay leaders in Conservative synagogues report[ed] increasing difficulty in recruiting other leaders." [73] By the 1990 NJPS, the denominational preference of adults born Jewish who still called themselves Jews was just under 7 percent for the Orthodox, about 38 percent for Conservative, and over 42 percent for Reform.[74] While this proportional drop among those calling themselves Conservative may appear relatively small in the twenty-year period since 1970, it is important to realize that the character of what was Conservative and Reform changed significantly throughout the postwar period. By the nineties, as we shall see, the Orthodox were far more religiously right wing while the non-Orthodox movements were far more religiously liberal, with a laity that often seemed practically interchangeable. Indeed, 39 percent of those who described themselves as Conservative Jews in 1965 Boston were in fact unaffiliated.[75] And by the later decades many of those who held Conservative synagogal affiliations also held Reform ones as well.

Mordecai Kaplan, who once saw in American Judaism a new

kind of civilization and who ended his teaching career at the Conservative Jewish Theological Seminary of America, probably had the people who were in the shrinking middle in mind when he urged an audience at the 1959 Conservative Rabbinical Assembly Convention not to allow their Jewish life to become eroded but rather to initiate a series of "religious imperatives" that more Jews would follow so that life here would recover its nerve. Among these were the rehabilitation of Israel as the spiritual homeland of the Jewish people, organic or more tightly bonded Jewish communities, better knowledge of Hebrew, and a revitalization of Jewish Sabbath and festival observance.[76] Of course, what he called for was precisely what was increasingly missing from the life of Jewish-Americans and even those in the middle. Toward the end of his life, the prophet of a new American Jewish civilization in the Diaspora had moved to Israel.

What happened to the middle? As the fifties gave way to the sixties, the number of these Jews of the middle level began to erode. The ethnicity they exuded, the Jewish practices they maintained mostly out of custom and historical convention, came to be associated with an older generation out of tune with emerging American Jewish models. In the polarizing atmosphere of the sixties and seventies, a world where one either took Jewish life and Judaism more seriously and actively engaged it or where one let meaningless rituals and old traditions fade, the middle level was hard to justify or sustain, nor was it always a comfortable place. Among the religious elites, those most active Jewishly, whose identity was wrapped up in being a Jew, to be Jewish required more than before—style was not enough—and so these elites looked on the people in the middle with contempt. On the other hand, among the large masses of Jews, Jewish identity demanded less—kosher was trivial. They looked at those who even tried to maintain a kosher style as senselessly trapped in old fashions and meaningless customs. With few who seemed to find meaning in their way of life, fewer and fewer Jews found the middle level attractive or meaningful. Moreover, the next generation, coming of age in the sixties and seventies and uncomfortable with a middle level, was pulling them with centrifugal force. Most of the parents were propelled outward toward less Jewish engagement, although a few were tugged by their Jewishly active children toward greater involvement.

One might thus understand the shrinkage of the middle as well as its hollowing out as the result of a combination of forces. These include a reinvigorated, more confident Orthodoxy that had demonstrated its capacity to be part of and survive in America (although in steadily diminishing numbers, as we shall see), that even after the tremendous losses of the Holocaust "reasserted its claim of being *the* authentic interpretation of Judaism" from the sixties onward.[77] This assertive Orthodoxy, which required greater activity than the middle allowed and which demonstrated that strictly kosher was quite possible in America, implicitly diminished the legitimacy and appeal of kosher-style. Accordingly, those in the middle could no longer claim to themselves, their children, or the rest of Jewry that what they were holding onto in their Jewish life was the maximum possible or more than enough. On the other hand, the liberal movements showed that minimal Judaism and a positive regard for Jewish heritage were quite sufficient for those not at home with Orthodoxy because they allowed people to call themselves Jewish without tying them up with details and outmoded traditions. An ideological justification of the moderate path was being eroded.

Add to this the fact that Conservative Judaism was itself torn between those within it who felt that its ideological essence was to allow for development and change, to be unorthodox, and those who felt that it should be slow to change, conservative in the most basic sense. The former often came from the laity, while the latter governed life at the seminary. This division resulted in a denomination that by the sixties and seventies, according to one insider's comic description, "had an Orthodox seminary that turned out Conservative rabbis who would have to minister to Reform Jews."

Still another drain on the middle was the cultural reality of the sixties and early seventies: the center was not a place to be in an American era that shunned moderation as a style of life. Led by the student extremism of the baby boomers, who shaped so much of the life in the period, and fueled by the protests—first for civil rights and later against the Vietnam War and nuclear weapons—Jews, who were prominent in these protest movements, found themselves embracing a way of life that was not at home with this middle-level style.

In this atmosphere, people were either for or against but not in the middle. Jews reflected this trend toward polarization in their own domains as well. Nowhere was this more true than among the young, who, as earlier noted, in great measure set the tone of the times. Some became more secular, leaving behind Jewish concerns as they increasingly involved themselves in American causes and life. Others, responding to the 1967 and 1973 wars in Israel as well as the emerging effort for the liberation of Soviet Jewry (a movement spearheaded by the young, who in 1964 organized the Student Struggle for Soviet Jewry), became more Jewish as they turned their student activism in the direction of their Judaism.

These were times that made much of the right and responsibility to choose how to act and among whom to be counted. Included in that choice was whether or not, as well as how, to be a Jew. "And that choice," as Calvin Goldscheider has put it, "has tended to become an either/or choice—with a range within both extremes and with fewer options available to remain within the middle." [78]

Accordingly, by 1975 it was clear to many observers that as the middle continued to shift overwhelmingly toward less Jewish commitment, with a minority going the other way, the story of the Jews in America during the years that would follow would become more and more an account of only two types: those Jews for whom a passive, minimalist Jewish-American heritage that was symbolic or latent was enough and those for whom being distinctively Jewish was an engaging, salient, and active component of who and what they were. To be more accurate, those I am calling Jewish-American heritage Jews were those who at best were ambivalent about their Jewish identity and involvements and at worst remained essentially ignorant of, although unwilling to deny, them.

There was of course a third group: those who completely assimilated into America, once and for always giving up their Jewish heritage. They include those who were born Jews but no longer identify themselves as such, a group that numbered over a million by the end of the 1980s. [79] Some may have converted, yet most simply stopped being Jewish or grew into something else. They are also those who chose to no longer live as Jews when they married non-Jews who did not convert. [80] While their numbers began to grow in these decades, their story has for the most part moved out of the orbit of Jewish life in America and need no longer be chronicled here. Although counted by some as part of Jewry in America, they were by their actions counting themselves out.

The paths of the remaining two groups who chose to stay Jews, who *do* concern us, have crossed and diverged a number of times. Many seem definitively to have left the active domains of Jewish life: "I was bar-mitzvahed, but don't ask me what I did because I hardly remember it any more; of course I'm proud to be a Jew, but let's not make too much of it." Others have begun from little more than a vague sense of Jewish heritage and moved to an intensive engagement with Jewish life, particularism, education, religion, and identity. The sixties and seventies, as we shall see, were decades when this movement became an important and visible part of the Jewish experience in America. Not only would the act of choosing to be Jewish become more crucial, particularly for those who were freed from the old tribal ties of ascription, but as several observers suggested already in the midseventies, these "choices in the future are likely to be less ambivalent, less ambiguous, and more decisively at one or the other end of the continuum." [81]

The middle did not disappear completely, but it lost its patina of permanence and solidity. Instead, it seemed far more unstable, a transitional channel through which Jews passed from one end to the other of the Jewish spectrum rather than a cultural resting place. There was movement toward the active pole because American Jews at times became very caught up, for example, in matters pertaining to Israel or the memorialization of the Holocaust, to name two outstanding vehicles for emphasizing Jewish identity in the last forty years. Others flirted with tradition, sometimes as part of the Ba'al T'shuvah movement, which marked a return to observance by numbers of former student radicals especially after 1967, or through supporting some outreach work by organizations like the Lubavitcher Hasidim. Still others came to an active Jewish identity through political action, on behalf of either Israel or Soviet Jewry.

It is worth noting that these polarizing trends among Jews were in some measure probably a reflection of a religious pattern taking place in America as a whole. Just as the rise in Jewish affiliation with synagogues in the fifties mirrored a similar increase among Christian Americans, so now this emptying out of the middle in the sixties and seventies reflected what the National Opinion Research Council (NORC) general social surveys of 1975–76 discovered: the most common religious switch that Americans made was not from one denomination to another but to having "no religion." Moreover, of all groups, the young adults were the ones most prominently switching out of religion.[82] As for those who chose the other extreme, there was a tendency, which would become even clearer by the eighties, to move toward a greater engagement with religion, particularly with its fundamentalist variety.[83]

There is another way to understand what became of the middle. Given the erosion of so much American Jewish life, what was once a kind of middle-level attachment increasingly seemed more at home on the margins of the right. Put differently, one might argue that when the Jewish path turned ever increasingly toward the left, toward minimalist attachments to heritage, those who still maintained some (although far from all) commitments to Jewish practices, distinctive ethnicity, and active identity and who thought this kept them in the middle of the road discovered that even this moderate way of Jewish life required greater effort and devotion and put them nearer the right side of the road. In a less identifiably Jewish America, any and all Jewish commitments were increasingly freighted with more symbolic and ideological meaning. The middle-level Conservative Jew of the thirties, forties, or fifties seemed like the far more religious grandparent in the seventies, eighties, and nineties. In a paradoxical way, what was less in those earlier decades was more in the later ones.

Jews and Education

Perhaps the contrasts between the two types of Jews and the reality of the weakening middle were most visible in educational aspirations and patterns. Among the "heritage Jews," for example, Jewish education became an increasingly peripheral enterprise.[84] Although the 1970–71 NJPS revealed that by the end of the sixties over 80 percent of American Jewish males and about 70 percent of American Jewish females had received some form of Jewish education, these numbers were inflated by the Jewish educational experience of the elders, who grew up at a time when some form of Jewish education was an expected feature of life in the Jewish ghetto. Among those between the ages of five and twenty-four (i.e., those born after the Second World War), however, only between 40 and 60 percent were getting a Jewish education. And the education they were getting was increasingly a watered-down version of what had been available in earlier years. "In 1946, 62.7% of students enrolled in supplementary schools attended five days per week; in 1958, 66% of the students attended three days and only 6% attended five days. By 1970 there were almost no five-day-a-week supplementary schools left."[85] Already in 1962 slightly over half the 589,000 students attending Jewish religious schools were in schools that met only one day a week, an increase over the proportion of those in the fifties getting such minimal education. Furthermore, only 3 to 4 percent of those in afternoon schools stayed on to graduate.[86] Jewish enrollment in Jewish education by 1966 was estimated at "549,000 or only slightly more than one-third of Jewish school age children in the United States at the time."[87] The proportions would hover around this figure for the remainder of the century. The fact was undeniable that for most American Jews, the decade of the sixties and even more so the years ahead marked a fading in the intensity of Jewish education, with "Hebrew school giving way to one-day-a-week schools," and one-day schools giving way to nothing.[88]

Although sociologist Bernard Lazerwitz could report in 1969 that "Jews of all identity levels but the lowest share an interest in the Jewish education of their children," the fact was that from the sixties onward the interest was overwhelmingly symbolic, as those with the lowest Jewish identity levels grew exponentially.[89] Jewish education for the most part remained restricted to the elementary level, dropping off "precipitously in the post bar/bat mitzvah grades."[90] By the end of the seventies, the data indicate "the proportion of all Jewish youth receiving any Jewish education drops from 69 percent of those in grades five to seven (the bar and bat mitzvah age) to 35 percent of those in grades eight to ten. It falls to 12 percent of those in grades 11–12."[91]

As for the products of this education, by 1969, Walter Ackerman, professor of Jewish education, could conclude persuasively that students were coming out of the supplementary schools knowing virtually nothing the schools claimed to be teaching.[92] And in the seventies, additional research demonstrated that only a very few of the students who went to these schools spent enough time in them to come away with significantly more knowledge than those who did not have any Jewish education at all.[93] More and more for this type of

Jew, "Hebrew school," as Leonard Fein has put it, became "mainly remembered as the place where Hebrew wasn't learned." [94]

Besides the obvious consequence of Jewish illiteracy and ignorance, there was another ominous implication in this Jewish educational erosion: "extensive and intensive Jewish education is generally correlated with Jewish endogamy." [95] More precisely, "a comparison of those with more than six years of Jewish education and those with less or none at all confirms that Jewish education is clearly associated with higher rates of inmarriage and lower rates of mixed marriage." [96] In fact, low levels of Jewish education correlated highly not only with outmarriage but also with movement from higher levels of Jewish activity to lower ones.

Yet while the Jewish education attained by the majority of American Jews was becoming diminished, actively Jewish Jews were building up and enhancing Jewish education. These were the Jews who had in the previous decade helped foster an increase of 131 percent in the number of students enrolled in Jewish education. [97] They were among those who, for example, in January of 1960, "pleaded for American Jews to raise more funds to meet the growing need for full-time religious education," which would have taken their children out of the public schools and back into a separate world. [98] They saw in the separate day school, where Jews were educated only with other Jews and where all learning (secular and religious alike) was accomplished in a Jewish context, a chance not only to enhance Jewish education but also to guarantee the separate solidarity of Jews— to "preserve a people" and "to make learning a vehicle for Jewish action," as Rabbi Joseph Lookstein, an Orthodox proponent of this system, put it. [99] By 1960 there were about 160 Jewish day schools (almost all Orthodox), with an enrollment of 48,000 and an annual budget of $35 million. In 1961, Torah U'Mesorah, an organization for Orthodox Jewish education, counted 278 day schools affiliated with it. That same year, the Conservative movement founded the first of what would be a growing network of Solomon Schechter Day Schools. In later decades even the Reform movement would open some day schools. In 1962, over 50,000 youngsters were enrolled in Jewish day schools; 8.5 percent of the Jews were receiving a Jewish education. By 1966, that number had mushroomed to 14 percent, and the World Council of Jewish Education had launched a program to establish one thousand day schools. As the Jewish education of the Jewish-Americans was fading, the education among these more active Jews was growing more distinctive and intensive.

This day school education was, however, not simply a version of the old-style yeshiva or *cheder* so ubiquitous in the Old World ghettoes. On the contrary, it often stressed the capacity of its students to marry Jewish particularism with civil belongingness, a marriage made possible by the American nominal and growing tolerance for pluralism. Even many of the Orthodox—so much identified with ghetto conditions in the past—picked up this theme. Thus, for example, many of their schools emphasized their ancillary (but increasingly important) goal of offering a high-quality education in what were often called "general studies." This allowed them "to educate . . . students in the two civilizations of which they are a part . . . the world of Torah, mitzvot, the Jewish people and its culture, Zionism and the State of Israel . . . , and with equal emphasis, . . . the disciplines and finest values of western civilization and the American democratic heritage."[100] Although these words come from the mission statement of an Orthodox day school, they probably articulate fairly closely the ethos of all day schools, regardless of denomination. The aim was to enable their students to succeed as active and committed Jews even as they immersed themselves in all that contemporary America promised.

To be sure, intensive Jewish education at the day school or yeshiva remained limited to a minority. Even among those who were actively Jewish, the most common form of Jewish education in America still remained the afternoon supplementary school, 92 percent of which were under congregational auspices.[101] The polarized Jewish education system, however, with most students in supplementary education that offered less and less and a small minority in day schools and yeshivas, paralleled the polarization of American Jewish life.

Education also reflected the continuing trends of Americanization and the move of Jews into the meritocracy. This is best seen in the developments in the domain of secular education, particularly at the university level, and in the allied data on professionalization. Throughout the sixties and into the next decade, enrollment of both types of Jews in American universities was up. Sociologist Chaim Waxman reported that already in the sixties, "89 percent of the native-born Jews surveyed had significantly exceeded their fathers' level of education . . . , far greater among native-born Jews than for any other group." [102] As already noted, by the end of the decade three-quarters of American Jews of college age were attending universities. In the years ahead the figure would rise to over 80 percent—but unlike that 80 percent of Jews who had received some Jewish education in their lives, this 80 percent would be exceeded in the years ahead while the other 80 percent was a peak that would not be reached again. When compared with the non-Jewish-American population, who had a significantly lower rate of college attendance of 34 percent, the figures are even more striking.

Jews were not only deeply involved as students, they were also playing an increasingly important role as university faculty. In 1969, "a survey conducted by the Carnegie Commission on Higher Education showed that those who admitted being Jewish comprised ten per cent of all university faculties in America." [103] By 1971, the figure jumped to 12 percent, while Jews made up over 20 percent of the faculty at elite colleges. [104] Indeed, although Jews remained a minority in American life, by the seventies no one thought of them as a minority in the university community; if anything, they were in danger of being perceived as the university establishment.

To be sure, American Jews had taken advantage of college in previous decades; already in the twenties, "New York's City College and Hunter College, both free schools, were estimated to have Jewish enrollments amounting to 80–90% of the whole student body." [105] Nor was this sort of education seen as conflicting with Jewish learning. Thus, in the fifties much was being made about a proposal to begin "selecting gifted young persons in high school who . . . manifested a real interest in Jewish problems and have acquired some background in Jewish culture" and seeing to it that they got a college education. [106]

In the sixties, however, as the first offspring of the postwar generation began to attend, the college experience of American Jews broadened significantly. No longer limited to the New York City colleges or to places like Yeshiva College, they went to the elite private as well as the large state universities, where they mingled with and sought to be absorbed in and by orientations that headed them toward a world increasingly removed from the Jewish orbit. Although administrators of these universities would no longer make statements like the one made by the president of Dartmouth, Ernest Hopkins, in 1945 that "Dartmouth is a Christian college founded for the Christianization of its students," the fact remained that in spite of the growing Jewish presence in them, these schools were still predominantly made up of a non-Jewish population and were not environments in which Jewish identity would flourish, at least not until the midseventies, when the Jewish studies explosion occurred (about which more will be said later).[107]

Many American Jews did not at first perceive that placing their young in an environment where Jewish identity would not flourish—or at the very least where it was overshadowed by campus life—might be a problem. Certainly most of the students themselves did not care. Hillel, the B'nai B'rith–sponsored Jewish student organization, never served more than a minority of the Jews on campus, even in its heyday in the early sixties. And even the so-called Jewish fraternities like Sigma Alpha Mu (probably the largest of them) were Jewish in membership but hardly so in the content of their activities and concerns. When not involved in the student activism so much a part of sixties life, Jews on campus concentrated on the opportunities that the university offered and the pathways to which it led in the world beyond.

Throughout the decade and into the seventies, college-educated Jews applied and got into professional schools of their choosing—law, medicine, business, and other graduate degrees—in numbers far beyond their proportion of the population. By the beginning of the seventies, in proportion to their numbers, about four and a half times as many Jews as non-Jews were going into medicine, dentistry, and health-related professions, while five times as many were going into the law. Overall, proportionately nearly three times as many Jews as non-Jews were going into all professions.[108] This was a change from the situation in 1950, when the *American Jewish Yearbook* reported that "Jewish students have had to apply to 10 times as many medical schools as white Protestants to get admitted." [109] Moreover, 31 percent were going into fields allied with the social sciences, over half of these into social work. No more would American Jews be predominantly merchants or union workers. And of course, a significant number were staying in the university world as professors.

This was an important change. Whereas their parents had been in the trade unions in the previous decades (in 1950, 30 percent of

the International Ladies' Garment Workers' Union still were Jews),
or they had made their way into sales, clerical work, or even middle-
management positions, these educated young Jews coming of age in
the sixties headed elsewhere.[110] Already large numbers of their older
siblings had had some success in this regard. By 1960, "some 25%
of employed Jews were in professional or semi-professional occupations," and the rate was even higher for the younger among them—
compared to slightly less than 14 percent for the rest of America.[111]
This process of training and professionalization which promised upward mobility also wrought significant cultural transformation.

As sociologist Everett Hughes has explained, the extensive training necessary for professionalization "carries with it as a by-product
assimilation of the candidate to a set of professional attitudes and
controls, a professional conscience and solidarity." [112] In general, he
concluded, "we may say that the longer and more rigorous the period
of initiation into an occupation, the more culture and technique are
associated with it, and the more deeply impressed are its attitudes
upon the person." [113] The more time Jews spent in the university or
in training for a career that was anchored in the American, rather
than the Jewish, domain, the further they moved from a core concern with their Jewishness. In short, as Hughes noted, for those involved in such professionalization, "the profession claims and aims
to become a moral unit." [114] To this Steven M. Cohen adds that "certain professions—particularly law, medicine, and college teaching—
can become a way of life and thus successfully compete with ethnicity as a basis for self-definition. As a result, individuals in these
professions may feel less of a need to link themselves to the Jewish
community." [115] For many American Jews, becoming good at their
professions, a lifelong ambition and pursuit, became at least as, if
not more, important than becoming a good Jew. Or, to put it differently, American professionalization was diametrically opposed to
Jewish tribalism.

On the surface, the pursuit of learning was not out of keeping
with established Jewish character; Jews certainly had a distinguished
history of scholarship and were comfortable with the idea of long
years in school. But this time it was different. No longer were they
spending this long period of training in a yeshiva meditating on the
Torah (as they might have in another place and time); now they were

thinking about other wisdom in the secular and open atmosphere of the liberal arts university. To be sure, they could have concentrated on Jewish studies, which were increasingly available at the university (unlike the case in the early postwar period), but most American Jews were not going to college to study Judaica.[116]

Jews and the Counterculture

By the close of the sixties, extended university education became for many young people not only a means of gaining professional training or a vehicle for getting a good job but an end in itself. The need to maintain student deferments from the universal military draft and to protest against the war in Vietnam sometimes served as an instrumental stimulus for this sort of prolonged learning, but the fact was that from about 1965, Jews had become enraptured with the university experience. Getting into a good college, and later a graduate or professional school, had become the single most important theme of Jewish adolescence and young adulthood.

Student status, however, often had unintended consequences. For one, it extended the "becoming stage" of life, leading to a kind of protracted narcissism and immaturity when students' only responsibilities seemed to be to enhance their personal growth. The question became: student status, terminable or interminable? Because Jews perhaps more than any other group sent their children to the university, they faced this question more insistently than anyone else.

For their Jewish parents, for whom the pressures of "making it" had been so important and who wanted to show how well they were able to provide for their children (as opposed to *their* Depression era or immigrant parents) and who hoped their children would acquire more education than they had and reach even greater heights, this kind of freedom not to have to enter the workforce at as early an age or as low a station seemed at first a blessing. Spending years amassing university degrees was something the parents initially tolerated and even encouraged.

This tolerance, however, was tested severely during the late sixties and much of the seventies when the young Jews in college ironically shunned their parents' life-styles and values, expressing greater solidarity with the student culture and generation than with their families, ethnic group, or established religion. Furthermore, in the context of the growing anarchy of 1960s and early 1970s America, generational differences seemed exacerbated. People spoke increasingly of the so-called generation gap as these students often defined the world outside their own as filled with people they perceived to be hopelessly misguided at best and adversaries at worst. Along with others of their university generation, they scorned the establishment, which they saw as belonging to another place and time. "Don't trust anyone over thirty" was a line that gained currency and expressed these feelings in these decades. This was particularly the case for the Jews, who, as noted above, in proportion to their numbers were spending far more time in school than most others and whose liberal political traditions made them feel at home with protest. Indeed, many young Jews were influential in sixties student culture, often taking leading roles in political student movements and in protests. Singers such as Bob Dylan (born "Zimmerman") and Phil Ochs, whose lyrics gave expression to these changing times, movements, and cultures, and leading protesters, such as Abbie Hoffman and Jerry Rubin, were—not surprisingly—young Jews.

While the involvement with student culture, personal development, and activism was something both types of Jews embraced, by the end of the decade it would become clear that the expressive form this involvement and activism took reflected the two Jewish identities. For the minimalist American Jews, activism and involvement came in the context of diminishing parochialism and increasingly American aspirations. In their schools, which during the sixties stressed the universality of man, most young American Jews felt no need to dwell upon Jewish problems. Rather, just as they had "abandoned Jewish concerns in search of careers in the larger society," now they did so "in the service of universal causes." [117] In short, they became *American* activists.

Although not tribalist in character, this sort of activism was not necessarily considered anti-Jewish. Many Jews who embraced this kind of activity on behalf of civil rights and later the peace movement or universal freedom argued that it was in tune with the best traditions of the Jewish-American liberal patrimony. [118] In 1961, when a new young liberal president, John Kennedy, announced that the "torch had been passed to a new generation" and urged America to think about "what together we can do about the freedom of man," young Jewish-Americans and many of their parents were especially receptive to these messages, as if the president spoke directly to them.[119]

During the sixties, initial actions on behalf of universal freedom were taken in the area of black civil rights. Although the *Brown v. Board of Education of Topeka* Supreme Court decision in 1954 striking down the separate-but-equal doctrine of public education was probably the first important postwar change in the struggle for black civil rights in America (along with President Truman's desegregation of the armed forces), the decade of the sixties was without question the period of most-accelerated civil rights activity. In February of 1960, American blacks, having seen the new start America had given its white citizens in the previous decade of plenty, asserted their right to share in this opportunity with sit-ins at segregated restaurants in Greensboro, North Carolina, and later on in other public establishments in the South. Subsequently, they moved on to boycotts of segregated buses, voter registration drives, and marches in order to gain their opportunities at the ballot box. These first nonviolent civil rights activities captured the conscience of white liberal America— and perhaps of no group more than the Jewish-Americans, who saw in the black quest for full equality an echo of the Jewish effort to be fully included in America. Recognizing that as a minority, their position was dependent upon how the society at large treated all minorities, many of these Jews (especially the college students) jumped into the civil rights movement, first helping to register voters in the South, later joining the protest marches, and finally even sharing in the martyrdom that accompanied these activities.

Concern for civil rights was not a new interest for Jews. Between 1930 and 1966, the National Association for the Advancement of Colored People had two Jewish presidents: Joel Spingarn and Arthur Spingarn.[120] Jews had even had their own experiences with southern prejudice; in 1915, the only Jew ever lynched in America, Leo Frank, was hanged in Georgia. Throughout the middle sixties, the active involvement of Jews in the black struggle for equality and advancement was striking. Nearly half the white civil rights attorneys in the South during the decade were Jews, more than half the white freedom riders were Jews, and "nearly two-thirds of the white volunteers involved in the Freedom Summer in Mississippi in 1964 were Jews," and two of them (Andrew Goodman and Michael Schwerner) were murdered.[121] The sit-ins, freedom rides, and voter registration drives became a passion of Jewish-Americans in the first years of civil rights activity. Jews gave generously to help fund the activities of the NAACP, the Congress of Racial Equality (CORE), the Southern Christian Leadership Conference (SCLC), and other civil rights organizations.[122] Except for the African-Americans themselves, it would be hard to find another ethnic group that so embraced the cause of civil rights.

However, their patrimony notwithstanding, it would be mistaken to say that for these Jewish-Americans, the civil rights struggle was perceived as a predominantly Jewish concern. In spite of the fact that many prominent rabbis participated in the civil rights efforts as an expression of their Judaism and often inserted matters of black civil rights into their synagogue sermons, for most Jewish-Americans involvement with the black struggle was viewed as part of their American experience, albeit nurtured by their Jewish heritage and their recognition of their minority status.

Later, when in the summer of 1964 riots broke out in New York's Harlem and Brooklyn as well as in Philadelphia, and the civil rights struggle moved to the North, Jews were increasingly painted as enemies rather than allies. By 1965, the major riot in the Watts neighborhood of Los Angeles dispelled some of the romance of the civil rights era for liberals and Jews. Jews were expelled from leadership positions in the civil rights movement. That year "for the first time in its sixty-year history, the *American Jewish Year Book* replaced its discussion of anti-Semitism in its lead articles with a section titled 'Civil Rights and Intergroup Tensions.'"[123] American blacks did not necessarily share the Jewish sense of their common destiny in the face of the American majority. On the contrary, in spite of the Jewish liberals who marched in Selma, Alabama, and elsewhere, African-Americans increasingly resisted seeing Jews as anything but part of the white American oppressive majority. As for the past Jewish involvement in the civil rights struggle, to many blacks the Jewish tendency to identify with the liberal, rather than the conservative, camp was largely explained as being motivated by self-interest.[124]

In many of the inner cities of the North, the areas of second settlement, where the civil rights crusades now focused their attention,

Jews and blacks confronted one another not as allies in a struggle but rather as uncomfortable neighbors.[125] By the late sixties more often than not, particularly in cities like Boston, Detroit, New York, and Newark that exploded in riots, Jews found themselves landlords in distressed neighborhoods where blacks were tenants, or shopkeepers where blacks were among the rioting customers. Or else, Jews, who were fleeing to the suburban frontier, were the ones selling their homes to blacks. Thus to many blacks, Jews were the incarnation of American "haves" while the blacks were the American "have-nots."

Perhaps nowhere did this emerging black/Jewish enmity become more concentrated and vivid than in the often acrimonious debate about community control of public education in the Ocean-Hill/ Brownsville district of New York City, where Jews (who were by now a plurality of the teachers) and African-Americans (from among whom most of the students and parents came) bitterly confronted each other. After this early dramatic competition came other more nuanced and hostile political contests. By the 1970s, the two groups, increasingly embittered, were often on opposite sides of certain affirmative action issues, particularly with respect to positions in the university world and the professions. Finally, perhaps the low point was reached when "in the 1980s, the nation's most prominent black leader, Jesse Jackson, appeared to most Jews to be anti-Semitic and to endorse positions hostile to Israel," while Louis Farrakkhan, a Black Muslim leader, found increasingly receptive African-American audiences for his comment that Judaism was a "gutter religion."[126]

Long before this, many of the liberal Jewish-Americans had shifted their activism from the civil rights struggles, where a string of legislative victories had been won, to a concern with the Vietnam War. This would be an arena of active political struggle in which Jews would play a prominent role as well. Yet many of these Jews did so by loosening their ties to their Jewish identity even as they recognized the role their Jewish heritage played in making them what they were: "I personally feel very torn about being Jewish," said Jerry Rubin, one of the most radical of young Jews in the sixties. "I know it made me feel like a minority or outsider in Amerika from my birth and helped me become a revolutionary. . . . But despite this . . . Judaism no longer means much to us."[127]

Young, Active, and Jewish and Ethnic

If one were to look only at the majority of American Jews and especially at the trends among the young, one might come away from
a survey of the sixties and seventies with a sense that the future of
American Jewry was genuinely in jeopardy. Indeed, that is the overwhelming impression when we examine the eighties and the start
of the nineties. Nevertheless, there were some signs of promise for
the American Jewish future, and they came precisely from that segment of Jewry that in most other respects seemed the source of
greatest concern: the same young people with advanced secular education, many of whom identified with the ethos of the sixties and
its counterculture. Some of these, however, came out of the decade,
not as American, but rather as *Jewish* activists. For the maximal-
ists, the actively Jewish Jews, the ethos of the counterculture would
be transformed into a scheme to counter the established culture of
assimilation, acculturation, and Jewish decline with something far
more patently and positively Jewish.

One segment of these Jewish activists still focused their attentions
on American issues, but they did so in a distinctively Jewish way.
Beyond simply nodding to their Jewish heritage of liberalism, they
used their Judaism as a medium through which their involvement in
American causes and the counterculture flowed. Not only did rabbis
and their congregants of all denominations, for example, choose as
Jews to march with Martin Luther King and to join in the mourning over his death, but also yeshivas, seminaries, and *havurot* (Jewish religious fellowships) provided a haven for those who wished to
avoid the Vietnam War draft.[128] Some synagogues became places of
sanctuary for draft resisters, and rabbinical students carried out anti-
war protests. In the struggle for the rights of farm workers to orga-
nize and improve the conditions of their labor, some Orthodox rabbis decreed grapes picked by nonunion workers to be nonkosher. It
has even been argued that activism on behalf of and "the overwhelming importance of Israel in American Jewish life during the 1970's
and 1980's was built partly on the confidence and political realism
gained through anti-discrimination and civil rights campaigns in the
immediately preceding decades." [129]

The other segment of Jewish activists, and in many ways the

far more historically important one for the Jews, turned, especially after 1967, toward Jewish matters rather than American or universal themes.[130] Expressing these sentiments, Richard J. Israel, a Hillel rabbi, declared: "I am no longer sure that it makes sense to sink as much into the American dream as we always have. We have some parochial Jewish needs that have to be taken into consideration as well, and not as low priority items."[131] It was noteworthy that some Jews, including those who were young and educated, were choosing to turn their attention to Jewish matters in spite of a rising intermarriage rate and the diminished involvement of most American Jews in Jewish life. While the overall trends continued in the direction of the division of American Jewry into active, maximalist and passive, minimalist elements, with most choosing the latter path, the focus of Jewish community attention moved toward the former group, who embraced and were embraced by a reinvigorated Jewish identity and involvement. To see young people going against the outward flow, to watch them move back toward Jewish life and culture, inspired optimism in some of those who had become concerned about the Jewish future in America. Although—like others of their generation—they embraced political activism and the desire for personal growth, they did not want this to be at the expense of their Judaism. In pursuit of their Jewish concerns, they often used many of the techniques and spoke in the terms that had become part of the sixties agenda. This meant using the rhetoric of protest and antiestablishmentarianism as well as emphasizing the importance of personal growth and continued learning. Like their Jewish-American counterparts involved in non-Jewish movements, they agreed that "the only important thing is how to revolutionize the establishment," and they were ready to "start from scratch."[132]

Many of these people found their voices in "an autonomous Jewish student movement" consisting "of loosely connected and independent Jewish student groups organized around such issues as support for Israel, Soviet Jewry, Jewish studies, and diverse protests against organized Jewry."[133] They saw a chance to galvanize and change the direction of Jewish life in America away from established patterns just as their less particularist counterparts were trying to do with American society in general. Thus, while some American Jews became caught up in liberal causes in American life, a young cadre

of actively Jewish Jews began to militate for more attention and resources for Jewish cultural life. They saw in America a diminished
Judaism that, "once it is denuded of [its] liberal values, is a silly
racism and unimportant socializing [that looks] for the Jewish names
in airplane crashes and the Jewish country club." [134]

Many of these new Jewish leaders evinced "a renewed interest
in the recovery of traditional Jewish religious customs and teach-
ings." [135] In 1966 college students could claim embarrassment at being
Jewish, but by the summer of 1971, the theme of the World Union of
Jewish Students meeting near Philadelphia was "Creative Jewing."
These students were able to reject "the prevailing Jewish life style
without rejecting Judaism and Jewish culture." [136]

To be sure, the Jewish establishment did not just give up its control to the young activists; many in it were turned off by the revolutionary and often confrontational sixties style of this new generation.
Yet the sincerity and commitment of the activists were often enough
to offset these matters of style.

Not only did they engage in political activism, they also looked
to enhance their spiritual and religious lives. Thus, in 1967, some
began what would be called the Havurah movement, which focused
on making a fellowship of Jewish learning and observance part of
the postcollege experience. First in Boston and New York and later
on in a variety of communities, *havurot* were established to enhance
Jewish education and spirituality for those who felt their elementary school Jewish education had failed them and who, after college,
wanted something more. They also emphasized the intimacy of a
Jewish community and reignited feelings of Jewish communal life.
Indeed, the idea of drawing upon Jewish sources within a tightly
knit community of Jews was perhaps the lasting contribution of the
havurot, whose design was by the end of the seventies absorbed
as a congregational activity by larger congregations who wanted to
arouse these same feelings among a membership that seemed to have
lost a sense of connectedness to one another and Jewish traditions.
Others turned their attention to the Hillel organizations on campus
and tried to revitalize them in dramatic ways. Rabbinical seminaries
reported an increase in the number and quality of applicants.

These actively Jewish Jews also focused on enhancing mainstream Jewish education, which many university students (who had

adopted the ethos of education) were convinced Hebrew school had failed to provide. In March 1969 some of these young Jewish student activists took over a Hillel national conference, urging that Jews "ban the country clubs" and instead "put money into Jewish education"—this at a time when researchers were reporting that "Jewish education has remained a peripheral enterprise for most American Jews."[137] In mid-November of that same year, another group of students forced themselves onto the agenda of a Council of Jewish Federations and Welfare Funds conference in Boston and "delivered an appeal for increased monies for Jewish education, a field that received less than 15 percent of federation funds in 1967."[138] They demanded increased Jewish subsidies for Jewish day schools and afternoon Hebrew schools that attempted to introduce meaningful innovations in their teaching and research to examine and improve what they viewed as the "wretched" state of those Hebrew and religious schools and to develop new curricula and teaching methods. They also asked for subsidies to raise the salary levels of teachers in such schools and to upgrade Hebrew teachers' colleges. One of their spokesmen "also made a plea for greater support for Jewish campus life and experimental communities that focussed on spiritual experiences," something that gave purpose to the personal growth that so many people in the sixties thought to be vital.[139] They exhorted the Jewish community to endow chairs in and departments of Jewish studies at universities along with academic scholarships that would encourage Jewish students to pursue these fields. And of course, they asked for greater support for the Hillel foundations to support the needs of Jewish students in an environment that they recognized took a heavy toll on Jewish identity and belonging. These were Jews who had come out of the decade and the university with the gnawing feeling that, as one of them put it, Judaism was being made superfluous; and they wanted to do something about it.[140]

They did. Jewish studies became a presence on the campus. In 1966, there were seventy such programs, a sevenfold increase in twenty years.[141] The number would grow in the seventies, even as the number of those who turned away from Jewish studies grew even more.

In a sense these demands by the Jewish activists revealed one of the paradoxes of the times. The vast majority of American Jews wanted less in the way of Jewish content in their lives. But those few who wanted more wanted *much* more, a richer Jewish life than had ever been part of American history.

Although these actively Jewish Jews were a relative few, their impact would ultimately be felt widely. This was simply because the Jewish establishment was far less imposing than the American one, and the opportunities for successful change and an ensuing Jewish renaissance in America stimulated by these young revolutionary activists were greater. As many American Jews abandoned the parochial domains and others were eased out by age and rival commitments, the young activists found themselves the new heirs of the American Jewish establishment. To a degree, these were the Jews who had answered the 1959 call of Mordecai Kaplan for a revitalization of Jewish life in America by stressing these religious, educational, and communal initiatives. Indeed, the Reconstructionist Rabbinical College, a legacy of Kaplan's ideas, would in the next decades be led by Arthur Green, a founder of the Havurah movement. Many of the revolutionaries of the sixties and seventies became the executives and heads of the American Jewish community in the eighties and nineties.

Jewish Feminism

If college students were the vanguard of Jewish activism and the Jewish counterculture during the late sixties and early seventies, young Jewish women evolved a key role as well, especially in defining their own special contributions to an active Jewish life. Emerging as well out of the campuses, Jewish feminism at first was simply a correlate to general Jewish activism. In 1971 a group of young women affiliated with the New York Havurah dubbed themselves Ezrat Nashim. The double entendre in their name (literally it means "help for women," but the phrase also refers to the area in the temple reserved for women) seemed to capture the double goals of the group: a self-help consciousness-raising group for and of women which would also enhance Jewish life. Ostensibly organized as a study group seeking to explore the status of women in Jewish law, Ezrat Nashim was made up of women in their twenties who had benefited from a relatively strong Jewish education during the fifties and sixties. Like their male colleagues in the Jewish counterculture, they distrusted the Jewish establishment. In response, they sought to repair it and to infuse it and American Jewish life with a meaningful new character. If their mothers had been satisfied with a subordinate role in Jewish life (or none whatsoever), particularly in the synagogue, where much of it was publicly expressed, these women wanted more. Coming mostly from the middle level of Jewish life and overwhelmingly tracing their roots to Conservative Judaism, they concentrated many of their energies and early efforts on non-Orthodox Judaism.

Already in 1955, Conservative Jews had begun to give women a larger part in Jewish life when the Committee on Jewish Law and Standards endorsed women's right to have *aliyot* (calls to rise) to the Torah reading, which had been limited to men. In 1968, the Conservative movement introduced the prenuptial agreement to guarantee women a binding *get* (Jewish bill of divorce) so that they would be free to remarry within the faith following the dissolution of their marriage. Until then, women were captives of their ex-husbands' willingness to grant a *get*. During the seventies, women wanted more.

At first Jewish feminists sought simply to extirpate sexist language from Jewish liturgy, lobbying the 1972 Conservative Rabbinical Assembly Convention for a change in the English translation of the new prayer book (changes that were formalized only in 1994 by the Conservative Committee on Jewish Law and Standards). All this was part of a desire to bring about a community-wide rejection of what they considered outmoded sex roles and demeaning Jewish images of women. Throughout the seventies, changes came quickly. By February 1973 a national Jewish women's conference in New York attracted over 500 women who wanted to be actively Jewish. That same year, the Conservative movement Committee on Jewish Law and Standards voted 9 to 4 to count women officially as part of the minyan, which in fact a number of liberal Conservative congregations had already been doing for years. The feminists and their supporters believed their goals were not just directed at the situation of women. Rather, they believed that "by rejecting obsolete sex-roles, the Jewish community will be more attractive to young people," thereby increasing the number of those who were actively Jewish.[142] Many of these actively Jewish women were "committed to a Jewish community where men and women are inherently equal" and demanded (as they put it in their publication *Lilith's Rib*) "the full, direct and equal participation of women at all levels of Jewish life—communal, religious, educational and political." [143]

The Reform movement responded to feminist concerns even more quickly. Already in 1972, it had broken a historical barrier by ordaining the first female rabbi, Sally Priesand. More would follow and by the 1980s approximately half the graduates of the Hebrew Union College Jewish Institute of Religion would be women. The Reconstructionists followed suit.

Yet for all of their successes, active Jewish feminists remain a minority. They are part of the minority of those American Jews who choose to be actively Jewish. By the end of the eighties, although feminists could point to "women rabbis, women scholars, women communal leaders" as evidence that they had succeeded in encouraging many Jewish women to become active Jewishly, it was still the case that most Jewish women, like most Jewish men, were content to be passive in their Jewish involvement. [144]

The Impact of the American Environment

Ironically, however important Jewish sources were for the enhancement of an active Jewish identity, the American cultural environment was probably no less (and maybe even more) important. Jewish feminism certainly was born out of a synergy of Jewish and American cultural trends. On the one hand, it arose out of the circumambience of the *havurot* and Jewish activism. On the other, it originated from the same wellsprings as the sixties and seventies student counterculture and later the American women's movement. No doubt the fact that these women had been exposed to a Jewish education no less intensive than their male peers throughout the postwar period was important, but the implicit message of the American meritocratic order—that all was possible for those who understood and worked hard—also played a part in their rising feminist consciousness.

Similarly, what reinvigorated many dimensions of Jewish identity was the fact that, following on the heels of a renascent black consciousness, a celebration of ethnicity emerged at the end of the sixties as a response to the decline of the WASP establishment, which the revolutionary atmosphere of the decade had ensured. This was what Michael Novak, in a book of the same name, called "the rise of the unmeltable ethnics." [145] Ethnic distinctions were more than tolerated in America; they were becoming featured. "For better or worse," as Daniel Bell opined, "the very breakup of the cultural hegemony of the WASPs and the growth of ethnicity as a legitimate dimension of American-life have . . . 'forced' . . . [Jews] to maintain an identity, and to define themselves in ethnic terms." [146] This no doubt had an impact on some American Jews, who saw that they could now emphasize their Jewish heritage and identity and use that as a way of locating themselves in the American national spectrum. In his introduction to the 1972 update of his classic study *American Judaism,* Nathan Glazer noted as much when he argued that "for the great majority of American Jews, Judaism means an *ethnic* commitment more than a transcendent faith." [147] How deep or substantive that commitment would be, whether it would add to the ranks of the actively Jewish Jews or simply become a matter of background and largely symbolic heritage, was, however, a separate question.

While the coming decades would provide an answer, by the end of the seventies, after the crest of American ethnic consciousness, it was clear that the reemergence of a vigorous Jewish sentiment, although an important element in the revitalizing of American Jewry after the sixties, whether among women or among the baby-boomer counterculture, and so vital for the future of American Jewish life, did not lead to a mass renaissance of enhanced Jewish involvement and identity. On the contrary, the two strains in Jewish life continued on their increasingly divergent paths. The good news was that the actively Jewish Jews did not disappear; the bad news was that they remained an ever more obviously minority element in American Jewish life, which more and more became dominated by the minimalist element.

Charitable Giving

Perhaps nothing so directly showed the impact of these two trends and the demographic modesty of the actively Jewish Jews than Jewish charity. Since the collection of the half-shekel by Moses in Sinai, Jews had used fund collection as a means of being counted as part of the community. To give of one's own resources for the needs of the Jewish community (or the unfortunate in it) was to be identified as an active member. This was no less true in America. Here, however, the collections also had a collective as well as a personal significance. In America the continuing success of Jewish fund-raising drives— from the UJA to money for Israel or for needy Jews throughout the world—was meant to serve "as a means of impressing public opinion with the cohesion, vitality, and unity of American Jewry." [148] Jews were very public about how much they collected, often announcing financial goals and their success at meeting them, much in the way that other American charities (the United Fund, for example) did. By the end of the sixties, both Jews and non-Jews looked at the bottom line of the collections as some sort of indicator of how much the Jews in America cared about their community.

Perhaps no collection more clearly articulated this than that raised by the Council of Jewish Federations and Welfare Funds (CJFWF), which supported Jewish communal concerns and which, by the 1960s, many considered a kind of quasi income tax on Jews. The relationship was simple: the higher the dollar figure of monies raised by the federations, the greater the measure and the more powerful the impression of the American Jews' voluntary association.

To be sure, there was also room for displays of personal commitment and status. Unlike the rule at Sinai, not everyone donated the same amount: for at least five decades, 80 percent of the money has come from about 20 percent of the donors. These often became the leaders, or at least the voices that were most clearly heard, within the community. The big givers sat on the boards of the federations and other philanthropic or community organizations.

Notwithstanding this differential rate of giving, higher amounts collected over the years could be seen as a measure of the ascendance of active Jewishness and the salience of Jewish concerns. Reduced collections, on the other hand, signaled a diminished sense of Jewish communal belonging or concern. In short, a strong community always raised more money; a disappearing or weakening one gathered less.

The numbers make clear that during the years when Jewish-Americans whose connection was little more than a matter of heritage became the dominant element of Jewish life in the United States, CJFWF fund-raising began to decline. In 1960, although the economy was doing well, the Jews raised only $128 million, down from the nearly $131 million of the previous year, a drop of 1.5 percent.

The next year the collection diminished over twice as much: 3.5%, down to $124 million. And although the figure in 1962 was about the same, it does not reflect the effects of inflation. In fact, not until the Six Day War (1967) did the number of contributors and the level of giving rise dramatically (repeating the striking increase in 1946 in the aftermath of the Holocaust).[149] After 1967, charitable donations continued to fall, except for an isolated increase after the 1973 Yom Kippur War. As Steven Cohen notes: "The 1965 nationwide total [of federation giving] reached $131 million; in 1974, following the Yom Kippur War, that sum amounted to a record $660 million. In 1975, however, the total amount raised nationwide plummeted to $475 million; it has remained there ever since, even as inflation has eroded the purchasing power of the charitable dollar."[150]

In part, the decrease has been due to the change in the career profile of American Jewry in the years following the 1960s. Jews, increasingly the products of university training and professionalization, were no longer shopkeepers and businesspeople exclusively or even overwhelmingly, which had significant consequences for philanthropy. For people in business or even shopkeepers, charitable giving publicly "symbolizes success to their peers. As such, they make donations in part to enhance their social esteem. Moreover, when a business person is solicited by a customer, a gift's size can influence his or her commercial prospects."[151] Professionals (the fastest-growing type of Jewish-American career), however, did not draw their prestige and community esteem from the amount of charity they gave away. "Moreover, certain professions—particularly law, medicine, and college teaching—can become a way of life and thus successfully compete with ethnicity [or religion] as a basis for self-definition. As a result, individuals in these professions . . . feel less of a need to link themselves to the Jewish community through charitable giving."[152] The changing education and growing professionalization of Jews thus led to diminished giving.

Moreover, as these changes helped move people into mainstream America, many Jews saw themselves in less and less parochial terms so that when they did give to charity, they increasingly gave to general, rather than to Jewish, causes.[153] Rich Jews who had made it in America were more likely to give to a secular university (their new alma mater, to which the ties were now stronger than those to the tribe), a symphony orchestra, a museum, or even the cancer society or United Fund than to a parochial, Jewish charity. Indeed, those Jews among the superrich who did continue to give to the Jewish world stood out more and more for their rarity. In real terms, although Jews still gave more than many other groups to charitable causes, Jewish collections for Jewish causes were declining and would continue to do so throughout the years ahead, reflecting the decline in Jewish parochial identification. In fact, from the end of the sixties onward, "non-Jewish charities [were] experiencing an exponential growth in support from Jewish patrons." [154]

Although the data about Jewish charitable giving in the sixties do not allow for a comparison between the money given by those who were actively Jewish versus the more passive Jewish-Americans, lessons learned since then have shown unequivocally that the more active a Jew is, the more likely he or she is to give. As Steven Cohen has shown, involvement in Jewish activities became twice as important a predictor of Jewish charitable giving between 1965 and 1975. [155] Indeed, by the end of the seventies it was clear that Jewish philanthropic activity was "becoming increasingly confined to those Jews who regularly act out their Jewishness," resulting in effect in "growing numbers of less-involved Jews turn[ing] away from [Jewish] philanthropy." [156] And even among these so-called committed Jews, the fact that they had to be solicited year after year with great propagandistic fanfare indicated the commitments of even these contributors were less than total. [157]

The fewer real dollars collected from the 1960s onward were thus a sign not of growing Jewish poverty (even though Jewish income has *not* always continued to grow in real economic terms throughout the last forty years) but rather of many Jewish-Americans moving further away from their heritage and Jewish involvement or at least a decline in its salience for them. [158] In Cohen's words: "Whereas in the past philanthropic giving was undertaken as a way of symbolizing economic success and securing social standing, today it is much more a reflection of Jewish commitment. [159]

Not surprisingly, this has been especially true for younger Jews (people in their twenties are "consistently infrequent contributors"), who, in the majority, have in almost every respect demonstrated diminished involvement in things Jewish. [160] In fact, one explanation

of the noticeable decrease in giving by the midseventies was that by
then "only middle-aged and elderly Jews regarded charitable giving
as normative" while those who would reach maturity during the
period would remain "permanently less inclined to give than their
predecessors."[161] By 1970, the NJPS showed that only 35 percent of
American Jewry had given to Jewish charities.

A Long Island rabbi recounts an anecdote from the midseventies that articulates this reality. Among his congregants was a holder
of Manhattan real estate who was able to and did give generously
to many of the Jewish charities that solicited his aid. His college-
educated son, in his late twenties, had made an even greater fortune
as a lawyer for a record distribution company. When the rabbi ap-
proached the son for a donation to some Jewish cause, the young
man explained, without even a scintilla of irony: "Rabbi, my father
gives to those charities; I have other priorities."[162]

Moreover, because by 1975, when these trends were clearly established, the Jewish community had already been transformed into its
bipolar form, with most Jewish-Americans being both less observant
and less involved in either organized Jewish life or any form of Jewish activity, the likelihood of a change in the future that would lead
to a new influx of funds seemed slim indeed. If anything, as the older
generation died out and in the absence of the new one becoming phi-
lanthropically oriented in a Jewish way, the numbers were likely to
decline even more. This left the burden of growing costs for Jewish
life increasingly on the sector of American Jewry that was committed
to living an active Jewish life. Put simply, fewer and fewer Jews were
being asked to shoulder a higher and higher cost of Jewish-American
life. From the midsixties onward, yeshivas and day schools, synagogues, Jewish community centers and Y's, and of course the State
of Israel as well as Jewish communities in distress (to say nothing of
Jewish campus organizations or Jewish studies programs at the university level) would have to look to a shrinking minority of the Jews
for help and funding. By 1985, a study by J. A. Winter and L. I. Levin
"showed that the donations of a family earning $40,000 annually
who gave $100 to the federation, bought High Holiday seats in the
synagogue and belonged to a Jewish community center would ex-
ceed the percentage of income the U.S. government assumes a family
would have given for *all* gifts and contributions."[163] This was a huge

and growing burden that the few could not be expected to successfully shoulder endlessly.

Throughout the seventies, the philanthropic and community organizations tried to camouflage these declining figures by comparing
absolute amounts rather than adjusting the figures to reflect inflation.
The motive here was to foster an impression of a cohesive and growing concern with Jewish life, an impression that was important for
maintaining political influence in America and for boosting morale
among those diminishing numbers who were actively Jewish. While
there were benefits in this tactic, it also led to the Jewish organizations fooling themselves, a feel-good strategy that led to a delayed
anxiety which would strike again by the 1990s when the decreasing
dollar amounts were felt acutely and the number of those who could
be counted among the actively Jewish seemed shockingly small.

Conclusion

By the end of the 1970s, American Jewry had firmly established its
bipolar character. While most Jews, who retained an attachment to
their heritage but made little of it, were relatively satisfied with what
had become of them in this country, they should not have been, as
the actively Jewish among them realized and kept reminding them.
The latter group sought not only to be more engaged as Jews but
also to attract greater numbers to their cause, demonstrating by their
Jewish life-style and goals how much more there could be to being
a Jew in America. But by the beginning of the next decade, they re-
trenched and, giving up on any great shift in numbers to an active
Jewish stance, began to speak of the quality of Jewish life rather
than its quantity. Perhaps less was more. If they could create a vital
and active Jewish identity for themselves, maybe that would sustain
the entire people. They tried to hide their anxiety about the future
under this hope, a hope nurtured by their growing influence in the
Jewish community's establishment. But as they would discover, the
few could not maintain the quality of Jewish life, the richness of its
institutions, or the vitality of its identity without a broad base of
economic and cultural support. The flow against the actively Jewish
way of life in America was too powerful to ignore.

3 Quality versus Quantity: *The Challenge of the 1980s and 1990s*

BY THE LAST TWO DECADES OF THIS CENTURY, THOSE WHO worried about Jewish life in America were no longer especially concerned about successful Jewish acculturation or even matters of dual loyalty, so much on the mind of American Jewry during the first half of the postwar era. These concerns had largely evaporated because America had changed. As already noted, by the late seventies, this country had moved away from its melting-pot ideal, where everyone was supposed to be alike, and given way to a salad-bowl America that legitimated an increasingly pluralist national character. The civil rights revolution of the sixties and the emergence of ethnicity as an American ideal during the seventies had made this country recognize that there was not simply one America but many. In this sort of multicomplexioned, multiethnic nation there could be no questions about the legitimacy of Jewish belonging. Even as support for Israel grew among American Jews in the aftermaths of the 1967 and 1973 wars, the question of dual loyalty seemed absurd in the context of ethnic diversity; if Jews were to be accused of dual loyalties, then so were Hispanics, Africans, Poles, Irish, Italians, and all the other ethnic groups who were now allowed and even encouraged to celebrate their cultural diversity and attachments to a mother country or church. In the United States of the eighties and nineties, "ethnic identity and religious identification have become in large part expected norms of individual identification."[1] To be an "unhyphenated American" these days is quite exceptional.

Moreover, as ethnic heritage became a part of the American scene, some Jewish symbols clearly became American symbols too. Everyone in America seemed to know what a bar mitzvah was; this Jewish coming of age was no less a part of the national experience than a kosher dill pickle or a bagel. "Chutzpah," "shmooz," and many other Yiddishisms had firmly entered into American English.[2]

Not only were Hanukkah menorahs appearing on city malls along with Christmas crèches, but on the Mall in the nation's capital on land donated by the federal government, a Holocaust memorial and museum were erected alongside the other symbols of American civil religion and national heritage. Similarly, during these last twenty or more years in New York, the state with one of the largest Jewish populations in the world, a week in which Jewish life is celebrated by a series of public events has become a feature of the cultural calendar. This happening, which is supposed to cut across all Jewish sectarian lines and is called simply Jewish Heritage Week, probably comes as close as anything can to being a Jewish civil religious sacred week. And everybody in the city knows when Jewish holidays are celebrated because on those days "alternate side of the street parking regulations are suspended" for all.

Yet, in this newly ethnic America there remained residues of the melting-pot ideal. They were embedded in the notion that while America allowed for ethnic, racial, religious, and cultural diversity, these differences were not expected to intrude upon the basic underlying common culture of Americanism which washed over all citizens. The ethnicity and cultural diversity permitted in the American salad bowl were to be symbolic at most, not really fostering a separate or parochial existence. Indeed, as sociologist Richard Alba has recently demonstrated, these ethnic elements are not sufficiently substantive in everyday life to hinder even intermarriage in white America.[3]

The point at which ethnicity becomes significant, or where the line should be drawn between acceptable diversity and too strong an attachment to cultural or religious differences, would be contested throughout the eighties and into the current decade. Whether the debate focused on intermarriage, cultural integration, bilingual education, ethnic quotas, civil rights for homosexuals, or public support for parochial schools, at the heart of the matter was the question of how different someone could be and still claim to be fully integrated into America.

Heritage Jews

For American Jews, this debate was not merely theoretical; it had practical consequences. Those who comprehended American tolerance for pluralism as symbolic and limited asserted consequently that Judaism and Jewish expression here would also have to be symbolic and limited. This minimalist expression, however, was not problematic for those I have called the heritage Jews because, having adjusted to the melting-pot ideal, they did not want or expect to do more as part of their Jewish identity even when America changed. If this new symbolic ethnicity meant they could don yarmulkes in public or cater their gatherings with kosher food or even make more of Hanukkah, that was fine. They might but would not necessarily do so. In fact, they did *not* demand American tolerance for a more active Jewish involvement. Instead, theirs continued to be a kind of vaguely cultural Judaism, "a much more open, yet more ambiguous and less binding parameter for defining a group."[4]

Nothing makes this more vivid than the finding from Steven M. Cohen's 1989 survey of American Jews that two-thirds of his respondents thought that the most essential element of being "a good Jew" was "to lead an ethical and moral life." Summing up this finding and others like it, Cohen concluded that by the end of the 1980s "a large majority of Jews (roughly two-thirds) feel committed to Jewish continuity and to their identity as Jews. Only about a fifth to a quarter, though, are committed to a particular Jewish content."[5] In other words, those I have called heritage Jews have continued to make a commitment without much content.

They have persisted in patterns set in the previous decade of at most celebrating a few rites of passage—most of which are generally bereft of specifically Jewish content even though they are nominally Jewish; these are the bar or bat mitzvahs that are little more than parties, Jewish weddings that have a rabbi officiating but little else of Jewish content, and Jewish funerals that lack most, if not all, of the specific Judaic rites associated with death and mourning. Large numbers of these Jews continue to light Hanukkah candles (77 percent), though commonly without consistency, or attend a seder (86 percent), albeit often one that is hardly different from a Thanksgiving gathering (which in the 1980s 92 percent of American Jews said they always or usually celebrate).[6] These are the Jews (the older more than the younger among them) who attend the synagogue at least once a year (88 percent) but not much more frequently and often without formal affiliation. They may attend a High Holy Day service, although they are not always certain how to participate. They may fast on Yom Kippur (61 percent) and even give to a Jewish charity, although only slightly more than half (59 percent) have. They get some Jewish education, but it is increasingly shallow and almost always limited to the primary school years, often no more than a few hours a week. Although "sentimentally pro-Israel," they are "not particularly active for or connected to Israel," know little about it, and most—especially the young—have still never visited there.[7] In fact, just 26 percent of the so-called core Jewish population polled in the 1990 National Jewish Population Survey (NJPS) claimed to have ever been to Israel; that figure rises to about 31 percent if we consider only those who call themselves Jews, to 37 percent in a more focused 1981 national survey of Jews, and to 42 percent among New York Jews in 1991.[8]

They insist on recalling the Holocaust but are not sure what lessons to learn from it. Thus, while they are sorry about those Jews who have been lost through murder and mayhem (three-quarters of those polled in 1989 said their feelings about the Holocaust had deeply influenced their feelings about being Jewish) and claim a concern for memorializing their lost heritage, they are (with far fewer expressions of regret) losing their children to high rates of intermarriage or to low rates of fertility.[9]

To be sure, there are Jews now who fall below even these minima. Thus, the 1990 NJPS found that about 14 percent of those who were fully Jewish (either born Jewish or converted to it) did not attend a seder of any sort (38 percent among those in mixed marriages), about 40 percent did not attend synagogue on High Holidays or fast on Yom Kippur, and about 23 percent of those entirely Jewish admitted that no one in their household ever lights Hanukkah candles. Fifty-seven percent of the Jews by religion reported never having lit Sabbath candles. Fifteen percent of this same population never celebrated a bar mitzvah. Even the relatively modest involvement of subscribing to a Jewish periodical was true for only 28 percent of those who identified as Jews.

For the harder practices—those requiring a greater commitment of time, money, or religious and ethnic energy—the numbers were even starker. Again, if we look only at those born as and still claiming to be Jews and those who converted to Judaism, about 38 percent did *not* contribute to a Jewish charity in 1989 and 89 percent did *not* attend the synagogue weekly. Only 45 percent claimed that most or all of their friends were Jewish. And of the 859,000 children under the age of eighteen in the core Jewish population, only about 400,000—*fewer than half*—were in the Jewish educational system at the end of the eighties.[10]

In spite of this low level of activity among the great majority of Jews, 87 percent of the entirely Jewish population nevertheless claimed at the end of the eighties that being Jewish was important in their lives, with about 60 percent of those saying it was "very" important.[11] Yet, as Nathan Glazer has argued and as these relatively low or simple levels of activity demonstrate, the fact that today's American Jews "are less embarrassed about their Jewish identity does not mean . . . that identity is a very weighty one, or exercises great influence over their behavior."[12] Indeed, as Steven M. Cohen found during this same period, the Jewish declaration of the importance of religion to them was not unique; almost half the non-Jews he surveyed also said that religion was "very important" in their lives.[13]

So, during the last two decades of this century, what did it mean to many of these Jews to be Jewish in America? When asked in the 1990 survey to answer this question, more of those who identified themselves as Jews said it was a "cultural group" (70 percent) or "ethnic group" (57 percent) than said it was a purely religious group (49 percent). Culture and ethnicity together make what I have been calling "heritage" the epitome of American Judaism.

In a 3 April 1993 column on beliefs, *New York Times* reporter Peter Steinfels, who found this kind of cultural and ethnic identity typical of many late-twentieth-century Americans of all faiths, quotes Richard Shapiro, who personifies this kind of Jew. Reflecting on his understanding of what it is to be a Jew, Shapiro says: "I don't know. It's some sort of connection to yourself and your family and your past. Jews seem to have this burden of something going back in time." It is a cultural burden Shapiro, like other heritage Jews, is willing to bear because, as he continued, it provides "something to touch base with."[14]

It is, however, often an indirect or very fleeting touch, as the following conversation I overheard in the early 1990s in a YMHA locker room between two such Jews demonstrates:

MURRAY: So, Morty, did you have a seder this year?
MORTY: To tell you the truth, I had three.
MURRAY: Three?!
MORTY: Well you see, for the first one I went to my son Brian. For the second I went to my daughter. And my other son, Phil, said to me, "Dad, you know we've had a skiing vacation to Vail scheduled for a long time and it comes out on the seder nights, so would you mind if we had a seder on the Sunday when we get back?" Naturally, I said no. So we had a third, very nice seder last Sunday night at Phil's. How about you?
MURRAY: Well, I'll tell you, we used to have them when the kids were young, you know. But now that they're grown and out of the house and so far away, it's just Gladys and me, so we don't bother anymore.
MORTY: Sure, I know what you mean.

For these Jews, the seder was important, but the specifics of its observance were not. Its greatest importance was as a link to the children, a matter of heritage to be passed on, yet one that could be outgrown, shuffled, and minimized.

Like others of their ilk who lacked a strong commitment to Jewish practice, these two men, although choosing to be members of a Jewish Y, were probably part of the 90 percent of American Jews in the 1989 Cohen survey who thought a Jew could be "religious" even if he or she is not very observant. Indeed, fully two-thirds of those Cohen questioned were so open and pluralist in their religion that they declared that they were "offended" by rabbis who told them precisely how to live their Jewish life, an attitude I suspect would have been held by the two gentlemen in the Y locker room. Nevertheless, these were Jews who by the 1980s had moved away from a middle level of observance and come to terms with their way of being Jewish. About 79 percent of the Cohen sample considered themselves to be "very good" Jews, and two-thirds said they were committed to Jewish continuity.[15]

Yet perhaps what is most striking is the conclusion reached by two-thirds of those surveyed that being Jewish did not make them any different from other Americans. So in the end, these Jews, so proud of their heritage (fully 96 percent claimed to be "proud to be a Jew") and so flexible with it, were Jews whose Judaism turned out to be their way of being Americans.[16] Their being Jewish did not make them unlike other Americans.[17]

Active Jews

On the other hand, for those who were convinced that America's new openness to pluralism was not superficial or merely symbolic but rather an ideological sea change from the melting-pot ideal, the possibility that an active and open expression of a distinctive Jewish life-style and a celebration of its traditions could be part of an American identity represented an opportunity unparalleled in the contemporary Diaspora experience. It meant they could now demand and hope to receive far more American support for uniquely Jewish involvement and identities. Among these people, this led to significant bursts of activity in Jewish life. They included an intensification of Jewish education—particularly in the growing numbers of those attending day schools, who now make up approximately one-third of those in the Jewish educational system.[18] It resulted in a more vigorous political struggle on behalf of Soviet Jewry, even when such activity created tensions with American foreign policies of détente. It manifested itself in an increasing involvement with and more aggressive lobbying on behalf of Israel, whose prominence in American Jewish affairs grew, in spite of the vicissitudes of the relationship with its changing governments. It meant at the very least synagogue membership as well as participation in some Jewish organization, and making some significant financial contribution to a Jewish cause. While American feminists tested America's commitment to gender pluralism, these actively Jewish Jews unlocked Jewish opportunities for women. And they were those who, returning to the faith of generations, newly rediscovered their Jewish identities, which their immediate forebears had sought to diminish.

In short, those Jews who believed in the depth of the new Ameri-

can attachment to pluralism and ethnic diversity took the occasion
to become more actively Jewish. They did so to such an extent that
even those with a pessimistic view of the future of Diaspora life had
to admit that at least during the last fifteen years, "Jewish life for
the most involved Jews is more interesting, more creative, and more
worthwhile than it was not too long ago."[19]

These people for whom "the perceived importance of being Jewish is highest" were, however, not satisfied to manifest their identity
simply as a matter of cultural or ethnic heritage; they wanted to express it religiously as well.[20] They were the ones who in their "creative Jewing" evolved new forms of Jewish worship and breathed
renewed life into many synagogues (like the groups that took over
the previously moribund Anshe Chesed and West Side Institutional
Synagogues on Manhattan's West Side or the Tremont Street Synagogue in Boston). Even in their feminism, the focus was often on
enlarging the religious rights *and* obligations of women so that they
would be no less responsible for Jewish activity than the men.

Many of these Jews continued to nurture their Jewish consciousness on the college campuses. Although the pulse of the Jewish movement on campus was no longer as vigorous as it had been in the late
sixties and seventies, when it first began its beat, and many young
people wandered away from Jewish involvement and identity during
their college years over the last two decades, the courses and academic programs in Jewish studies born in the 1960s and 1970s were
now a firmly established feature of the American universities; and
there was no shortage of distinguished faculty in them, even if the
numbers of students who took the Jewish studies courses remained
modest. Some Jews augmented their college educations with years in
institutions dedicated to Jewish learning, many (but not all) of them
in Israel, where they not only acquired more knowledge but developed a more acute Jewish identity and often a stronger bond to Israel.

Among Jewish lay leadership, not commonly distinguished by
their awareness of the importance of Jewish education during the
first half of the post–World War II period, the last fifteen years have
witnessed a growing recognition of the essential importance of Jewish learning and practice. Not only do they now see a need to support
such Jewish learning and practice, but they also share a conviction

that to lead the Jews properly one must be more fully Jewish. Thus, for example, by the 1980s most of the members of the most powerful lay body of the New York Federation of Jewish Philanthropies (the Distribution Committee) had higher levels of Jewish education, synagogue membership, and survivalist Jewish attitudes than their predecessors in the sixties.[21] Perhaps even more striking was the theme of the federation's General Assembly in 1993: the need for more Jewish education. This was a remarkable turnaround for an institution that in 1969 had to be "taken over" by students to even get talk about Jewish education on the agenda.

Finally, among those embracing the notion of an American ethnic diversity, we discover during the 1980s and early 1990s an Orthodox Jewry who by nearly all measures of active Jewish identity score higher than any other Jewish group, asserting their presence with a triumphalism and confidence unmatched in their American experience.[22] In spite of their relatively small number of adherents (Orthodoxy continues to be the smallest of all the Jewish denominations), they continued to build day schools and yeshivas and support synagogues. Proportionately more Orthodox Jews traveled to Israel than Jews of any other denomination, and they even took over many of the executive or staffing positions of some of the central institutions of American Jewish life, such as the Conference of Presidents of Major Jewish Organizations, major federations, and the American Jewish Committee. Some, like Habad Hasidim, were even out recruiting among the general Jewish community and claiming huge successes. And in April of 1990, over twenty thousand Orthodox gathered at Madison Square Garden to celebrate the ninth Siyum haShas, the completion of the seven and a half year cycle of daily study during which the entire Talmud is reviewed.[23]

In brief, looking at this side of the spectrum, one discovers during the last fifteen years an American Jewry that trains more rabbis, consumes more kosher food, devotes more time to prayer or Jewish studies, publishes and buys more Jewish books, produces more Jewish plays, and teaches more children to speak Hebrew and study Jewish texts than at any time in the American past. These are Jews who show that for some there is commitment *and* content in American Jewish identity. Focusing on these people, dubbed by some sociologists the "Jewish elites," one might see only signs of vitality and forget the anxieties about the Jewish future.

The only cloud on the horizon seemed to be the matter of numbers. The actively Jewish Jews were far outnumbered by their minimalist, "heritage" counterparts. Moreover, when the former were not congratulating themselves on their triumphs, they admitted to themselves that they were a shrinking minority. Then the question of Jewish survival—rather than matters of successful acculturation or matters of dual loyalty—became paramount.[24] Indeed, for some this concern about Jewish survival in America, ripening since the sixties, has become even more important than what that survival was supposed to ensure. Leonard Fein has called this concern "survival as vocation."[25]

Yet the question of survival is not simply whether or not there will continue to be Jews in America; most demographers now agree that people who call themselves Jews, although shrinking in numbers, will continue to be a part of American life for the foreseeable future. What the character of their Jewish identity will be *is*, however, in question. Hence the concern of survival is not whether the Jews as a people or an ethnic group will survive in America but, as Calvin Goldscheider has put it, "which subsections or segments will survive."[26] Put differently, as we come to the end of the twentieth century we wonder not so much about the survival of the Jews but about the nature of the survival; we wonder about the survival of Judaism.

Certain facts are undeniable. Not only are the two types of Jews who constitute the two faces of American Jewry asymmetric in number, but the imbalance is unlikely to change in the years ahead. Although those among whom the quality of Jewish life is high are an increasingly smaller proportion of American Jewry, many of them have nevertheless increasingly set the agenda of Jewish life here (in part because, as I will argue later, most Jews have abandoned such parochial involvements and concerns).

The key questions, however, are whether these few can continue to exert such influence and define the character of American Judaism, and whether they can continue to be actively Jewish while the majority drifts away toward a peripheral involvement with Judaism. And if the Judaism with which the majority identify is so diluted that it is substantively and perhaps even structurally different from the

Judaism practiced by the active minority, will more than one Judaism survive or will this variance lead to a Judaism so divided against
itself that survival will be meaningless? Put differently, in the matter
of the survival of American Judaism *can we depend on the quality of
Jewish life, high though it may be, to ensure the survival of Judaism
if we do not have the quantity?*

To answer these related and key questions it is best to look more
closely at today's American Jewry, about whom we have more sociological data than ever before in history. Such an examination turns us
toward what most researchers agree are the seven major domains in
which Jewish development has been most affected during the 1980s
and 1990s. These are issues of *demography,* especially concerning
population growth and fertility. They also include matters of *generational variation,* more specifically how the young either differ from
or resemble their forebears. The third domain is the evolution of
Jewish *residential patterns and migration,* particularly the questions
of where and with whom Jews now live, something that throughout
the post–World War II period has been of great significance in determining and reflecting the character of American Jewish life. The
fourth concern is with *marital patterns,* especially the matter of Jewish outmarriage. The fifth domain concerns *Jewish identity,* or how
Jews perceive and characterize themselves. The sixth area is Jewish
institutional or organizational life, including and especially the matter of Jewish education. Finally, we shall consider the state of Jewish
political power and influence, perhaps the domain in which Jews
have measured their greatest strength in these last years.

Population Growth and Fertility

Obviously the first issue to consider with regard to population
growth and fertility is the precise number of Jews in America. The
1990 NJPS figures demonstrate the complexity of determining who
is to be counted as a Jew. Among those counted, those who were
born Jews and who currently identify themselves as Jews numbered
4.2 million. These people are the only Jews who would unequivocally be recognized as Jews by everyone in the Jewish community. In
addition to these people, the survey counted 185,000 Jews by choice

(i.e., converts of some sort) and 1.1 million people who admitted to being born as Jews but who currently claimed no religion. This last group tended to be heavily populated by young people. Together these three groups constitute what the researchers have called a core American Jewish population of 5.5 million. When compared with those counted in the last survey, in 1970, which found about 5.4 million self-described American Jews, this represents a growth of about 1.8 percent, strikingly smaller than the 22.4 percent growth in the overall U.S. population in the same period.

In addition, the 1990 survey counted 210,000 who were born or raised as Jews but claimed to have converted out of the faith, 415,000 adults of Jewish parentage or descent who currently identified with some other religion, and 701,000 children under eighteen years of age who have "qualified Jewish parentage" (an obscure bit of jargon, at best) but who are being raised in a religion other than Judaism. This last category has proved to be the most vague, since only 40 percent of the number actually have a parent who was born Jewish and the rest have some forebear who was Jewish, although who he or she was and how far back in time are not clear. (Senator Barry Goldwater, raised and living his entire life as an Episcopalian but with a Jewish father, would have been counted as one of these Jews.) Finally, the survey also counted 1.35 million Gentile adults who were in a household that had a Jew in it.

While these sorts of distinctions were not drawn in previous surveys, the general assumption is that in the past statistics have been gathered only for those who identified as Jews. Comparing the 1990 figures with those of the previous decades, one could either see shrinkage in the 4.2 million figure of universally defined Jews (62 percent of the total count), see relative stasis in the 5.5 million core population, or else be struck by the extent to which the numbers of Jews who were now part of the community included those marginally Jewish (19 percent in all) as well as those not Jewish at all (16 percent of all the households surveyed).

These ambiguities notwithstanding, the 1990 NJPS population count made vividly clear that it is no longer possible to calculate the number of Jews in America without counting Gentiles and without counting those whose affiliation with and identification as Jews are open to question. Here was vivid demographic evidence of an overall convergence between Jews and the host society. The notion of a distinct Jewish community is now far more difficult to support demographically than at any time in American history. Jews have become more and more like the non-Jewish-Americans around them. Indeed, over the years, "there has been a reduction of differences in terms of family, marriage, and childbearing patterns, as well as in social class, residence, occupation, education, and culture," and Jews are increasingly "less likely to vary demographically from American non-Jews." [27]

In part this has been a product of the fact that nine out of ten Jews in America are now born here, and "half are at least two generations removed from the immigrant experience." [28] The fact is "the American Jewish community is today overwhelmingly descended from one major wave of immigration that lasted from the 1880s to the 1920s. As a result, the 1920s, 1930s, and 1940s had their most marked impact on the second generation, while the 1950s, 1960s, and 1970s had it on the third generation." [29] Although in the past much of the Jewishness of American Jewry—in both its religious and its ethnic dimensions—could be accounted for by the presence of the foreign born among them, this subpopulation has largely declined in numbers and influence. The proportion of foreign born in the core Jewish population as of 1990 was down to 9 percent.[30] Even in the New York area, which traditionally has had the highest proportion of Jewish immigrants, figures from 1991 indicate that over 83 percent of the Jewish adults were born in the United States. Except for the relatively few post-Holocaust immigrants, the Israeli immigrants of the late seventies and early eighties, and those from the former Soviet Union (the latter two groups estimated at no more than 300,000 during the last twenty years), all of whom in the 1990 survey total about half a million, American Jewry is a community of the native born.[31] Moreover, of these three immigrant groups, only the first exhibited relatively high religious activity and significant numbers who in America sought to stress their Jewishness.

Even more crucial than the matter of immigration for fleshing out the demographic picture is the matter of birthrates. In fact, "the growth of the Jewish population in America has been uneven over time and largely the result of net immigration rather than natural increase." [32] Throughout the last forty years, American Jews in the main have demonstrated that "Jewish couples want, plan, and have small families."[33] In fact, in part because of their great investment in education and mobility, "the timing of childbearing . . . is delayed longer among Jews than non-Jews."[34] The result of all this has been that "the Core Jewish Population . . . has had low fertility over most of the past 40 years."[35] In effect, although America has become the world Jewish demographic leader, this is actually a result of the combined impact of forty years of mass immigration between 1880 and 1920 and the destruction of European Jewry in World War II rather than a result of Jewish fertility.

While the surveys of the seventies revealed a Jewish birthrate of between 1.5 and 1.7 children per family, the figures from the 1990 NJPS show almost no change in the core Jewish population, between 1.5 and 1.6 (the 1990 figures coming from women between the ages of thirty-five and forty-four, i.e., those at the end of their childbearing years). Jewish women forty-five years old and older in the core population exceeded replacement levels *only* at the height of the baby boom, and even then, as we saw, the Jews did not have as large a boom as the rest of America. In fact, "fertility among Jews is low in absolute level, as well as relative to other subpopulations," with Jews having a consistently lower birthrate than the rest of white America.[36] Indeed, throughout the "recent decades, Jewish population growth in America has been slower than the growth in the total American population."[37] Thus, for example, while Jews between the ages of thirty-five and forty-four had just under 1.6 children born per woman as of 1990, women of the same age in the U.S. white population had 2, a 25 percent higher rate.[38]

Given this low growth in American Jewish fertility and barring large-scale immigration, Israeli Jewry will likely outnumber American Jewry by early in the next century. Is it thus any wonder that a 1992 article entitled, like the *Look* magazine article in 1964, "America's Vanishing Jews" was published? This new piece appeared, however, in an Israeli publication, the *Jerusalem Report*.[39]

Although the population figures do not distinguish between those actively Jewish and those not, the numbers suggest that low birthrates are the norm for most of Jewry. Beyond that, of the more than 3 million households represented in the 1990 survey, the indications were that being Jewish seemed to lead to smaller household size.

While the 867,000 mixed households in the sample (i.e., in which at least one member of the family was a Gentile) had an average size of 3.2 people, entirely Jewish households, which made up about 57 percent of the sample, averaged only 2.2 persons per household, a "cost" of one child per family.[40]

Indeed, "the major sources of higher fertility ideals and larger family size are among the self-segregated religious Jews in a few metropolitan areas of the United States."[41] Only among this segment of committed Jewry which has in a variety of ways "rejected the integrationist ideology and behavior of the vast majority of American Jews," and which emphasizes traditional roles for women and the centrality of the family as well as supporting a general stance of nonacculturation, have "large family size values and behavior . . . been retained and supported."[42] Simply put, birthrates remain highest among the Orthodox. Yet even here, the figures are not unequivocal. Although most of those who called themselves Orthodox (about 60 percent) had just under three children per family, about 17 percent of those identifying as Orthodox reported birthrates of around replacement level, and about 22 percent, the most traditionally observant, were at the high end, with just over four children per family.[43]

Taken together, these two facts suggest that what growth there is in family size within the greater Jewish community occurs principally among that 6 to 10 percent of American Jews who call themselves Orthodox (and especially the 30 to 40 percent of the most observant among them), at one end of the spectrum, and among those who are in mixed marriages (or at least have Gentiles in the household), at the other end.

In sum, as these figures make clear, the current fertility profile of all American Jews, like the population figures in general, points to a small number of American Jews, who, as the total number of Americans steadily rises, will become an even smaller proportion of the national population. Moreover, a growing fraction of that population will be living in households that also include non-Jews. And, as already indicated, among the remaining identifiable Jews, those actively pursuing their Jewish identity and supporting it will continue to be the smallest segment. If a meaningful Judaism is to survive in such a future, less will have to be more.

But can less be more? Can we argue that American Jews are better off with a Jewish community of small numbers whose involvement is intensive and intimate? This argument first of all assumes that those who remain will be actively Jewish Jews, but in fact the likelihood is that, for at least a generation or more, the majority will be Jews of high pride and minimal involvement, those I have called the heritage Jews. Yet even assuming that these Jews will inexorably move to the periphery and ultimately out of the Jewish orbit, leaving only the actively Jewish Jews responsible for and populating the American Jewish community, would this "higher quality" Jew be enough to sustain Jewish life in America? A brief look at some economic realities is crucial for an answer.

Although it is true that even in the economic downturn of the early 1990s, Jews as a group have higher incomes than many other ethnic groups in America, this statistic only tells a part of the story. Jews, or more specifically actively Jewish Jews, need more money because an active Jewish life is expensive to sustain. For example, in 1992, day school education, synagogue and Jewish community center membership, attendance at a Jewish summer camp or a brief trip to Israel, and a donation to a Jewish charitable organization would, according to a 1992 American Jewish Committee report, at minimum cost between $18,000 and $25,000 per year for a family of four. The report probably underestimates these costs, especially among those Jews who are paying multiple day school tuitions, each of which alone can range between $5,000 and $10,000 annually. Moreover, it does not figure in the higher costs of a kosher food diet and lifestyle. "To afford this level of Jewish living and giving," this report concludes, "such a family would require an annual income of $80–125,000, depending on the region of the country."[44] Those figures are conservative estimates. But the median income for American Jewry of about $50,000 is significantly below this; and in fact, when controlling for inflation, it is lower now than it was in 1970, as the table below (which shows the figures for Jews by denomination) illustrates.

In fact, according to the 1990 NJPS, only about 20 percent of American Jews had incomes of $80,000 or more per year, and less than 7 percent had incomes above $125,000. Even looking at the New York metropolitan area, where some of the richest Jews live, although the counties of Nassau ($67,900), Westchester ($65,000), Suffolk ($61,600), Staten Island ($57,400), and Manhat-

MEDIAN INCOME BY DENOMINATION: 1970 VERSUS 1990

	Orthodox	Conservative	Reform	Other
1970	$13,963	$19,209	$20,584	$17,649
	[$45,379]	[$62,429]	[$66,898]	[$57,360]
1990	$40,098	$50,396	$60,608	$50,143

Note: The numbers in brackets are 1990 dollars, factor of 3.25. The factor of 3.25 is based on the Consumer Price Index, which suggests that $1 in 1970 was worth $3.25 in 1990. See Ronald G. Ehrenber and Robert S. Smith, *Modern Labor Economics: Theory and Public Policy,* 4th ed. (New York: HarperCollins, 1991), p. 31.

tan ($55,400) had higher median incomes than the national average, the costs of living (including Jewish living) there were higher too. Although these Jews might feel their economic situation was "reasonably comfortable," as most did, they could feel this only if they were paying a minimal amount to support their Jewish identity and involvement.[45]

Perhaps nothing more strikingly demonstrates the effect income has on Jewish involvement than the figures on synagogue affiliation. According to the 1990 NJPS data, that affiliation (although low across the board) is highest for those with annual household incomes of $80,000 or more (just under 50 percent) and hovers at about a third for all those groups with annual incomes of $60,000 or less, with a slight increase to about 38 percent among those at or near the median income. Obviously, the cost of synagogue affiliation (as much anecdotal information about the unaffiliated confirms) is a factor in American life. In one report, 60 percent of the unaffiliated in metropolitan St. Louis and a similar proportion in the MetroWest region of New Jersey (the counties adjacent to New York City) said that "the high cost of involvement in organized Jewish life . . . was what kept them from joining" synagogues.[46] That there is a larger constituency to be had is perhaps most convincingly shown by the fact that in the 1990 NJPS only 36 percent of those who reported that they fasted on Yom Kippur said they were affiliated with a synagogue.

Given these incomes, which by 1990 show erosions since 1970 of 10 percent for the Orthodox, 19 percent for the Conservative, 9 percent for the Reform, and 14 percent for those Jews who did not identify with any one of the three major denominational groups, and given that the cost of Jewish institutional life is rising, and finally given that there are fewer actively Jewish Jews supporting these Jewish institutions that now firmly sustain the American Jewish community, can we really make the argument that less is more? Put differently, to those who say quality is more important than quantity, the demographer and economist who look at contemporary American Jewry and who learn from the sociologist that the actively Jewish Jews are diminishing in numbers must say there can be no quality if there is no quantity. Actively Jewish Jews will not be able to support the institutions which bolster and nourish Jewish life if they do not enlarge their numbers. Moreover, they will be unlikely to find support for those institutions elsewhere—certainly not from the rest of America, which, however tolerant it may continue to be about ethnic and religious diversity, has always been scrupulous about the financial separation of religion and state. While American Jews, as I have suggested, will continue to provide philanthropic support for American universities, museums, symphony orchestras, the United Fund, and other non-Jewish causes, neither the American government nor American philanthropy is likely to financially support Jewish institutions, in spite of their increasing needs and their crucial importance for the future of Jewish life here.

Accordingly, when observers rhetorically ask, "Would the quality of American Jewish life be improved if there were an additional million Jews?" analysts looking at these facts must reply, "Yes, it would be improved, but only if this one million were fully committed to their Jewish identity and hence to supporting Jewish activity and Jewish institutions." Those making the "let's worry about quality rather than quantity" argument fail to acknowledge the fact that having a community made up of smaller numbers of engaged Jews will inevitably limit the possibilities of a developed Diaspora Jewish life since with a smaller base, the community will have neither the human nor the economic resources to support a rich Jewish life.

In a sense, the problem of resources also explains how Israel has become a more hospitable place for actively Jewish Jews. Beyond the obvious positive atmospherics of life in a sovereign, Hebrew-speaking Jewish state with its rich history and enhanced Jewish consciousness, Israel offers an important demographic and economic support that America cannot match. In Israel, the taxpayers—secular Jews as well as non-Jews—help sustain many Jewish institutions upon which actively Jewish Jews depend. These include the public religious schools, synagogues, and a myriad of institutions from community centers to yeshivas, supported either by national political parties or by the government (which does not separate religion from state as does America). With so much of the "Jewish bill" picked up by others, the Jewishly active can be sustained even if they are relatively few. But America, with its inability to tax or draw upon the many for the benefit of the few actively Jewish Jews, can offer nothing even close to this sort of support.

Having said this, the obvious next question is, "Would bigger numbers be enough to ensure the future of American Jewish life?" The simple answer is, "Yes, if they are committed and actively Jewish Jews." Or, as demographer Sergio DellaPergola has aptly put it: "Jewish continuity is not a mere biological-demographic fact but also depends significantly on the nature of the Jewish identification and its *transmission from one generation to the next*."[47] It is thus to generational variations we next turn.

Generational Variations

Before considering the matter of generational variations and transmission, a few words about the age structure of American Jewry are in order. During the eighties, Gallup Polls demonstrated that overall "Jews are older than the rest of the population," and, specifically, "the proportion of Jews over age 50 averages 8 percentage points higher than the rest of the population." What's more, these "age differences between Jews and other Americans have been increasing."[48] In 1980, 21.7 percent of American whites, but only 16.2 percent of American Jews, were under the age of fourteen. On the other end, only 11.8 percent of the American white population, but 15.5 percent of the Jewish, were over sixty-five.[49] The 1990 NJPS data are even more striking. While the total population of 8.1 million enumerated in the survey reveals a little over 20 percent under age fifteen and almost 14 percent over sixty-five—almost identical to the white American population—when the "core Jewish population" is considered alone, a different picture emerges. Here just under 19 percent are under fifteen, and over 17 percent are over sixty-five (this excludes institutionalized Jews, who were not formally part of the survey and tend to be older rather than younger). This is over one-third more elderly persons than the 12.5 percent in the total American population in 1990.[50] "This difference extends even to the old aged; almost 8 percent of the Jews were age 75 and over, compared to 5.5 percent of the whites." Ironically, *the greatest Jewish population growth has been in the number of aged*. The risks of this are clear: communities do not sustain themselves by increasing the proportion of their aged.

What about the Jewish character of the children or, more generally, the generational variations in Judaism? All groups concerned with survival must necessarily look to the next generation for hope. Ritual practice seems a neat starting point since it is distinctively Jewish and its exercise signifies commitment with content. The data suggest that "children's ritual practices tend to replicate those of their parents."[51] But this is not as hopeful as it sounds at first. Instead, we discover that it shows us that as the parents have diminished their ritual practice (and their Jewish activity in other domains) so too have their children, only more so. That is perhaps the single most consistent fact about Jewish generational reality during the four and a half decades reviewed in these pages.

To be sure, there is some indication that this decline in observance was greater in previous generations and is leveling off now. "Where the prewar second generation abandoned many of their immigrant parents' ritual practices, the postwar second generation largely retained their parents' level of observance."[52] There is thus, according to at least one researcher, some moderation in the weakening in some aspects of Jewish identity and involvements, even some evidence "of stabilization among younger adult age-groups" after declines among their generational forebears.[53] Of course, part of this may be explained by noting that the decline in observance in the past was so great that the current apparent leveling off may be partly the result of there being less left to stop doing than there was in the past, and what is left (as I have argued earlier) is a kind of symbolic heritage that American life allows for and even sanctions as a means of being part of multicultural contemporary America.

Looking at the diminished involvement of the young in Jewish activity, some have argued that no valid evaluation of generational variations in Jewish activity, identity, and involvement can ignore the role that life cycle plays in this process. The young, this argument runs, who generally have fewer attachments, may be less Jewishly involved or identified only while they are young and will return to the synagogue and community when they become parents, especially "when offspring attain school age."[54] Involvement will intensify with age. Joining a synagogue, for example, is the "Jewish activity which is most sensitive to changes in family life cycle, reflecting the family centeredness of the American synagogue."[55]

In response to this argument that young Jews will become more affiliated and involved over time as they enter into family life and establish their own households, one may, however, note that the young—more than any other segment of the Jewish community— have been moving into alternative Jewish sorts of households, a category which increased over 100 percent between 1965 and 1975, growing from 15 to 38 percent of the population. These include single-parent families, mixed households of Jews and Gentiles, and unmarried couples. By 1990, the proportion of traditional Jewish families was quite small: only 14 percent of Jewish families contained a married Jewish father and mother with children. Indeed, "the most common type of household found in the [1990] survey was a Core Jewish person living alone."[56] The significance of these changes cannot be minimized since "almost all declines in measures of Jewish involvement during the ten-year period [of 1965–75] could be attributed to the rise of alternative families . . . and by 1975, these sorts of families had grown more distant from Jewish life than their counterparts in 1965."[57] Put simply, if Jews continue their abandonment of the traditional family setting which in the past has stimulated increased Jewish engagement, that later-in-the-life-cycle involvement may never happen or may at best be significantly attenuated.

The change in life-styles, however, is not the only factor here. Already in 1978 sociologist Steven M. Cohen concluded that in general "there is a nearly steady, but definitely precipitous drop in Jewish involvement as one descends the age ladder" and that decline "cannot . . . wholly be written off to life cycle effects."[58] In 1987, Cohen repeated his judgment that by "any visible standard, younger adults are simply less involved in Jewish life than those just 20 or 30 years their senior," although, as noted, the decline was not as precipitous.[59]

Finally, after looking at all the recent data, DellaPergola said more or less the same thing in 1991: "With very few exceptions, the trend is one of further weakening when passing from older to younger age groups."[60] The famous maxim by historian Marcus Hansen that what the child wishes to forget the grandchild wishes to remember is just not borne out by the data.

This generational decline can be seen in a variety of indicators. Consider institutional or organizational affiliation. Throughout the 1980s "most American Jews under 30 belong[ed] to no Jewish institution as compared to less than a third of the middle-aged."[61] Even when there is institutional affiliation, the differences between generations are clear. Thus, for example, as revealed by the 1990 NJPS, among the so-called core Jewish population, 25 percent of those under the age of thirty affirmed that they were "currently" a synagogue member, while 35 percent of those over thirty were. Asked if during the past twelve months they had volunteered for work in a Jewish organization, 19 percent of those over thirty in the core population claimed to have done so, compared to only 12 percent of those under thirty. To be sure, both of these figures are small, reflecting the minority status of the actively Jewish (whether young or old) in the American community. Even in the relatively effortless commitment to subscribe to a Jewish periodical, those under thirty were about half as likely to do so as those over thirty.

In a trend begun in the late sixties and seventies and continued into the next decades, young people give less often to Jewish charities. People in their twenties are consistently infrequent contributors; and when the young do give, they are more likely to give to causes other than Jewish ones.[62] In the 1990s this is still true. In fact, even among New York Jews, only about 15 percent of Jews between the ages of eighteen and thirty-four gave exclusively to Jewish charities, while 20 percent of this same age group gave exclusively to general charities.[63] This was and is not simply a measure of income, since income largely affects the decision on the size of a contribution while Jewish activity and involvement are what correlate with the fundamental decision to give. Hence, if the young do not give these days, this says more about who they are than what they make.

The young tend "toward greater social intimacy with non-Jews."[64] Of those under the age of thirty, only about 24 percent, according to the 1990 survey, said all or most of their friends were Jews (compared with the almost 45 percent of those over thirty, and 55 percent of those between fifty-five and sixty-four, who made this claim). And of course, as we shall see in greater detail later, the young are more likely to intermarry than their forebears.

By 1989, a solid majority of American Jews were once again expressing concern about anti-Semitism in America (in the 1990 data nearly 80 percent of those responding to the question agreed that anti-Semitism was a serious problem in the United States). Indeed, basing his conclusion on the findings of his 1988 survey, Steven M. Cohen suggested categorically that the "perception that Gentiles are anti-Semitic is a core element of modern Jewish identity." [65] This feeling was engendered in part because of the increase in black/Jewish hostilities (in 1992 more than twice as many blacks, 37 percent, as non-Jewish whites were found to have anti-Semitic views), a decline in the American positive image of Israel, and the resurgence in the political influence of the Christian religious right.[66] To be sure, American anti-Semitism, at least according to a survey by the Anti-Defamation League of B'nai B'rith, had declined by the 1990s, down from 29 percent of Americans in 1964 to 20 percent in 1992.[67] Yet whatever the causes for Jewish concern about anti-Semitism, the evidence was that "younger people were less concerned than their elders." [68]

With regard to Israel, so much a part of the late-twentieth-century ethnic consciousness of American Jews, by the end of the eighties more older than younger Jews had visited there. Even more importantly, younger Jews evinced less attachment to Israel and fewer pro-Israel attitudes than their older counterparts. Gone were the youthful euphoric ties to Israel that characterized the early post-1967 war period. A 1986 survey "was the first to report lower levels of attachment to Israel by younger adults." [69] To be sure, majorities of both groups still supported Israel, and as Steven M. Cohen discovered in a 1989 survey, "over a third of American Jewish adults have been to Israel; over a third have family and over a third have friends in Israel." But although "over two-thirds, in various ways, claim to feel passionately committed to Israel," and about a third of the population "is most passionately committed to Israel and displays that commitment actively in one or more visible ways," the depth of this support as well as the size of the majority among younger Jews was significantly lower than among the older segment of the population.[70] Cohen could state, *"with a substantial degree of confidence, that younger Jews are indeed less pro-Israel than older Jews."*[71] While some of this could change as a result of the growing popularity of teen group trips to Israel, the fact remains that as of this writing, younger Jews as a whole express weaker attachments to Israel.

Even with regard to marital stability—long a hallmark and supporting pillar of Jewish life in America—the 1990 figures demonstrate that the younger segments of the population are more likely to have been divorced, a sign that even in this practice younger Jews are increasingly behaving like American non-Jews.[72]

What all these indicators affirm is that today the younger Jews are not just overwhelmingly native born, they are native Americans, integrated into American society and as such more distant from public and civil Judaism and its more parochial manifestations of traditional observance and identity and even from an ethnic or political connection to Israel. If they represent the future of Judaism in America, it is a future that is significantly less Jewishly intense and involved. It may even be one where the relatively minimal level of celebrating Jewish heritage or enthusiastically supporting Israel may not be reached by many of these young people as they mature. In fact, as Nathan Glazer correctly points out, "it is not yet clear what will be the shaping historical events for the fourth generation," those about whom these pages are most concerned.[73] That these events will have to do with their being Jewish, however, is increasingly less likely.

Are there no exceptions? What about the actively Jewish Jews? Evidence here suggests that their young are in many instances not dropping away—or at least not as precipitously—from Jewish engagement but are instead playing important roles in much of the activity. As we have already seen, not all actively Jewish Jews are alike. Some are active in Jewish social or communal affairs; others are active in ritual or religious matters.

Among the most consistently active in Jewish life are the Orthodox. This is demonstrated by Cohen, who devised a scale of "Jewish activity" and found that the Orthodox had twice their proportion in the population among those who were actively Jewish.[74] Accordingly, a look at generational variations among them is revealing. We have already pointed out the higher fertility of Orthodox Jews. With regard to observance, as Cohen and I reported in 1989, "increasingly, the adult children of Orthodox parents claim to be Orthodox themselves, practice a higher level of observance, and report having attended a yeshiva or day school."[75]

If we compare Orthodox rabbis and Orthodox rabbinical students, we find that in the late 1980s, the students scored at least as high as the rabbis in measures of Jewish identity and involvement.[76] Although both groups scored about ten percentage points higher than all other rabbis and rabbinical students from other denominations, those others (also, obviously, among the most actively Jewish of American Jews) evinced high measures of Jewish identity and involvement, with the young displaying essentially no less a Jewish profile than their seniors.

Beyond the Orthodox and the ranks of rabbinical students, there is some indication that when their parents are active and involved Jewishly, young people tend to replicate that involvement. In fact, from his data on 1980s Jewish America, Steven M. Cohen argues that "measures of Jewish involvement register just as high (or just as low) levels among young adults as among their parents."[77] The younger generation repeats the levels of faith in God, ritual observance, and Jewish familism that their parents display. Thus, where Jewish activity is present, generation does not play as crucial a factor as where it is absent. Put differently, a positive view of Jewish heritage or even symbolic ethnicity will probably not be enough to keep the young Jewish. Being an actively Jewish Jew, however, will. Hence the matter of generational differences brings us back to the primary claim: to ensure the future of Jewish life in America, there will have to be more actively Jewish Jews.

Residential Patterns

Although American Jews have abandoned the idea and often the reality of a ghetto, Jews have lived with other Jews for much of their history in this country, as indeed throughout the Diaspora. This has had benefits because living near or with other Jews is still perhaps the best recipe for maintaining Jewish identity and continuity. As Calvin Goldscheider has put it: "in terms of the vitality of local

Jewish communities, migration and population redistribution are of greater significance perhaps than any other demographic factor."[78]

Once the Jewish ghettoes were no longer enforced either by ordinance or by economic circumstances, and particularly in the growing openness of America after 1950, Jews began to disperse. That openness is dramatically demonstrated by the Gallup Poll's finding that by the 1990s, 91 percent of the Americans polled said they would like to have Jews as neighbors—whether they meant it or not is immaterial here.[79] In this atmosphere of stated support for integrated residential patterns, many Jews felt that to live primarily with other Jews conflicted with the American ethos of integration. Perhaps more importantly, it frustrated the Jewish obsession with mobility. For Jews in this country, moving up meant moving out. Specifically, among Jews, "early residential independence coupled with later family formation" became a dominant feature of maturation.[80] Grow up, get an education, get married, and move away was the normative pattern. By the 1960s and 1970s, as the college campuses throughout America attracted more and more young Jews, moving away sometimes came earlier, as part of getting an education. The young Jew who went away to the university to make something of himself or herself often never came back permanently to the parental home or community.

This passion for mobility, as we have seen, played a role in the development of Jewish suburbia. By the end of the century, however, Jews could and began to move further afield. During the eighties and nineties, in increasing numbers, young American Jews on the move up the social scale and looking to make their own way have continued to move away from where they grew up, away from the large centers of Jewish population, especially the East Coast and New York. This extended movement began with an extraordinary spurt in the 1970s. Whereas 83 percent of American Jews lived in the East in 1970, only 60 percent were there by the beginning of the next decade. During that same period the number of Jews in the West grew threefold, to 18 percent of American Jews, with a similar surge in the South.

As reported in the 1990 NJPS, the movement in the next decade was even more striking. *Nearly half the Jewish population changed their residence between 1985 and 1990.*[81] Both the West and the South posted net gains in population while the Northeast and the Midwest showed losses. But these two new regions of Jewish growth were also the areas that began with the fewest Jews. Hence recent mobility patterns indicate more than mobility; they betray a move from dense to relatively sparse Jewish communities, where ties to non-Jews would necessarily become a larger component of Jews' lives.

Undeniably, in the eighties and nineties, about half of the American Jewish population still lived in the metropolitan areas of New York (where Jews still make up 13 percent of the total population), New Jersey, and Connecticut, a region where only one-fifth of America's non-Jews make their home.[82] Nevertheless, recent patterns of mobility suggest that it is likely that significant numbers of contemporary Jews will, at least for the foreseeable future, be living in areas of low Jewish concentration. Since "Jewish survival is likely to be most pronounced in the large metropolitan centers of Jewish concentration—old and new"—this new pattern of life on the residential periphery of Jewish communal life probably represents the greatest threat to Jewish continuity and survival.[83]

To be sure, some, like Sidney Goldstein, have argued that migration "may also have positive effects on the vitality of Jewish life by bringing additional population to smaller communities or to formerly declining ones, thereby providing a kind of 'demographic transfusion' needed to help maintain or develop basic institutions and facilities essential for a vital Jewish community."[84] For the most part, however, this seems not to happen, except (as I will elaborate later) when Orthodox Jews move to such areas.

The effect of residence is clearly reflected in Jewish marital patterns. Thus, for example, the male mixed-marriage rate "outside New York is about double that found in the New York area."[85] Similarly, during these decades, approximately 80 percent or more of the marriages in Baltimore, Boston, and Essex and Morris Counties in New Jersey (just over the Hudson River from New York), all areas of relatively dense Jewish urban/suburban population, were inmarriages, whereas in San Francisco and Dallas, where Jews are relatively fewer and more separated, the proportions are 60 percent and 66 percent, respectively.[86] Likewise, in Denver and Phoenix, areas of relative Jewish scarcity, 61 percent of married Jews under thirty are married to non-Jewish partners. This is not simply a western motif; in Los Angeles, where the number of Jews is much higher, the figure is far lower, at around 30 percent.

Living with other Jews does not affect just rates of intermarriage; it also plays a role in fertility. The evidence is that areas of high Jewish concentration have higher birthrates.[87] On the other hand, since "neighborhoods of major centers of Jewish concentration have become heavily weighted toward the older segments of the age pyramid," the higher birthrates come from a smaller proportion of young Jews who are living in these areas of high Jewish concentration.[88] Put differently, we may say that those young Jews who choose to have more children are also the ones who are living in areas of high Jewish concentration, but there are relatively few such young people making this choice.

This also suggests that such demographic growth as does occur will be on the periphery, where the families are more likely to be of mixed parentage and the Jewish involvement is more likely to be at a lower level. Thus, in the 1990 NJPS we find almost as many household members under the age of eighteen in the South as in the Jewish Northeast (11 percent versus 11.7 percent, respectively).

In fact, beyond the matter of the effect of residence on intermarriage patterns, there were important differences between those Jews who lived in the Northeast (especially those in and around the heavily Jewish-concentrated New York area) and those who lived elsewhere. Nowhere do these show up more than in the data collected in the 1981 Greater New York Jewish Population Survey. Thus, for example, about 90 percent of New York Jews claimed to attend a Passover seder and 75 percent said they lit Hanukkah candles, a figure that was even higher when those without children (like Murray) were excluded from the sample. Fully two-thirds of the New York Jews claimed to go to the synagogue on High Holy Days and to fast on Yom Kippur, versus 59 percent and 61 percent, respectively, among the Jewish core population reported on in the national survey.[89] During the eighties, in Queens and Long Island, "90 percent of youngsters 10–12 years old belonged to families whose adult respondents said they were synagogue members."[90] Although the 1990 NJPS did not ask that question, it revealed that 44 percent of households with children under twelve were members of synagogues. Two-thirds of New York Jews reported having a mezuzah on their doors, while only 57 percent in Phoenix did.[91]

The figures for 1991 in the New York metropolitan area generally confirm these patterns. Thus, 92 percent of Jewish adults claim to attend a seder, 84 percent light Hanukkah candles, 61 percent attend the synagogue on High Holy Days, and 68 percent claim to fast on Yom Kippur. And in perhaps one of the most dramatic illustrations of the significance of living in an area where Jews are concentrated, the 1990s data show that while 45 percent of the national sample said most of their close friends were Jewish, 63 percent of the Jewish New Yorkers did.[92] Out of close Jewish friendships, communities and futures are made.

One last point needs to be made about Jewish continuity and residential patterns. The fewer Jews there are in a community, the more difficult it is to sustain the basic Jewish institutions which act as the structural supports for Jewish life and continuity. These institutions are bolstered by usage and financial support even as they synergistically sustain the Jewish community. In areas of Jewish sparsity where Jewish institutions—most importantly synagogues, community centers, and schools—nevertheless do exist (often against the odds), they are often dependent on economic and human support from sources other than those who utilize them. This makes their continued existence very precarious, and accordingly it makes the circumambient Jewish community, such as it is, equally precarious.

Outmarriage

Jewish outmarriage is a topic that has grown in importance during the years since 1950. Over the last decade or so, concern about intermarriage (within the context of the anxiety over Jewish survival in America) has overshadowed almost all the older outstanding Jewish concerns about political anti-Semitism and economic discrimination.[93] This has been not only because minorities in general tend to display anxiety about exogamy but also because, as their numbers and active members dwindle, outmarriage has become an ever greater phenomenon among American Jews. Whereas only 9 percent of those married before 1965 married Gentiles, that number grew to 25 percent by 1974, and 44 percent by 1984. Since 1985, 52 percent of those Jews marrying have married Gentiles, the first time in

American history when more Jews are marrying Gentiles than Jews. Moreover, "since 1985, twice as many mixed couples (born Jew with a Gentile spouse) have been created as Jewish couples (Jewish, with Jewish spouse)."[94] In spite of these figures, Jews are not the most likely to be in mixed marriages compared to other religious groups. N. D. Glenn reports that on the eve of the eighties, while about 20 percent of American Jews were in mixed marriages, this was the situation of 38 percent of Catholics, almost 58 percent of people with other religious affiliations, and 81 percent of individuals who identified with no religion.[95] Only Protestants, at slightly over 16 percent, had a lower rate, but since "Protestant" includes a wide variety of denominations, this low rate may hide the fact that there were rising rates of Baptist and Presbyterian or other interdenominational Protestant marriages. To counter this apparent "advantage" among Jews, researchers have pointed out that the relatively lower overall intermarriage rates for Jews are the result of the relatively high inmarriage rate among older Jews. The younger generation, as earlier noted, is not nearly as endogamous.

Looking at these figures, at least one researcher, however, sees some room for optimism in the fact that the ascending outmarriage rate of young Jews seems to be leveling off now among the youngest. He points out that "contrary to reports of rapidly rising intermarriage, among those 25–39 the younger respondents report rates that are almost identical with those of their elder counterparts."[96]

To this, the cynic might rebut that a leveling off of intermarriage at a high rate is not really cause for celebration. After all, the 1990 survey data indicate that 32 percent of those born Jews are not married to someone who was also born Jewish (quite a bit higher than Glenn's figure of only a decade earlier). Moreover, this 32 percent contains only 4 percent who converted; the rest (28 percent) have remained Gentiles. In fact, since World War II, while the number of outmarriages has risen, conversions have declined: from 22 percent in the fifties, 11 percent through the seventies, and 9 percent in the last decades.[97] Also, the portents of increasing rates of intermarriage are there; in Cohen's 1989 national Jewish survey, 61 percent admitted to having had a romantic relationship with a non-Jew.[98] Like the rest of America and in spite of the concern among some of them, Jews increasingly accept the idea that "bonds of love take precedence over bonds of faith, bonds of ethnicity, and occasionally even bonds of color." [99]

All this outmarriage (with its minimal conversion rates) signifies not only a Jewish demographic erosion but also a cultural drift toward the rest of America. That is, not only do "high rates of outmarriage threaten directly demographic survival of small minority populations," but they also "symbolize, as perhaps no other indicator, the conflict between universalism and particularism, between assimilation and ethnic continuity in American society." [100]

The most obvious result of this increased outmarriage and consequent cultural drift is that throughout these last decades non-Jewish elements have increasingly been woven into the fabric of Jewish life. One of the most notable findings of the 1990 survey, as earlier indicated, was the large proportion of people who, strictly speaking, did not fully qualify as Jews but who nevertheless found their way into the Jewish household, community, and census.

This coupling of non-Jewish and Jewish families not only emerges from but leads to even greater cultural and religious drift. In the first place, it precipitates more outmarriage. [101] Thus the 1990 NJPS revealed that among those with two Jewish parents, 36 percent were in mixed marriages, while among those with only one Jewish parent, fully 95 percent were married to a non-Jewish spouse.

Cultural drift, however, means more than simply that children of an intermarriage will themselves be more likely to intermarry. It means that in a single household and family there will be movement and intimate affiliation between different (and sometimes discrepant) ethnic and religious identities, particularly (but not exclusively) on the part of children in mixed families. Often as a result, the boundary between what is strictly or legitimately Jewish and what is not tends to become fuzzy at best and at worst disappears altogether. The stereotypical Hanukkah celebrated with a Hanukkah bush or the family that easily moves between Christmas dinner at one set of grandparents and Passover seder at the other perhaps symbolically captures this sort of cultural drift most vividly. But there are other manifestations, not necessarily limited to mixed-marriage families. These include the "surprisingly high" attendance of American Jews at non-Jewish religious services: 37 percent claimed to have gone at least once during the year (and among secular Jews the rate was

49 percent). In another survey, 40 percent said they felt close to a non-Jewish American "to a great extent."[102]

Cultural drift is also manifested in the changing attitudes that Jews have to the reality of outmarriage. When Marshall Sklare and Joseph Greenblum examined Jews on the suburban frontier in the late 1950s, 43 percent claimed they would be somewhat unhappy if their child married a non-Jew, while 29 percent said this would make them "very unhappy."[103] That outlook has changed. Throughout the seventies and even more so in the years that followed, attitudes toward intermarriage have become significantly more tolerant.[104] By the end of the 1980s, 79 percent of the NJPS respondents claimed they would support or accept the marriage of their child to a non-Jewish person. In Cohen's 1989 national survey, a quarter of those polled said it was "not important" to them that their children marry Jews.[105] To be sure, the move toward Jewish/non-Jewish integration was a two-way street; Gallup reported that over 75 percent of Americans likewise now approve of the idea of Jews and Gentiles marrying, up from 59 percent in 1968.

While tolerance is a good thing, and something we as Americans have been taught to value in our increasingly multicultural society, it in fact magnifies the cultural drift in intermarriage. In the past, outmarriage would have normally signaled an end to Jewish identification or allegiance among those with a non-Jewish spouse, but in these closing decades of the twentieth century, this is no longer necessarily the case. Although more Jews are entering mixed marriages, they are not always simultaneously abandoning their ties with the Jewish community. This Jewish link among the outmarried has been evident at least since the late sixties, when, as reported in the 1970 NJPS, over 50 percent of couples in mixed marriages reported raising their children as Jews. In 1990 the survey found the number down but still significant: 28 percent were being raised as Jews.[106]

Even more remarkable than what was happening to these children—not all of whom qualified as Jews by strictly halachic standards—was the fact that often non-Jewish spouses also began to participate in Jewish life, although they did not in most cases convert to Judaism in order to do so. Like so many American Jews, these Gentile spouses blurred the boundaries—both social and religious—

between Jews and non-Jews. They too could share in Jewish heritage (as, we have seen, Jews sometimes shared in non-Jewish heritage). With an American Jewry more tolerant of intermarriage, this kind of linkage was more possible than in the past.

As a result, the exogamy of American Jewry was being seen in a different light. To some observers as well as to some Jewish leaders, intermarriage was no longer to be considered a recipe for disaster presaging the end of the Jewish people in America but only its transformation. Thus, Calvin Goldscheider, perhaps the foremost proponent of this view, contends that "it is difficult to argue that young intermarried households are disassociated from Jewish communal life and the networks of the Jewish community when 60 percent say that most of their friends are Jewish, 40 percent say most of their neighbors are Jewish, 54 percent define themselves into established religious denominational categories, and almost two-thirds observe religious family rituals." [107]

The story of Lisa Dicerto, a woman who spent her formative years taught by the Dominican Sisters of St. Mary of the Springs but who married a Jew, is perhaps emblematic of this trend of cultural drift and the blurring of religious boundaries. Writing in a magazine called *America,* which like the country for which it was named addressed people of all faiths, Dicerto described how she, still a Catholic (and apparently still keeping her non-Jewish last name), went about making a Passover seder for her Jewish family and how she related to Judaism. "I bought a Jewish holiday cookbook and planned an old-fashioned menu, complete with Kugel and Matzoball soup." She also described how she shared in the experience of High Holy Day prayers, noting that she would "never forget the feeling of warmth and spirituality that washed over me when, during a prayer [on Rosh Hashanah] John [her husband] put his Tallis, the blue and white prayer shawl, around both of us." She could admit that at that moment, "I felt as prayerful then as I do in my own church." Like many non-Jews who have found their way into the Jewish family and community and who have begun to share in Jewish heritage, Lisa Dicerto concluded that her intermarriage had been good for her own faith too: "Not only do I enjoy learning about Judaism, but I have also felt a resurgence of love for my own faith." [108] That someone would regularly come to the synagogue and in reverence make the sign of the cross out of renewed faith, unthinkable in another era of Jewish history, was no longer impossible.

Lisa Dicerto is not alone. "Tom and Lynn O'Brien had agreed before they were married that the family religion would be Judaism, even though Tom was Catholic," began a 1993 report in the *New York Jewish Week*. "When they consulted with Rabbi Charles Agin of the Free Synagogue of Flushing, Tom was asked if he planned to convert. He answered no. 'Fine,' said the rabbi." Ten years later the O'Briens are "active members of the congregation."[109] In America at the end of the twentieth century, Judaism's transformation was extraordinary; it verged on an absolute metamorphosis.

So much had the non-Jewish elements entered into Jewish life that the largest denomination in American Jewish life of the eighties, the Reform, as well as the Reconstructionists, an offshoot of the second-largest denomination, Conservative Jewry, had formally accepted the principle that all offspring of mixed marriages could be considered Jews. This doctrine was at odds with time-honored halachic standards that demanded that the mother had to be Jewish if the child was automatically to be considered a Jew. Nevertheless, given that de facto many children of mixed marriages were acting like and often being treated like Jews, this de jure move by the liberal religious movements seemed more like ratifications of reality than stimuli for change. After all, by the last decade of the twentieth century, hardly a family could be found in America that had not in some way been touched by intermarriage. Recall that the 1990 NJPS counted 1,350,000 Gentile adults living with the total Jewish population. The presence of all these non-Jews within the Jewish family and community means, among other things, that not only the children of intermarriage "have legitimate alternative identities," but so do their intermarried parents.[110]

To those inclined to see hope in this continuing link to Jewish life among the mixed married and their non-Jewish family members, one must reply that if this linkage results in such a cultural drift and transformation of American Jewry that its heritage becomes indistinguishable from other ethnic heritages in America, the result may not be worth celebrating. While maintaining linkage may make the trauma of intermarriage bearable by Jewish families and individuals, it may, in the long run, prove to be devastating for the cultural integrity of the Jewish people.

Jewish Identity

Jewish identity is of course an amorphous concept. Without launching into a deep philosophical discussion about what it truly means, one can stipulate that at the very least it refers to a willingness to publicly mark oneself as a Jew and tie one's sense of self with the Jewish people, their history, practices, and destiny. When Jews were not free to assert an individual identity, to choose where to live or whom to marry, when their right to select a career or to pursue any kind of education was systematically blocked, Jewish identity remained essentially a matter of fate. In America, however, where such restrictions were never enforced, or at least not sanctioned by the powers of the state, Jewish identity became far more a matter of choice. Like the one in four American adults who according to Gallup "has changed faiths or denominations at least once," people born as Jews no longer see their Jewish identity as an unchangeable given.[111] Never has this been more true than in the decades since 1950, when in practice as well as theory America opened itself to Jews.

The key issue confronting those who expressed a Jewish identity in these decades has thus been the need to survive by choice and not only by virtue of birth or institutional involvement. Since the late 1960s, as we have seen, increasingly "that choice has tended to become an either/or choice—with a range within both extremes and with fewer options available to remain within the middle."[112]

Moreover, Jewish identity for many American Jews, as we have also seen, is no longer something associated exclusively with religion, long the most acceptable and hence common way American Jews had for characterizing themselves. Instead, Jewish identity seems to have moved increasingly toward ethnicity or heritage and culture, while being a "good Jew" has been defined in vaguely moral terms.[113] In fact, 69 percent of those reported on in the 1990 NJPS (and even more of those who were "Jews by choice" or those who were born Jews but who claimed no religion at the time of the survey) identified themselves as a national group, a culture; and as already noted in Cohen's 1989 national survey, the most widely agreed-upon essential for being a good Jew was the vague notion of leading a moral and ethical life.[114] While such an identity may be sufficient to sustain a group when it is a clearly defined nation, a sovereign majority in its own land, it is far more tenuous an identity for persons of a minority group who simultaneously view themselves as having more than one national culture. The latter is the case for American Jews, who see themselves as Americans perhaps as much if not more than they see themselves as Jews. To maintain this bicultural identity with the least discomfort and cultural conflict, many, if not most, American Jews have thus made these two cultures interchangeable. That is why they so often speak of a "Judeo-Christian" culture in America. Of course, the best way to tie these two religions and cultures together is not to focus on the doctrinal and ritual differences but to say that the essential in both is to lead a moral and ethical life.

Yet a careful reading of Judaism and Jewish history indicates that the two cultures are not interchangeable. Judaism, for example, does not set democracy as an ideal above all others, whereas America does. Or, to take another example, Judaism places a premium on the community above the individual, whereas America places the individual's life, liberties, and pursuit of happiness above all else. Certainly with regard to Christianity, Judaism has many points of opposition. All these cultural conflicts must however be overlooked in the quest for a comfortable American-Jewish identity. In the process, most American Jews have made the cultural adjustments to the Jewish side of their identity.

Some other Jews, a minority—most notably the Orthodox and particularly the insular *haredim* (ultra-Orthodox) among them—have, however, chosen to handle the contradictions between Jewish and American cultural or ethnic identity by disassociating themselves from or even denying those American cultural ideals or social circles that they view as inimical to their Jewish identity. They have evolved an identity that moves them to associate overwhelmingly with Jews like themselves. Albeit still very much Americans—particularly when compared with their Israeli counterparts—these Jews have an identity that emphasizes that, as one such Jew put it, "Judaism is a separatist religion."[115] This is seen, for example, in friendship patterns. Thus, in contrast to the 45 percent of all American Jews over thirty and 24 percent under thirty who in the 1990 survey said that all or most of their friends were Jewish, among Orthodox Jews 70 percent of those older than thirty and 79 percent of those under thirty reported that most or all of their friends were Jewish. Moreover, according to another study of Orthodox Jews in the late 1980s, the insularity of these patterns and of the identity they signify was even greater when one realizes that most of those Jewish friends whom Orthodox Jews claimed to have were also Orthodox Jews.[116]

Beyond the cultural kind of Jewish identity, other American Jews have turned political ideology into the predominant aspect of their Jewish identity. Thus, in the eighties, a nationwide survey of American Jews by the *Los Angeles Times* substantiated the view that liberalism (or a variant thereof) is central to many American Jews' understanding of their Judaism. Interviewers asked, "As a Jew, which of the following qualities do you consider most important to your Jewish identity: a commitment to social equality, or religious observance, or support for Israel, or what?" Half answered "social equality." The rest were equally divided between the other options.[117] While the number of Jews claiming an attachment to liberalism has diminished over the years, Jews are still among the most liberal of white ethnics in America. Even in the midterm elections of 1994, while America turned to the Republican right, 78 percent of the Jews voted for Democrats.[118]

Although some American Jews espouse a political Jewish identity that defines them as supporters of Israel, the evidence suggests, as Nathan Glazer sums it up: "Less and less of the life of American Jews is derived from Jewish history, experience, culture, and religion. More and more of it is derived from the current and existing realities of American culture, American politics, and the general American religion."[119] This is perhaps the aspect of Jewish identity that the Gentiles who are part of Jewish households can most easily embrace.[120]

Finally, there is a Jewish identity that has demonstrated a capacity to persevere throughout most of Jewish history, even though for a time in the early 1960s it seemed about to disappear in America: the Jew as a victim or potential victim of anti-Semitism. For some, this identity manifests itself in a quiescent vigilance against defamation. Perhaps this is the identity of the 57 percent of Jews who in 1989 agreed with the proposition that "American Jews could one day face severe anti-Semitic prosecution." [121] For others, this sort of identity expresses itself in political action oriented toward defensive or even offensive measures against anti-Semitism. The ubiquitous appearance of Holocaust memorials throughout America is one of the means by which many of these Jews, both the quiescent and the activist, have symbolically articulated their Jewish identity and their opposition to anti-Semitism. Who knows?—in the decades ahead, the Holocaust Museum in Washington may become the single most outstanding monument to Jewish identity in America (and its most visited shrine). Of course, if it does, it will be a monument to Jews as victims—not necessarily something upon which to build a future.

In spite of the marginalization of Jewish activity and involvement among most American Jews in these last decades, there are those who argue that nevertheless a real desire remains to maintain a Jewish identity and continuity, to maintain attachments to some sort of Jewish heritage. But as one scans the variety of ways in which this desire for Jewish identity displays itself, one must conclude, as does Nathan Glazer, with respect to most Jews today: "It is not a very strong desire, however, and it adapts itself to the needs of integration in the United States. . . . It makes few demands and is largely cut off from historic Judaism in terms of belief and practice." [122]

Perhaps a coda with regard to the relationship of Jewish identity to marital stability is appropriate. For some, Jews are simply those who have stable family lives. Overall, the data indicate that while Jews are divorcing more in the 1980s and 1990s than they did in the past, they still maintain a "relatively high rate of marital stability," with almost 84 percent of the so-called core Jews reported on in the 1990 survey having been married only once at the time they were polled.[123] Looking more closely at the findings, one discovers that those "classified as Jewish by religion reported 13.6 percent of their first marriages broken by divorce," but at almost 25 percent, "the rate was twice as high among secular Jews," those whose Jewish identity was at most a matter of heritage or considered an accident of birth.[124]

Institutional or Organizational Life

There is no question that during the years since 1950, American Jewry has been engaged in institution building. We have already seen the growth in the number of synagogues. To this we can add the surge in the number of day schools and yeshivas, university Jewish studies programs, summer camps, Jewish magazines, and Jewish community centers and Y's (especially throughout suburbia); a thriving Anglo-Jewish press in practically every major Jewish population center in America; the emergence of political action committees, Zionist associations, Jewish professional groups, Jewish communal organizations and voluntary associations, Jewish campus organizations, Jewish community relations boards, and of course the ubiquitous federations which collect and disburse large amounts of aid. Some of these institutions were generated by the interests of growing numbers of Jews; others were meant to provoke such interests.

Although Jews were certainly instrumental in building these institutions, they did not always maintain a constant supply of people to support them, either as member/volunteers or as financial backers. Thus, for example, with regard to synagogues, the 1983 National Gallup Polls found that "Jews are significantly less likely than their neighbors to be identified with religious institutions"; in fact, "Jewish enrollment is 60 percent of the national figure." [125] By 1989, only a third of those in the Jewish core population reported that they or someone in their household belonged to a synagogue. Ironically, "within the core group, membership was highest (56 percent) among households in which the respondent was a Jew by choice," suggesting that the human imports were likely to be more important for Jewish institutional life than is commonly recognized. [126]

In a similar vein, only 21 percent of the entirely Jewish population in the 1990 NJPS sample reported that they volunteered for a Jewish organization in 1989 (the figure for those under the age of thirty in this same core population was an even lower 12 percent). Indeed, more American Jews (39 percent) claimed to have volunteered for a secular organization during the year. Only 19 percent of the core Jewish population over thirty participated in activities at Jewish community centers or Y's, and even fewer (9 percent) of those who were younger. (Although the figures for New York Jewry were higher—slightly over 25 percent—this was still a strikingly small proportion.) [127] Even the relatively easy act of subscribing to a Jewish periodical was something only about a quarter of the over-thirty adults, and less than half that proportion of those under thirty, did.

In his 1989 national survey of Jews, Steven M. Cohen found similar trends. Only 46 percent said they currently belonged to any Jewish organizations other than a synagogue, 80 percent said they were not at the time questioned serving on a board or committee of a Jewish organization, and 53 percent said that since the age of twenty-one they had never served in such a capacity. Only 33 percent felt in any way attached to a local Jewish community center or Y.[128]

Finally, while day schools and yeshivas now have more students than ever before (about 130,000), and not only from among the Orthodox, their rising costs, which are not covered by tuition revenues and are not sufficiently deflected by the decreasing philanthropic donations from a shrinking base of givers, have made many of these institutions sink under the weight of their own success.[129] On the other hand, supplementary schools, at an enrollment of just under 270,000, although still the single largest Jewish educational resource for American Jewry, serving about 60 percent of the Jewish school population through the 1980s, with about a third of these in one-day-a-week institutions, find themselves in many cases underenrolled.[130] And all are having an increasingly difficult time finding competent faculty trained in Jewish studies.

Perhaps most noteworthy in the matter of institutional or organizational involvement during the last decade and a half has been the decline in membership—or at least in the active participation—in Jewish voluntary associations whose major goal had been to ensure the social welfare, political liberty, and economic opportunities of American Jews. Institutions like the American Jewish Committee, American Jewish Congress, and a variety of Jewish community relations councils saw their supporters and participants dwindle during these years (after all, fewer than half of American Jews in the 1980s claimed to have ever belonged to any Jewish organization).[131]

Paradoxically, this drop in membership was at least in part a result of the organizations' successes in achieving their goals during the preceding decades. Once they had achieved many, if not all, of their policy goals, they found it difficult to mobilize or even attract members on a continuing basis. Thus, throughout the period when Jewish political influence grew (see below), there was a steady shift of members and contributions from these organizations and institutions. It is therefore no surprise to learn that by the 1990s such venerable institutions as the American Jewish Committee and American Jewish Congress were retrenching, downsizing, and even flirting with the idea of merger and that their membership was increasingly made up of an aging Jewish population.[132]

Those organizations that did manage to hold onto their members or even grow slightly—primarily women's organizations—often did so by changing their raison d'être, becoming, for example, focused on Jewish education, self-help, or consciousness-raising rather than the outmoded or already achieved previous goals. Hadassah is perhaps one of the best examples of this latter recipe for institutional survival (although even it is not as robust as it was even a generation ago).

Probably no institution more graphically displays the problems of affiliation and support than the synagogue. Already noted is the relationship between income and generation with synagogue membership. But there are other developments during the 1980s and 1990s that have led to declining synagogue membership. Thus, with migration away from the Northeast and Midwest to the South and West came a degeneration in synagogue affiliation. In the Midwest and Northeast belonging to a synagogue was far more likely (48 percent and about 42 percent, respectively) than in the South and West (about 35 percent and 29 percent, respectively). Moreover, those who moved after 1980 were about a third less likely to be synagogue members than those who had moved in the earlier decades. Fewer than half of those in the core Jewish population who said they attended synagogue on High Holy Days (59 percent) claimed a current synagogue affiliation. Synagogues have had to do more with less during these years.

All this flux has led in the last decade to a crisis of sorts for many Jewish institutions. While some feel the need for greater support and more members keenly, others are overwhelmed by patterns of utilization which are either too great for the resources available or too small. Some search for greater financial subsidies, while others try to enlarge their pool of subscribers or staff. In a sense the crisis of quality versus quantity—so much a part of Jewish life in these closing years of the century—is most vivid in the Jewish institutional domain.

Political Influence

An anxiety often expressed by those who perceive the declining numbers of Jews is that as the Jewish proportion of America shrinks its political punch will correspondingly become weakened. A diminished political influence, in turn, would result in an imperiled Jewish community. This dread is of course built upon the unspoken but abiding assumption that as a politically powerless minority the Jews run the risk of once again assuming their historical position as a pariah people—even in such an open and presumably tolerant nation as America. Yet, as Goldscheider correctly notes, "American Jews have never constituted a numerically large segment of the population, nor has their political and economic power been a simple function of population size."[133] Glazer extends this argument that political influence "does not depend on numbers alone" by pointing out that "certainly no one would argue that Jewish influence was greater in 1927 [when American Jews peaked at 3.6 percent of the population] than it is in 1985, despite the proportionate decline in the percentage of Jews."[134]

Indeed, throughout the years considered in these pages, American Jews have steadily enlarged their political influence despite their declining numbers. They have done this not only at the level of national politics but also at state and local levels. There are now Jews in positions of power in both houses of the Congress. As these words are being written, the two senators from California, the nation's most populous state, are Jewish women. This era saw a Jew, Henry Kissinger, become one of the most powerful secretaries of state in American history. Three Jews served on the United States Supreme Court during the period, and in 1993 and 1994 a fourth and fifth were confirmed by the Senate. There have been Jewish governors even in states like Vermont with tiny Jewish populations. Jews sit in city halls and on town councils. A Jew, Walter Annenberg, was appointed ambassador to the Court of St. James. Although none has been president or vice-president, by 1987 89 percent of Americans said they would elect a well-qualified Jew as president.[135] Thus, there is no elective or appointive office in America to which Jews today cannot aspire.

Perhaps even more impressive, the political clout of Jews is not limited to those whose Judaism is simply a matter of background heritage. Actively Jewish Jews, including even the Orthodox, have successfully exerted political power. The often effective lobbying efforts of Agudath Israel, the Union of Orthodox Jewish Congregations of America, Habad Hasidim, and the National Jewish Commission on Law and Public Affairs are ample testament of this political muscle. Moreover, Orthodox Jews have also entered the national political arena without giving up or even weakening their Jewish commitments. Thus we find the Orthodox Joseph Lieberman of Connecticut in the U.S. Senate and a yarmulke-wearing Ari Weiss as House Speaker Thomas "Tip" O'Neill's chief legislative aide.

Indeed, perhaps more than any other aspect of Jewish life in America in the approximately four decades in question, the political is one of enormous achievements. To be sure, there have been some setbacks, to which Jews seem particularly sensitive. Thus, in the American Jewish community small losses often psychologically overshadow great victories. Perhaps that is why such organizations as the American Jewish Committee and the American Jewish Congress frequently try to gauge the opinions of the nation on matters of Jewish political influence.[136]

These polls have, at least of late, provided a picture of some ambiguity. Thus in 1992, the American Jewish Committee published a survey that showed that nearly half of all New Yorkers and about 21 percent of a national sample believe Jews have too much influence. These figures are higher than the 11 percent in 1964 and the 13 percent in 1972 who believed Jews held too much influence.[137] What this seems to show is that with rising power will come an increase in the number of people who take exception to that power. Given the choice of having political power that is resented and not having any at all, the former seems the distinctly better option for a minority such as the Jews. In the political domain, at least for now, the relationship between quantity and success is in question. Less has led to more.

Of course, one might argue that part of the growing political influence of Jews is connected to the increasing numbers of American non-Jews who are now related to and part of the Jewish community. These people may serve to amplify the connections Jews have to the American body politic. Yet, for the most part, those who serve as the leaders of Jewish political influence are the Jews themselves.

Orthodoxy in the Eighties and Nineties

One of the reactions that many American Jews have had to the anxieties of their shrinking numbers and precarious condition as reported in the 1990 NJPS and other surveys throughout the last few years has been to suppose that while things may be going badly for many of them, at least Orthodox Jews are holding their own. Indeed, one writer has gone so far as to suggest that for more-assimilated Jews, the Orthodox, and perhaps more so the ultra-Orthodox, "are a nostalgic source of comfort and an assurance that, despite their own abandonment of the ways of their . . . progenitors, the pristine Jewish spiritual past has managed to survive in the lives of these pious few."[138] There's even a black joke among some liberal Jews that with the rapid assimilation this generation is seeing, in the years ahead most of the remaining Jews will be wearing black hats and coats, earlocks and beards. (I say "black joke" since three-quarters of surveyed American Jews did not agree that Orthodox Jews or Hasidim were "the most authentic Jews around," and 84 percent were offended by Orthodox Jews who "show no respect for the way they [the non-Orthodox] choose to be Jewish.")[139] Given what I have said so far in these pages about Orthodox Jews and given my own years of work in the sociology of Orthodoxy, I therefore cannot conclude these reflections on American Jewry without a closer look at how these most actively Jewish Jews are doing and what this says about their future.

Certainly, as already indicated, in many facets of Jewish life and involvement, the Orthodox have cause to celebrate. "Orthodox of the younger generation have higher fertility norms and behavior than the non-Orthodox."[140] They have the lowest rate of intermarriage; about nine in ten of them are married to Jews, and of those relative few who have intermarried, a quarter have spouses who converted to Judaism.[141] They are most likely to visit Israel or to have strong ties to it, scoring higher in their attachments than any other denomination in Jewish America. In 1989, the majority of the 14 percent of American Jews who said they were seriously considering living in Israel were Orthodox.[142] More than any other group, they give to Jewish causes: 87 percent.[143] (To be sure, more than any other Jews, they give predominantly to Orthodox Jewish causes.)[144] The Orthodox have the highest proportion of predominantly Jewish friends (albeit most of them Orthodox like themselves). Cohen even found them to score highest of all denominations in feelings of ethnic pride and level of communal involvement.[145] Although they commonly live in areas of highest Jewish density, when Orthodox Jews have moved to the periphery of the Jewish community, they have managed to do something that few other of their coreligionists could: they have changed the communities into which they have moved rather than become changed by them. Thus, because they cannot or will not acquiesce to a diminished level of Jewish life, no matter where they live, the entry of Orthodox Jews into small Jewish communities has frequently promoted greater religious and ethnic participation in these places.[146] They have been able to make areas of Jewish scarcity flourish. Habad Hasidim are perhaps the most prominent, but by no means alone, among the Orthodox in this regard.

In their family lives, they can point to a lower divorce rate than their coreligionists and than much of the rest of America. Orthodox Jews are wealthier and far better educated than in the past. Many of them have entered the ranks of the professions, achieving political power and prosperity—apparently doing all this without sacrificing their Orthodoxy. The existence of Orthodox physicians, lawyers, politicians, CEOs, and professors is no longer astonishing. On the contrary, at least among the modern Orthodox of America, it is common. According to the 1990 data, about 52 percent of Orthodox Jews had at least one to three years of college. For those who came to America after 1950, the era of Orthodox triumphalism, the figures were even higher, a whopping 81 percent. The same survey shows that by 1989, 32 percent of Orthodox Jews were professionals and about 11 percent were managers. As for those Orthodox who arrived in the United States after 1950, the proportions were even higher: two-thirds were either professionals or managers.

Along with enhanced secular learning, their synagogue, day school, and yeshiva building and enrollment have expanded dramatically. They have made kosher food widely available.

Orthodox Jews have achieved unprecedented political power in America. They lobby successfully to have their interests and needs supported. They exert political influence both within the Jewish community and in government, at both local and national levels. They know their way around a variety of political institutions and corridors of power. It is no longer surprising to see politicians courting their vote, and lobbying in Congress by various Orthodox organizations is today routine, no less than seeing the president, a governor, or a mayor donning a yarmulke. All this has led to an infusion of confidence among the American Orthodox, in sharp contrast to the timidity that often characterized the movement in the first two-thirds of this century.

While there are many ways to account for this confidence, the most likely explanation appears to come from a confluence of three developments. First is the fact that although most observers predicted its imminent demise, Orthodoxy in America defied those predictions and did not disappear. Confounding expectations yields confidence. Put simply, when everyone expects death, even the most fragile of lives seems to be a great triumph. Second, the same American Jewry that in the first half of this century predicted the demise of the Orthodox now ironically finds itself confronting its own rapid assimilation and evaporation. While other American Jews are suffering the ravages of intermarriage and declining Jewish involvement, the relatively overwhelming endogamy and intensive Jewish activity of the Orthodox loom larger and more impressively. Finally, the political influence and power of the Orthodox in Israel, which, in spite of their relatively small numbers, was enhanced during the years of the Likud governments, stimulated a vicarious confidence and parallel political awakening among American Orthodox. In America, moreover, as non-Orthodox Jews abandoned Jewish concerns and activity, their positions of authority and power within the shrinking Jewish establishment were filled by those who remained actively Jewish, most prominently (although by no means exclusively) the Orthodox.

Although the character of this Orthodox triumphalism is complex, it is thus possible to condense it into four decisive and essential features: (1) American Orthodoxy's refusal to wither as predicted along with its apparent ability to maintain continuity, (2) its unbending fidelity to halacha and Jewish tradition even in the open and pluralist American cultural environment, (3) its success in institution building and maintaining economic stability, and (4) its growing political influence.

All this is the apparent triumph of Orthodoxy during these last four decades. But is the triumph real or can we see within Orthodoxy some weaknesses that, while different from those we have seen among American Jewry in general, suggest that even among these most intensively Jewish people within the American Jewish universe, there are signs of decay or at the very least deterioration, signs that the triumph is not without some deficiencies?

The Numbers

An obvious starting point is the population figures. For at least the last twenty-five years, estimates have put the number of American Orthodox Jews at somewhere between 10 and 12 percent of the approximately 5.5 million American Jews, or at about 660,000. Of these about a quarter have been identified as *haredim*, with the rest being "modern Orthodox," a group now divided into a minority that is nominally Orthodox at best and a large majority that is sometimes called "centrist," falling as it does between the extremes of the absolute parochialism of the *haredim* on the one hand and simple affiliation with the label "Orthodox" on the other. This was good news, especially after the predictions at midcentury that Orthodoxy was a relic of the past, soon to fade from the American scene, a case of what sociologist Marshall Sklare in 1955 called "institutional decay." [147]

Yet while the Orthodox failure to disappear might be a source of satisfaction, the 1990 NJPS also disclosed some ominous numbers. For all their expressions of triumphalism and predictions of a rosier demographic future, the Orthodox remain today the smallest of all major Jewish denominations—only the Reconstructionists are fewer. That survey puts all Orthodox at about 7 percent of the 5.5 million born Jews who identify their current religion as Jewish, or about a total of 385,000.[148] The numbers are even smaller when we look more closely and discover that only about 66 percent of those approximately 7 percent who call themselves Orthodox in the 1990 survey always keep kosher, have separate dishes in their homes for meat and milk products, or claimed a current synagogue affiliation (three basic requirements that many would assume are a sine qua non of authentic Orthodoxy). This would yield about 254,000.

The more recent 1991 New York UJA-Federation Jewish population survey finds numbers that seem to echo these smaller population sizes. American Orthodox Jews, who still overwhelmingly live

in the New York metropolitan region, are reported to be at about
14 percent of the 1.4 million New York Jews, or about 200,000.[149]
Even assuming that only 60 percent of American Orthodoxy lives in
and around New York, that leaves a national total of about 330,000,
or about 6 percent of the 5.5 million core Jewish population (born
Jews + Jews by choice + those who though born Jews say they have
no religion) and 8 percent of those 4.2 million who identify themselves as Jews by religion.

Seeking to explain these lower than expected numbers, some
point to the well-documented refusal of the more insular right wing
to participate in social surveys, especially those conducted by organizations that these Orthodox view as suspect, such as the university
or the federations, which are perceived to be dominated by the non-
Orthodox. If, to compensate for the *haredi* element that was not
counted, we add another 25 percent to this figure, we arrive at a total
of about 413,000 American Orthodox Jews, or about 7.5 percent
of the core Jewish population and 9.5 percent of the Jews by religion. Even the most optimistic count puts the Orthodox at 481,000,
or about 9 percent of the core population. These figures certainly
contradict the notion of a triumphal demographic revival among the
Orthodox.

As of this writing, the fact remains that overall the proportion of
those calling themselves Orthodox in America represents no growth,
and perhaps even a decline, in the numbers that have commonly
been assumed. Moreover, this demographic stagnation and decline
has been going on for a while. In Boston, for example, between 1965
and 1975 the proportion of Orthodox shrunk from 14 percent to
5 percent. The data from the 1990 survey confirm this pattern. The
413,000 I count represent a 59 percent decline from the 1990 NJPS
figure of "one million adults reported raised as Orthodox."[150] Put
differently, while about 25 percent (by the NJPS count) of the slightly
more than 4 million people who were born Jews and still identify
themselves as such were (by their own claims) raised as Orthodox,
only 7 or 8 percent still identify themselves as such. To be sure this 25
percent rate of allegiance is higher than the 20 percent of Orthodox
who in 1954 told Gallup that they expected to remain Orthodox—
but not by much.[151] These numbers must surely come as a shock to
all those who claimed that in the last half of this century, American

Orthodoxy was somehow immune to the erosion that characterized the rest of Jewish America.

To this diminished Orthodoxy must be added the fact that what was always a kind of Orthodox "demographic transfusion" into the American Jewish community—immigration—is no longer something the Orthodox do in any significant numbers. Most of the Orthodox migration that occurs today is to Israel and not to the United States.

Certainly, there are ways of looking at the statistics and finding good demographic news. Thus, for example, offering optimism for the future, Sidney Goldstein notes that by 1990 among those who identified themselves as Jewish by religion, almost 10 percent of those between eighteen and twenty-four years of age called themselves Orthodox, twice as many as the 5 percent on average between the ages of twenty-five and sixty-four who did so. These higher numbers among the youngest group, moreover, were closest to those of the Jews at the other end of the age scale, the almost 12 percent of those over sixty-five who called themselves Orthodox, suggesting that the old maxim that "what the son wishes to forget the grandson seeks to remember" may at least be true among the American Orthodox.[152]

Looking more closely at these figures, one finds some indication that the young are indeed maintaining a higher allegiance to their Orthodox origins than those of earlier generations. Among those aged eighteen to twenty-nine, 63 percent of those raised Orthodox were currently Orthodox. This is a rate more than twice as high as that for the thirty to forty-four age group who were raised and remain Orthodox (30 percent) and five times higher than that for the forty-five to sixty-four age group (13 percent).

In support of this reading of the situation of the young are the data that Cohen and I reported in 1989. As noted earlier, we found that "increasingly, the adult children of Orthodox parents claim to be Orthodox themselves, practice a higher level of observance, and report having attended a yeshiva or day school."[153] Indeed, in the last decade many of the young Orthodox display religious attitudes that put them to the right of their elders—and these are attitudes that reflect not only a stronger commitment to Jewish life but also a willingness to act in ways that emphasize Orthodox Jewish identity or involvement.

Although perhaps a most extreme case (but convincing for precisely that reason), if we compare Orthodox rabbis and Orthodox rabbinical students—surely both groups being among the most actively Jewish Jews in America—we find that in the late 1980s, the students score no lower, and sometimes even slightly higher, than the rabbis in measures of Orthodox Jewish identity and involvement.[154] Thus, for example, 100 percent of the Orthodox rabbinical (yeshiva) students polled strongly agreed that being a Jew was one of the most important aspects of their lives, while 96 percent of the Orthodox rabbis took the same position. When asked how they felt about the statement that "halacha must sometimes be compromised to save the Jewish people," 55 percent of the Orthodox rabbis disagreed while fully 70 percent of the Orthodox rabbinical students took the hard line and disagreed (for comparison, the figures for those who disagreed in the other movements were from 5 to 15 percent among the rabbis and 4 to 47 percent among the students). When asked which sorts of Jews best ensure the continuity of the Jewish people, 68 percent of the Orthodox rabbis chose the Orthodox while 88 percent of the Orthodox rabbinical students did so (majorities of all the other respondents said "no single denomination" ensures Jewish continuity). This attitude resonates not only with a stronger sense of Orthodox allegiance but also with an intense sense of Orthodoxy's superiority among its young.

To this denominational self-assurance should be added the fact that in certain places the Orthodox proportion of the population is greater than in others, often giving an impression of being more sizable overall. This is certainly the case in places like New York, where in 1982, they were counted at 11 percent, but by 1991 they were again up to slightly over 14 percent.[155] Moreover, when politicians or other public officials want to signify that they share a concern for or seek the support of American Jewry, they often do so by being photographed or aligning themselves with visibly Orthodox Jews—commonly *haredim*—who are meant somehow to symbolize all Jews. This iconographization of the visibly Orthodox has also amplified the public perception—both among the Orthodox and among other Jews—of their growing strength.

But this self-assurance among the young, these higher proportions in some places, and photo opportunities mask the reality. Thus, no one can really be certain that the higher levels of Orthodoxy among the young will be maintained as they grow older; certainly they were not for previous generations of American Orthodox Jews. With regard to the demographics, for example, the 13 percent figure of New York Jewry for 1981 translates into about 206,000 people, while the apparently higher 14 percent figure of 1991 betokens only about 201,000, since the number of Jews in New York decreased in those ten years. And everyone who thinks even for a moment about the realities of American Jewish life realizes that the bearded Hasid is not the face of most Jews, even in New York City.

What about the purported gains that the Orthodox are supposed to have made in attracting new members? The figures indicate that about 90 percent of those who are now Orthodox were raised as such, demonstrating that for all the noise about the success of Jewish outreach or the Ba'al T'shuvah movement (the so-called returnees to Orthodoxy), very few have been switching into Orthodoxy, Habad Houses and Mitzvah Tanks notwithstanding.[156] Of the 10 percent of the Orthodox who were raised in another denomination, chances are that most of them entered the denomination as a result of marriage to an Orthodox Jew.

These demographic trends suggest that the Orthodox in America may not have been so successful in holding on or adding to their numbers during the last forty years, at least not as successful as many assumed they were. Nevertheless, in the years ahead, if as they mature their young continue the high rate of confidence in and allegiance to the Orthodoxy that they have already displayed, the Orthodox may slowly gain back at least some of the numbers they have lost. That they will in any foreseeable future constitute the majority of American Jews, however, is implausible.

One may look at these small numbers and see another aspect of the Orthodox in America. From this perspective, the essence of the story is not the demographic erosion or potential growth of Orthodoxy but rather its changing character. This outlook actually sees good news in an American Orthodox population whose size has contracted, for that contraction demonstrates that the ante for being considered Orthodox has gradually been raised. Whereas in the past, people who attended public school, who kept kosher most of the time (but not always), and who were affiliated (no matter how tenuously) with an Orthodox synagogue could and did call themselves "Orthodox," in the last twenty-five years the Orthodox life-style has demanded greater Jewish activity and commitment, including but not limited to full-time day school or yeshiva education, stringent adherence to halachic standards of the most demanding sort, and more than simple synagogue affiliation. Those who look at the reality this way argue that the numbers counted in the past were inflated by the inclusion of nominally Orthodox Jews. Given the more demanding criteria of today, fewer Jews may feel able to call themselves Orthodox. But these few who do, many of whom are young, are a hard core that will not decline any longer.

The young Orthodox Jews coming of age today, this argument continues, reflect greater commitments. In time, they will replenish the numbers in the movement, and these adherents will be truly Orthodox. The low population figures thus are to be seen as a trough in a curve that will inevitably rise again, based on a continued movement of Orthodox Jews toward the religious right, which in turn will lead to higher fertility (for the more Orthodox have more children) and negligible denominational defection. The present, this argument concludes, is a smaller, more rigorous, leaner, and therefore exclusivist Orthodoxy in America which in time will grow. Better a small and loyal hard core than a larger and more diluted population.

But can less be more? Can a small Orthodoxy sustain itself long enough to grow? We have already seen that in the case of the general Jewish community, having fewer Jews from whom to draw resources puts an enormous burden on those who choose to be actively Jewish. This is no less true in the case of Orthodoxy. Nothing can better illustrate this than the matter of Orthodox institution building and economics.

Institution Building and Economic Stability

Without question, for all their demographic stagnation or decline, the Orthodox have been tremendously successful in building their institutions in America. The movement is smaller, but its plethora of institutions indicates it is by no means less vital. The institutions of the day school and yeshiva, pioneered by the Orthodox, are multiplying. At last count, about 130,000 were attending day schools and

yeshivas, and the number of such schools exceeded 300. The Orthodox have proportionately more synagogues (many of them small)
than any other Jewish denomination. They have created a variety of
national organizations, many of them umbrellas for an even greater
number of local ones. These include such groups as the Union of
Orthodox Jewish Congregations of America, Association of Orthodox Jewish Scientists, Agudath Israel of America, Association of
Orthodox Jewish Teachers, and National Council of Young Israel.

But institutions cost money and require human resources to maintain them. In particular, the proliferation of yeshivas and day schools
has placed a huge financial burden on the Jewish community in general and especially on the Orthodox. The broken-down building of
the old-time yeshiva has been replaced by a modern edifice that may
still have a mortgage debt and certainly has increased maintenance
costs. The day school that tries to provide high-quality religious and
general studies requires a far more sophisticated faculty than did
the cheder. The *melamed* now draws a higher salary and benefits
package. To support these schools, tuitions have exploded, in some
cases going above $10,000 per student, more expensive than atten-
dance at some state universities. Indeed, some argue these costs are
so burdensome that they have actually "accomplished what zero-
population-growth ideologists never would have—the decline of the
modern Orthodox birth rate." [157] Elissa Blaser, a program specialist
at the Covenant Foundation, which gives grants for excellence in
Jewish education, offers anecdotal evidence: "In my travels around
the country I've found there are many middle-class Jewish families
who are only having two children instead of three or four because of
the cost of day schools." [158]

The *haredi* world has been building educational institutions at
extraordinary speed, including the *kollel*—a yeshiva for married students that provides a stipend for its associates so they can support
large families and an Orthodox life-style (still the most expensive of
Jewish life-styles) and that has costs that can run upward of $30,000
per year per participant. Institution building has been a hallmark of
haredi identity and a symbol of their vitality. These academies, however, absorb enormous sums of money; they do not generate them.

While the Orthodox may expect some funds from the various
federations and national Jewish charities (and some, especially the

haredim, have even found ways to get aid from the U.S. government through the Education Department), these contributions can never fully sustain these many institutions. Indeed, the day schools and yeshivas alone could easily devour all the funds available and still lack sufficient economic means to continue operating without a deficit. That would leave synagogues and voluntary associations looking for additional monies. Hence, at least with regard to institution building, less is not more. The shrinking membership base, a function of the dropping numbers of people who are calling themselves Orthodox, should lead to a realization that in its institutional life, Orthodoxy sits in a very precarious position. Moreover, the *haredi* wing of Orthodoxy is in an even more shaky economic situation, having higher expenses per capita and per institution and generally far lower income than any other sector of American Jewry ($14,702 per household per annum in Kiryas Yoel, for example, a well-known American *haredi* settlement, and one in the news because of its dependence on New York State assistance). Their situation has led some *haredi* institutions and individuals to find licit and sometimes illicit ways of receiving income from public sources like welfare, medicare, and other funds for the indigent.[159]

Ironically, the tremendous success of the Orthodox institution building is thus the very source of its undoing. To dismantle what has been built for lack of support would be a failure of massive proportions. To try to sustain it by taxing the same Orthodox people who are being asked to support all the other Orthodox institutions is, however, also to court disaster. Perhaps this is why increasingly Orthodox Jews have begun supporting the idea of tax vouchers for parochial schools, blurring the boundary between religion and state. Yet in doing this, they run up against one of the cardinal principles of American Jewry and American law, both of which have always sought to keep that boundary very clear. Given that boundary, the likelihood of finding much more in the way of support from tax levy funds is small indeed. (The Orthodox in Israel, though proportionately a larger part of the population at about 15 percent, actually face many of the same economic realities, but there they can count on government support—especially for their education, the single largest expense—which may be one purely economic justification

for an Orthodox aliyah.) Thus, the Orthodox in America will essentially have to sustain themselves. But can they?

Some suggest that American Orthodoxy's richer adherents will
help to support the financial needs of the movement, especially if it is
smaller and leaner. But can this really happen? A brief look at some
economic realities is crucial for an answer.

We have already seen earlier in these pages that the median annual income of the Orthodox (in 1990 slightly more than $40,000)
is the lowest of all Jewish denominations, as it has been throughout the last forty years. Moreover, controlling for inflation, it is even
lower now than it was in 1970. Orthodox Jews as a class have not
become richer vis-à-vis the general American Jewish population in
the last twenty years. Yet the costs of being Orthodox—maintaining its institutions and life-style—have if anything grown over this
same period. Nor have the Orthodox a large number of wealthy adherents available to help offset these costs. In 1990, about 10.5 percent of Orthodox Jews reported having an annual family income of
about $80,000 or more, compared with about 17 percent of the total
Jewish population reporting the same level of income. The data demonstrate that the percentage of Orthodox Jews with "high income"
(over $40,000 in 1970 dollars and over $130,000 in 1990 dollars)
actually decreased in the last twenty years. Even if Orthodox Jews
do become richer, their communal expenses will continue to rise.
Unless more people enter into the movement or more of the rich give
more of their money to Orthodox causes, this will make it prohibi-
tively expensive to be Orthodox in America.

How expensive? Considering that the completed Orthodox Jewish household size on average in America is about 5, with the more
traditionalist households at 7 or more, we can compute some of the
figures.[160] A rough estimate of the annual Jewish costs such families would incur include synagogue membership ($750), day school
education (between $5,000 and $10,000 per child), Jewish community center or other voluntary associations membership ($400),
charitable donations ($1,600), and attendance at a Jewish summer
camp (between $2,000 and $4,000 per child).[161] The total of such
expenses ranges between $23,750 and $72,750 on average, depending on family size and region of country. Moreover, these expenses

do not include the undeniably increased costs of kosher food and of housing, which for most Orthodox Jews is in urban areas where prices are relatively high. Nor do they include the costs of an occasional trip to Israel, subscriptions to Jewish periodicals, a bar or bat mitzvah celebration, weddings, and the other "luxuries" which have largely become part of the obligatory pattern of American Orthodox life. Taken together, these are massive (some might say, impossible) financial burdens for a group whose median income is about $40,000. In effect, the Jews with the lowest median income in America, the Orthodox, have the highest Jewish expenses precisely because of their more intense and active Jewish pattern of life. Is it any wonder that when asked by the New York population survey if they felt "prosperous," "comfortable," or were just "getting along" or "poor," New York's Orthodox Jews, who were most likely to make these minimal Jewish commitments, were also the most likely (over 30 percent) to feel they were just getting by or poor? [162]

Finally, given the fact that *haredim* by virtue of a life-style which emphasizes extended time in Jewish education and large family size tend to need far more money than they can produce and the fact of their growing proportion within the Orthodox movement, an even greater economic burden will be placed on the Orthodox as a whole. This is something that all the *meshulachim* (emissaries) who collect for Orthodox institutions have begun to recognize. "You travel a hundred miles even for fifteen dollars," as one such fund collector told me. It is also not surprising that *haredim* and *haredi* institutions in America have been scrambling frantically for funds in the last few years—not always avoiding questionable means, as illustrated by the recent Pell Grants and GAO audit scandals, which revealed *haredim* drawing on government funds for which they did not qualify.

Given this picture of shrinking numbers and high expenses without the money to pay for them, one might conclude that for the Orthodox in America, the near future is at least as frightening as it is for all the rest of their coreligionists. Without real growth, the Orthodox will find it hard to remain steadfast in their ways. They will not be able to support the institutions which bolster, nourish, and symbolize a vigorous Jewish life. Moreover, they will be unlikely to find support for those institutions and ways of life from elsewhere—certainly not from the rest of America, which, however tolerant it may continue to be about ethnic and religious diversity, has always been scrupulous about the financial separation of religion and state. Nor will they likely find aid coming from non-Orthodox American Jews, who will continue to provide more of their philanthropic support to American universities, museums, symphony orchestras, the United Fund, and other non-Jewish causes. And when these other Jews do support Jewish causes, they are unlikely to select the Orthodox ones (which are still viewed as overly sectarian by most) in spite of the increasing needs of the Orthodox. Still today, most non-Orthodox Jews continue to view the Orthodox negatively as "narrow-minded, isolationist, and intolerant." [163]

As bleak as this economic picture is, it does highlight something quite remarkable about the Jewish commitments of the Orthodox. The fact that, in spite of these economic burdens and their uncertain demographic future, the Orthodox have continued to be highly involved in their Jewish life says volumes about the depth of their devotion to such an active Jewish life and the rewards that they see in it. To be Orthodox today and into tomorrow is no small matter. This demanding attachment certainly merits the attention that those concerned with Jewish continuity in America have given the Orthodox.

Yet all this does not deny the basic fact that, without real demographic growth, strength becomes weakness. When institutions sap instead of sustain a group, there is decay, not triumph. Or as the old Jewish proverb puts it: *im ein kemach, ein Torah* (without funds, there is no way to promote the Torah).

Of course, the Orthodox could go out and try to recruit new followers, to enlarge their base of supporters, although if they opened the books and showed the costs of joining, they might find few ready to pay the price. While some do try to attract new Orthodox, the outreach and recruiting efforts of Orthodoxy to this point, as the previously cited numbers make clear, have shown little demographic success. For the most part preferring to turn inward and maintain the boundaries between themselves and other Jews, the Orthodox— except for Habad Hasidim—have never really taken up proselytization with gusto in America.

There is one more putative Orthodox success story in America that should be considered: the day school. As mentioned, these institutions are perhaps the single most striking symbol of Orthodox vitality and its capacity to root itself in America while ensuring its future. But what do we find when we look more closely at these schools?

The emphasis on secular education and professionalization among large numbers of the so-called centrist Orthodox, those who stress their capacity to be loyal to the tradition without being overly insular and parochial, has also brought changes in their schools, the crucial pipeline that nourishes Orthodox life. In the first place, these schools are now, more than ever, emphasizing secular achievements over Jewish studies, a trend that, as earlier noted, has accelerated during the last forty years. Equipping their students to get into a good college and then make a good income rather than developing observant and Jewishly educated Jews is often effectively the goal of these schools. When day school graduates subsequently do achieve success in the secular world, the temptation to ease into a pattern of life that embraces the culture of that world is particularly powerful. One must assume that at least some formerly Orthodox Jews have yielded and may continue to yield to this temptation. Dramatically betokening such cultural drift is the fact that among those Jews who received a day school education (admittedly not a totally Orthodox population although a preponderantly Orthodox one), 43 percent of the males and 22 percent of the females reported a non-Jewish spouse in the last decade.[164]

By itself, the emphasis on a high-level secular education in some day schools need not necessarily lead their graduates to abandon their Orthodox origins, if the Jewish studies teachers provide a parochial counterpoint to the attractions of secular culture. However, another of the results of the shift of so many Orthodox Jews into the mainstream of secular culture during these last forty years has been, first, a tacit devaluation of Jewish education as a profession, except among the *haredim,* where being a yeshiva head or teacher is still an esteemed position, and, second, a draining from the available pool of Jewish educators those who are committed to a centrist Orthodoxy. Today, therefore, those who have remained the Jewish educators in Orthodox institutions often are either people who chose not to embrace the culture of the outside world, America (by and large those who cleave to the religious right, often the ultra-Orthodox), or those who could not make it in that outside world. The former are persons who, while perhaps Jewishly inspiring, do not share the ideology and values of centrist Orthodoxy. The latter, on the other hand, are dominated by those who "stayed behind" and are often considered incapable of providing a dynamic and inspiring Jewish education. These then are the people who are supposed to act as cultural and religious counterpoints to those who would pursue secular American culture with abandon. But what sorts of counterforces can they be?

Assuming that those who are Jewish educators because they can be nothing else soon drop out of the picture—failures do not generate continuity—we can predict an Orthodox Jewish education that will either pull the young further to the religious right through the effect that their ultra-Orthodox teachers have on them or, failing that, turn them away completely from an Orthodoxy so at odds with the life their parents lead and the values they hold dear. For all the success in day school creation, then, the Orthodox, by virtue of the sorts of lives they have chosen to lead in America, have also built some problems into that very school system of which they are so proud.

Hence, those who look to the Orthodox to serve as a kind of insurance policy for Judaism in America, who count on them to certify kashrut, write Torah scrolls and mezuzahs, staff the needs of Jewish education, and provide a safeguard for tradition, must consequently realize that they cannot count on the Orthodox to continue taking care of themselves. And when these most involved and active of Jews are in trouble, what optimism can there be about all those who are less involved and whose Judaism is less intensive, whose commitments may crumble under the weight of economic realities or erode under the tides of assimilation? Moreover, if the Orthodox, who score so high in Jewish involvement, are in distress, does this mean that American Jewish life will ultimately fall completely into the hands of those for whom minimal involvement and vague heritage are enough? If the Orthodox in America are in trouble, are not all American Jews in trouble?

Conclusion

In a sense, those who chose to identify themselves as Jews yet remained in America after the 1950s, and especially after 1967, when an enlarged and more secure national homeland in Israel beckoned, reflected an implicit optimism about the possibilities of Jewish life here. Moreover, as long as they persist in staying here, they continue to affirm this confidence. Although emerging from an extreme case, an example of this attitude was expressed in a 1993 prediction from a member of one of the thirty remaining Jewish families in Butte, Montana (down from a peak of 500 in the 1940s). Speaking with a kind of die-hard optimism about the Jewish future in his town, he declared: "As long as there is one family, there will always be a temple in Butte. It will never bite the dust." [165] A version of this hopefulness is undoubtedly signified in the opinion held by the 61 percent of American Jewry who at the outset of the eighties agreed (the extent of the optimism may be even greater, since only 13 percent disagreed) that there was a "bright future for [Jewish] life in America." [166]

To be sure, the form in which this Jewish confidence has manifested itself has varied. For a majority, as they became inextricably bound up with America, it was evidenced in their widely held assumption that even with a minimal level of Jewish activity enough of what was valuable in the Jewish heritage would be preserved. A student rabbi occasionally flown in to run a service in Butte, a seder once a year (while the children are young) in New Rochelle, Sunday school in Chicago, a sense of Jewish pride in Seattle demonstrated by attendance at a lecture series on Jewish themes—these were sufficient. They all seemed to imply that "it was easy enough to be a Jew in America," at least at some low level of Jewish identification. One could therefore conclude: "America was good to and for the Jews."

The other group, a minority, was also optimistic about being Jewish in America, for they continued to try to assert, express, and practice being Jewish in America, regardless of the obstacles. They persevered in celebrating parochial involvement, even if this meant going against the cultural grain of American integrationist ideology. They demanded more involvement and content in Jewish commitments, even if it sapped many of their financial resources. Their conviction that in their choice to be active and involved they could ensure Jewish continuity and vitality sustained them. And even when some of them gave their Jewish identity and activity an equal, if not superior, ontological personal meaning than their strictly American attachments and activities, even when they acted like insular religious sectarians, in doing so openly here, they tacitly demonstrated that they trusted in America's tolerance of their distinctiveness and desire to maintain their way of life. They believed that as Americans, they were entitled—perhaps even encouraged—to be good Jews. This certainly also displays a great faith in what America promised.

The question, of course, that all these sociological reflections revolve about is whether that optimism of American Jewry has been justified. Or, to repeat my inquiries at the outset of these pages: Has this been a place that preserved and protected Jewish life? Is it a place in which a Jewish future is ensured? Does Judaism survive, as well as the Jews?

As already noted, in order to respond to all these questions in the affirmative, some have had to change their perspective as well as the standards of measuring what it means to be Jewish in America. Perceiving life out of their sense of a deep-rootedness in and assimilation to this country, they have suggested that anxieties about the American Jewish future—as about the past—are unwarranted; Jews in America will survive but will be transformed, reconstituted in political, economic, and cultural styles that will provide new bases for cohesion and continuity. They see cultural recognition, the growth of opportunity, political influence, and the absence of persecution or sanctioned discrimination against Jews as the ultimate achievements and elements of an American Jewish success story.

On the other hand, those who have maintained that anything short of a fidelity to traditional Jewish tribalism and observance will end American Jewish history and make it little more than a "part of American memory as a whole" worry about survival and cannot therefore answer these questions always in the affirmative.[167] If their remaining here trying to lead full Jewish lives to ensure survival in America signifies their optimism, their continuing and simultaneous anxieties about the possibilities of that survival are an equally powerful counterforce. These are the people after whom Charles Liebman so aptly entitled his book *The Ambivalent American Jew*.[168] They see being Jewish in America as a challenge.

To the transformationists one is tempted to point out that a Jewish education that is largely trivial in its contents, a growth in the membership of less-demanding Jewish denominations at the expense of

those that require a greater commitment of observance and Jewish involvement, an increasing difficulty in finding both Jewish leadership
and Jewish educators, a large offering of Judaica in the university but
something short of large enrollments in such courses, a diminishing
density in Jewish residence, a falling number of Jewish philanthropic
collections, a ballooning intermarriage rate with a declining number
of the non-Jewish spouses converting to Judaism, low fertility and a
reduced population, many of whom are aging and dropping out of
Jewish activity, all point to a transformation of American Jewry that
demonstrates that "a significant and enduring trend toward lower
levels of Jewish identification is indeed under way,"[169] and that cannot inspire confidence among any but the hopelessly naive optimists.

Jewish heritage and pride are simply not enough, even when they
result in political influence and symbolic ethnic visibility. If those
raised as Jews "continue to think of themselves as Jews regardless of
how they behave," this is, in the words of one observer who views
Jewish life in America in pessimistic terms, nothing less than "a
form of collective assimilation that takes place in stages."[170] Such an
attitude would transform being Jewish in America to denoting little
more than a community of origin, an ethnic and religious starting
point from which the paths diverge to almost anywhere one chooses.
While there is a "basic sociological wisdom" that "the community of
birth is stronger than the community of choice," certain choices can
restructure the community of birth.[171] When being Jewish becomes a
matter of choice rather than a sense of unchangeable destiny, it may
become no more grounded in meaning than is, say, Ronald Reagan's
Irishness.

As for the public displays of Jewishness that render Jewish life
far more visible than in the past and that some point to with optimism, these do not presage a rosy future. The Hanukkah menorahs
and Holocaust museums, the kosher food on airlines, the Israel Day
parades, and Jewish book fairs are not enough. Rather, as Charles
Liebman argues, these public displays project "a false image of Jewish vitality," a kind of "residual Jewishness," or a hollow Judaism.[172]
To be meaningful barriers against the sweeping tide of America,
Jewish choices in the future will have to be "less ambivalent, less
ambiguous, and more decisively at one or the other end of the continuum."[173] Yet without large numbers willing to make those decisive

choices, the few who do dare to make them will, barring some radical and unforeseeable shift in the winds of history, feel their Jewish life in America is precarious at best. There will probably continue to be such Jews: the compulsion to survive in all sorts of host societies is a trait acquired by generations of the Diaspora experience. It will not easily evanesce. But is this enough upon which to hang the future?

In a sense, one might conclude that those who left America for Israel more than anyone else have unequivocally answered this question in the negative. In their aliyah they were saying Jewish life, however expressed or active, could not flourish in America and that to remain fully a Jew one needed to be in and part of the Jewish homeland, with all its problems and Jewish contradictions. Certainly among the Orthodox, who have the highest rate of aliyah of any segment of American Jewry, who think about it more seriously than any other American Jews, and who have been sending their young there for extended stays and education for at least the last ten years, the Jewish yearning for Israel looms ever larger. But they are not alone. Many of those Americans whose commitments to their Jewish identity burns brightest and who have gone to Israel are among the most shining examples of what a Jew can be. To meet them is to be encouraged about the Jewish future and its link to the past.

Are the days of Jews in America numbered? Will American Judaism become so transformed as to be unconnected with all that preceded it? There are no unequivocal answers; each Jew will have to answer for himself or herself. What is clear as I write these last words is that the Jews in America will continue to have two hearts, show two faces, and turn toward two directions. One of those hearts beats with the rhythms of Jewish life, and its face turns ever more frequently toward the Jewish core, even though the feet underneath it seem still firmly planted in American soil. But the other face, the larger of the two, turns toward the West and America and its heart pounds to an American beat. Its footsteps lead into American life, and Israel and Jewish tradition are but a distant melody that still echoes in the mind, sometimes louder, sometimes softer. Whether this song will be enough, in the din of American life, I cannot say for certain.

As for me, an active Jew standing here in Seattle, I can only quote the great poet Yehuda Ha-Levi, who throughout his life longed for his return to Zion: "My heart is in the East but I am in the far-thest reaches of the West." If I am to be certain that my children and their children will continue to be actively Jewish, then the boat that brought my family here to America in 1950 may still have another trip to make.

Notes

Prologue

1. Lucy Dawidowicz, "A Century of Jewish History, 1881–1981: The View from America," in *American Jewish Yearbook, 1982* (hereafter cited as *AJYB*), p. 10.

2. Arriving on 20 May 1946, the first ship carrying displaced persons to America was the *Marine Flasher* (see Morris U. Shappes, *A Pictorial History of the Jews of the United States*, rev. ed. [New York: Marzani & Munsell, 1965], p. 258).

3. *New York Times*, 20 Jan. 1950, p. 5, and 19 Jan. 1950, p. 1.

4. *New York Times*, 19 Jan. 1950, p. 7.

5. Elliot Cohen, "An Act of Affirmation," *Commentary* 1 (Nov. 1945): 3.

6. Charles Dickens, *A Tale of Two Cities* (Boston: Colonial Press, 1867), p. 1.

7. These people are those who are born Jews and identify their religion as Judaism and those who identify themselves as Jews by choice. See Barry A. Kosmin et al., *Highlights of the CJF 1990 National Jewish Population Survey* (New York: Council of Jewish Federations, 1991).

1. Starting Over: *Acculturation and Suburbia, the Jews of the 1950s*

1. Bernard Bailyn, Robert Dallek, David Davis, David Donald, John L. Thomas, and Gordon Wood, *The Great Republic* (Lexington: D.C. Heath, 1985), p. 792.

2. Alvin Chenkin, "Jewish Population of the United States, 1955," in *AJYB, 1956*.

3. Albert I. Gordon, *Jews in Suburbia* (Boston: Beacon Press, 1959), p. 9.

4. Ibid., p. 1; and *U.S. News and World Report*, 10 Aug. 1956.

5. Morton Keller, "Jews and the Character of American Life since 1930," in Charles Herbert Stember et al., *Jews in the Mind of America* (New York: Basic Books, 1966), p. 270.

6. Ibid.

7. David Riesman, *The Lonely Crowd* (New Haven: Yale University

Press, 1950); Joseph Berger, "Emigrés in Suburbs Find Life's Flip Side," *New York Times*, 24 Jan. 1993, p. 30. Although the article discusses the new suburbanites of the 1980s, its descriptions are no less true for the 1960s.

8. Gordon, *Jews in Suburbia*, p. 60.

9. Ibid. For a full discussion of the difficulties that this mother/housewife role entailed for the suburban woman, see Helena Z. Lopata, *Occupation: Housewife* (New York: Oxford University Press, 1971).

10. Berger, "Emigrés in Suburbs Find Life's Flip Side," p. 30.

11. See Gordon, *Jews in Suburbia*, p. 64; and Lopata, *Occupation: Housewife*.

12. Lopata, *Occupation: Housewife*, p. 51.

13. Berger, "Emigrés in Suburbs Find Life's Flip Side," p. 30.

14. See Gordon, *Jews in Suburbia*, p. 69.

15. Address delivered at the United Nations, 26 Sept. 1961.

16. Ben Halpern, "America Is Different," in Ben Halpern, *The American Jew* (New York: Theodor Herzl Foundation, 1956); reprinted in M. Sklare, *The Jew in American Society* (New York: Behrman House, 1974), p. 78.

17. Bailyn et al., *The Great Republic*, p. 795.

18. Ibid.

19. Rabbi Morris Kertzer, "What Is a Jew?" *Look*, June 1952, p. 10.

20. Ibid., p. 11. See also Milton L. Barron, ed., *The Blending American* (Chicago: Quadrangle Books, 1972), p. vii ("Especially noteworthy are the ambivalent attitudes toward intermarriage held by Americans.").

21. Kertzer, "What Is a Jew?" p. vii.

22. The exact number of Jews in America has always been unclear. (1) No accurate census has been possible, because the government does not ask about religion when conducting censuses. (2) The open nature of American ethnic identity has enabled all sorts of people to call themselves Jews whether or not they fit the traditional definition of who is a Jew. (3) The counts taken have usually been made either by relying on the reports of Jewish leaders (who have a vested interest in inflating the count of those they purport to lead) or by counting the affiliated (most commonly by counting those who appear in the synagogue on Yom Kippur or who are listed as members of some other Jewish organization or institution). But in March 1957, for the only time since 1950, the Census Bureau asked a sample of Americans fourteen years old and older their religious preferences, and from that count a fairly accurate projection of the number of Jews in America was possible. The number they came up with was 5,030,000. Given that the census did not count those who were brought up as Jews but no longer considered themselves such, did not count children under fourte, and did not count Jews in the armed forces, that number should probably be raised by about 200,000. See U.S. Bureau of the Census, *Current Population Reports: Population Characteristics*, ser. P-20, no. 79, 2 Feb. 1958; and Jack J. Diamond, "A Reader in the Demography of American Jews," in *AJYB, 1977*, pp. 284–86.

23. Reprinted in *Menorah Journal* 43, nos. 1–2 (1955): 3.

24. Quoted in *Time,* 15 Feb. 1963, p. 21.

25. Sklare, *The Jew in American Society,* p. 69.

26. David Wyman, *The Abandonment of the Jews: America and the Holocaust, 1941–1945* (New York: Pantheon Books, 1984). While no one would argue that the Americans had any complicity with the Nazis, the facts remain that only 10 percent of those who could have been allowed in as refugees were permitted to enter (a poll taken during the war showed that 78 percent of Americans did not believe that such refugees should be allowed in even after the war's conclusion) and that the Americans (with the full support of the U.S. State Department) refused to bomb Auschwitz or take any steps to end the slaughter when they first received conclusive evidence of the Jewish death camps in 1942. Even as late as 1948, after the world knew about the horrors of the Holocaust and the Displaced Persons Act had been passed and was being implemented, while 53 percent of Americans polled said they would limit the number of German immigrants allowed into this country, 60 percent said they would limit the number of Jews allowed to immigrate (Charles Stember, "Attitudes toward Association with Jews," in Stember et al., *Jews in the Mind of America,* p. 147).

27. Stember, "Attitudes toward Association with Jews," p. 104; Theodore Solotaroff and Marshall Sklare, "Introduction," in Stember et al., *Jews in the Mind of America,* p. 9.

28. Halpern, "America Is Different," pp. 86, 85.

29. Irving Howe, *The World of Our Fathers* (New York: Harcourt Brace Jovanovich, 1976), p. 615.

30. Gordon, *Jews in Suburbia,* p. 16.

31. Alvin Chenkin, "Jewish Population in the United States, 1957," in *AJYB, 1958,* Appendix Table 2, p. 23.

32. Mark Zborowski and Elizabeth Herzog, *Life Is with People* (New York: International Universities Press, 1952). The publication of this book at the beginning of the fifties can be seen as a kind of sociocultural reminder to them of what they were on the verge of changing.

33. Gordon, *Jews in Suburbia,* p. 16.

34. N. Glazer, "Social Characteristics of American Jews, 1654–1954," in *AJYB, 1955,* p. 11. Most of the rest lived in the Northeast—quite a change from 1890, when Jews were in every state in the Union except the Oklahoma Territory. See John S. Billings, *Vital Statistics of the Jews in the United States,* Census Bulletin 12 (1890).

35. C. Morris Horowitz and Lawrence J. Kaplan, *Report of the Demographic Study Committee of the Federation of Jewish Philanthropies* (New York, 1959), p. 21.

36. Ibid., p. 41.

37. Arthur Hertzberg, *The Jews in America* (New York: Simon & Schuster, 1989), p. 321.

38. Sklare, *The Jew in American Society,* p. 72.

39. Judith R. Kramer and Seymour Leventman, *Children of the Gilded*

Ghetto: Conflict Resolutions of Three Generations of American Jews (New Haven: Yale University Press, 1961).

40. Joseph W. Eaton, "Controlled Acculturation: A Survival Technique of the Hutterites," *ASR* 17 (1952): 338.

41. Steven Polgar, "Biculturation of Mesquakie Teenage Boys," *American Anthropologist,* n.s., 62 (1960): 233; Horace Kallen, "The Foundations of Jewish Spiritual and Cultural Unity," *Judaism* 6 (Spring 1957): 110–18.

42. Erich Rosenthal, "Acculturation without Assimilation? The Jewish Community of Chicago, Illinois," *American Journal of Sociology* 66, no. 3 (Nov. 1960): 275–88.

43. Herbert J. Gans, "The Origin of a Jewish Community in the Suburbs," in Marshall Sklare, ed., *The Jews: Social Patterns of an American Group* (New York: Free Press, 1958); reprinted in Marshall Sklare, *The Jewish Community in America* (New York: Behrman House, 1974), pp. 38–39.

44. N. Glazer, "What Sociology Knows about American Jews," *Commentary* 9 (Jan.–June 1950): 279.

45. As an Israeli, Tartakower felt impelled to add that American Jewry also remained focused on "the state of Israel as its political as well as moral center." But as time went on, this became more a matter of wishful thinking than a description of empirical reality. See Aryeh Tartakower, "New Trends in Jewish Sociology," *Jewish Social Studies* 12, no. 2 (1950): 116.

46. Ralph Linton, ed., *Acculturation in Seven American Indian Tribes* (New York: Appleton, Century, 1940), p. 519.

47. Thomas K. Fitzgerald, "Education and Identity: A Reconsideration of Some Models of Acculturation and Identity," *New Zealand Journal of Educational Studies* 7, no. 1 (May 1972): 49. On dominant and subordinate culture, see also A. F. C. Wallace, "Cultural Composition of the Handsome Lake Religion," in W. N. Fenton and J. Gulick, eds., *Symposium on Cherokee and Iroquois Culture,* U.S. Bureau of American Ethnology Bulletin 180 (Washington: Government Printing Office, 1961), pp. 139–51.

48. Eaton, "Controlled Acculturation," p. 339. The so-called ultra-Orthodox understood this danger and accordingly distanced themselves from "modern Orthodoxy," while continually criticizing both its strategies for survival and its leadership.

49. Gordon, *Jews in Suburbia,* p. 16.

50. Gans, "Origin of a Jewish Community in the Suburbs," p. 26.

51. Ibid., p. 33.

52. Ibid., p. 38.

53. Kramer and Leventman, *Children of the Gilded Ghetto,* p. 213.

54. *New York Times,* 20 Jan. 1950, p. 5, and 19 Jan. 1950, p. 1. See also Egon Mayer, *From Suburb to Shtetl* (Philadelphia: Temple University Press, 1979), pp. 3–19.

55. Horowitz and Kaplan, *Report of the Demographic Study Committee of the Federation of Jewish Philanthropies,* p. 339.

56. "[I]f [an individual] identifies with the host society, he should favor

assimilation [i.e., unilateral absorption]" (E. A. Sommerlad and J. W. Berry, "The Role of Ethnic Identification in Distinguishing between Attitudes toward Assimilation and Integration of a Minority Racial Group," *Human Relations* 23, no. 1 [1970]: 24).

57. Gordon, *Jews in Suburbia,* p. 65.

58. Calvin Goldscheider, "Demography and Jewish Survival," in M. Himmelfarb and V. Baras, eds., *Zero Population Growth: For Whom?* (proceedings of American Jewish Committee Conference on Population and Intergroup Relations, held in New York, N.Y., in 1975) (Westport, Conn.: Greenwood Press, 1978), p. 132.

59. Milton L. Barron, "Intergroup Aspects of Choosing a Mate," in Barron, *The Blending American,* p. 43.

60. Calvin Goldscheider, *Jewish Continuity and Change* (Bloomington: Indiana University Press, 1986), p. 29.

61. See Marshall Sklare's comments about Orthodoxy in his *Conservative Judaism,* 2d ed. (New York: Schocken, 1972), p. 43.

62. A. Roy Eckardt, "The New Look in American Piety," *Christian Century,* 17 Nov. 1954, pp. 1395–97. See also Will Herberg, *Protestant Catholic Jew,* 2d ed. (New York: Doubleday, 1960), p. 1.

63. Jacob Sloan, "Religion," in *AJYB, 1955,* p. 188.

64. Herberg, *Protestant Catholic Jew,* p. 84.

65. Cited in ibid.

66. *Encyclopedia Judaica,* vol. 15, p. 1643; Will Herberg, "The Post-war Revival of the Synagogue," *Commentary* 9 (Jan.–June 1950): 315.

67. That Wright had no idea about the nature of Jewish prayer was apparently not deemed an obstacle to choosing him to design this synagogue on the American suburban frontier. His design of a building to look like Mount Sinai and to give those inside a feeling of their insignificance draws more from Christian cathedrals than from synagogues, which stress human assembly and communal bonding.

68. David de Sola Pool, "Judaism and the Synagogue," in O. Janowsky, *The American Jew: A Composite Portrait* (Freeport, N.Y.: Books for Libraries Press, 1942), p. 52.

69. Two who did not assume that this sort of synagogue was enough are, for example, B. Berry, *Race and Ethnic Relations* (Boston: Houghton Mifflin, 1951), p. 217; and Robert Bierstedt, *The Social Order,* 2d ed. (New York: McGraw Hill, 1963), p. 176.

70. Herberg, "The Post-war Revival of the Synagogue," p. 315; and see also Hertzberg, *The Jews in America,* p. 321.

71. *Encyclopedia Judaica,* vol. 15, p. 1643.

72. Hertzberg, *The Jews in America,* p. 323.

73. David Reisman, "Introduction," in Elliot E. Cohen, ed., *Commentary on the American Scene* (New York: Knopf, 1953), p. x.

74. Herberg, "The Post-war Revival of the Synagogue," p. 323.

75. Ibid.

76. Everett Stonequist, "The Marginal Character of the Jews," in I. Graeber and S. Britt, *Jews in a Gentile World* (New York: Macmillan, 1942), pp. 302, 306.

77. Charles Liebman, *The Ambivalent American Jew* (Philadelphia: Jewish Publication Society of America, 1973), p. vii.

78. Milton M. Goldberg, "A Qualification of the Marginal Man Theory," *American Sociological Review* 6, no. 7 (1947): 53.

79. William B. Helmreich, *The World of the Yeshiva* (New York: Free Press, 1982). On the narrow range of students even an institution like Yeshiva College attracted during the fifties, see Jeffrey S. Gurock, *The Men and Women of Yeshiva* (New York: Columbia University Press, 1988), pp. 165–67.

80. Fred Massarik, "Trends in U.S. Jewish Education: National Jewish Population Study Findings," in *AJYB, 1977*, pp. 246–47.

81. Ben Seligman, "The American Jew: Some Demographic Features," in *AJYB, 1950*, p. 35.

82. See *AJYB* for the years 1948 through 1952.

83. Uriah Engelman, "Jewish Education," in *AJYB, 1960*, pp. 48, 58.

84. Seligman, "The American Jew," in *AJYB, 1950*, p. 35.

85. Engelman, "Jewish Education," in *AJYB, 1960*, p. 58.

86. Massarik, "Trends in U.S. Jewish Education," in *AJYB, 1977*, p. 242.

87. For a fuller description of the process, see Samuel Heilman, "Inside the Jewish School," in Stuart Kelman, ed., *What We Know about Jewish Education* (Los Angeles: Torah Aura, 1992), pp. 303–30.

88. Dawidowicz, "A Century of Jewish History, 1881–1981," in *AJYB, 1982*, p. 67.

89. George Lebovitz, "Satisfaction and Dissatisfaction among Judaic Studies Teachers in Midwestern Jewish Day Schools" (Ph.D. diss., University of Cincinnati, 1981).

90. The phrase, an old saying, comes from Reisman, "Introduction," in Cohen, *Commentary on the American Scene*, p. xxii.

91. To be sure, as Paul Ritterband and Harold Wexler document (*Jewish Learning in American Universities* [Bloomington: Indiana University Press, 1994]), there were some professors as early as the 1880s who taught subjects within the context of Semitic philology and biblical studies that might be considered "Jewish," but the real explosion of what would be called and perceived as "Jewish studies" did not begin to happen until the late 1960s (about which more below). See also Arnold J. Band, "Jewish Studies in American Liberal Arts Colleges and Universities," in *AJYB, 1966*, pp. 3–30.

92. A. G. Duker, "Joshua Starr," *Jewish Social Studies* 12, no. 1 (Jan. 1950): 4.

93. Sherry Gorelick, *City College and the Jewish Poor: Education in New York, 1880–1924* (New Brunswick, N.J.: Rutgers University Press, 1981).

94. Mark Zborowski and Elizabeth Herzog, "The Place of Book Learning in Traditional Jewish Culture," in M. Mead and M. Wolfenstein, *Childhood in Contemporary Cultures* (Chicago: University of Chicago Press, 1955), p. 119.

95. Barry Chiswick, "The Labor Market Status of American Jews: Patterns and Determinants," in *AJYB, 1985*, p. 145.

96. Morris U. Schappes, *A Pictorial History of the Jews of the United States*, rev. ed. (New York: Marzani & Munsell, 1965), p. 289.

97. Barry A. Kosmin et al., *Highlights of the CJF 1990 National Jewish Population Survey* (New York: Council of Jewish Federations, 1991). The numbers vary slightly, depending on whether one includes those Jews who call themselves Jews and those Jews who say they have no religion.

98. Eli Cohen, "Economic Status and Occupational Structures," in *AJYB, 1950*, p. 65.

99. Schappes, *Pictorial History of the Jews*, p. 265.

100. Ibid.

101. Glazer, "Social Characteristics of American Jews, 1654–1954," in *AJYB, 1955*, p. 26.

102. Bureau of the Census, *Statistical Abstract of the United States* (Washington, 1970), p. 11.

103. Diamond, "A Reader in the Demography of American Jews," in *AJYB, 1977*, p. 295; Seligman, "The American Jew," in *AJYB, 1950*, p. 31; *Encyclopedia Judaica*, vol. 15, p. 1639; Cohen, "Economic Status and Occupational Structures," in *AJYB, 1950*, p. 65.

104. Everett C. Hughes, *The Sociological Eye: Selected Papers* (New York: Aldine Atherton, 1971), p. 327.

105. See Diamond, "A Reader in the Demography of American Jews," in *AJYB, 1977*, p. 295.

106. Trying to ascribe an optimistic element to the data about the Jewish move to the suburbs, Erich Rosenthal suggested that it might result in a spurt in the birthrate to fill the larger suburban homes ("Jewish Fertility in the United States," in *AJYB, 1961*, p. 26). Was he ever wrong about fertility in the suburbs!

107. Ibid., p. 4.

108. A. Chenkin, "Jewish Population in the United States, 1959," in *AJYB, 1959*, pp. 10, 12.

109. Calvin Goldscheider, "Demographic Transitions, Modernization, and the Transformation of Judaism," paper presented to the Council for the World's Religions Conference in Toledo, Spain, 10 Nov. 1989, p. 2. See also Calvin Goldscheider, "A Century of Jewish Fertility in Rhode Island," *Rhode Island Jewish Historical Notes* 10, no. 3, pt. B (Nov. 1989).

110. Chenkin, "Jewish Population in the United States, 1959," in *AJYB, 1959*, p. 6.

111. See, e.g., Donald J. Bogue, *The Population of the United States* (Glencoe: Free Press, 1959).

112. Chenkin, "Jewish Population in the United States, 1959," in *AJYB,*
1959, p. 12.

113. Goldscheider, "Demographic Transitions," p. 2.

114. Goldscheider, "Demography and Jewish Survival," p. 137.

115. Robert Gordis, *Judaism in a Christian World* (New York: McGraw
Hill, 1966), p. 186.

116. Clark E. Vincent, "Interfaith Marriages: Problem or Symptom?"
in Barron, *The Blending American,* p. 188; E. Rosenthal, "Extent of Jewish Outmarriage in the U.S.A.," in Werner Cahnman, ed., *Intermarriage and
Jewish Life in America* (New York: Herzl Press, 1963).

117. Cited in Andrew Greeley, "Religious Intermarriage in a Denominational Society," *American Journal of Sociology* 75, no. 6 (May 1970): 950.

118. A. Schwartz, "Intermarriage in the United States," in *AJYB, 1960,*
p. 104. See also Erich Rosenthal, "Jewish Intermarriage in Greater Washington," in *AJYB, 1963,* p. 33.

119. Rosenthal, "Jewish Intermarriage in Greater Washington," in
AJYB, 1963, p. 33.

120. S. M. Lipset, "Jewish Sociologists and Sociologists of the Jews," in
*Papers and Proceedings of the Tercentenary Conference on American Jewish
Sociology, 11/27–28/54,* in *Jewish Social Studies* 17, no. 3 (July 1955): 177.

2. The Emergence of Two Types of Jews:
Choices Made in the 1960s and 1970s

1. Milton Gordon, *Assimilation in American Life* (New York: Oxford
University Press, 1964).

2. *New York Times,* 21 Jan. 1962, p. 14.

3. Bureau of the Census, *Statistical Abstract of the United States,* prepared by the Data User Services Division (Washington, 1993).

4. Barry Chiswick, "The Labor Market Status of American Jews: Patterns and Determinants," in *AJYB, 1985,* p. 139.

5. See Alvin Chenkin, "Jewish Population in the United States, 1967,"
in *AJYB, 1968,* pp. 280–81; Chiswick, "Labor Market Status of Ameri-
can Jews," in *AJYB, 1985,* p. 139. See also Henry Feingold, "Foreword," in
Edward Shapiro, *The Jewish People in America,* vol. 5, *A Time for Healing:
American Jewry since World War II* (Baltimore: Johns Hopkins University
Press, 1992), p. xii.

6. Chiswick, "Labor Market Status of American Jews," in *AJYB, 1985,*
p. 138.

7. Ibid., p. 145.

8. Shapiro, *The Jewish People in America,* vol. 5, p. 122.

9. One of the sardonic jokes exchanged in Jewish circles, where the
ironies of assimilation were often expressed, was that America was a land of
opportunity for Jews, even if it often required some extraordinary transfor-

mations. The proof? "If a Jew ever runs for president in America, chances are he'll be an Episcopalian." The nomination of Barry Goldwater turned the joke into a reality. When in 1972, Milton Shapp (née Shapiro), the former governor of Pennsylvania, ran for the Democratic presidential nomination, his Jewish religion seemed almost unnoticed, as it is in the 1994 plans of Senator Arlen Spector, also of Pennsylvania.

10. See Dawidowicz, "A Century of Jewish History, 1881–1981," in *AJYB, 1982,* p. 74.

11. Chiswick, "Labor Market Status of American Jews," in *AJYB, 1985,* p. 152.

12. Ibid., p. 153.

13. See Lopata, *Occupation: Housewife.* Although Betty Friedan's *The Feminine Mystique* was published in 1963, women began to rethink their roles intensively more toward the end of the decade. An apron popular by the end of the decade had printed on it the question: "For this I needed 4 years of college?!"

14. Nathan Glazer, "On Jewish Forebodings," *Commentary* 8 (1985): 36.

15. Milton Gordon, "Marginality and the Jewish Intellectual," in Peter Rose, ed., *The Ghetto and Beyond* (New York: Random House, 1969), p. 35.

16. *New York Times,* 16 Jan. 1960, p. 11.

17. Hertzberg, *The Jews in America,* p. 321.

18. Peter Rose, "Small Town Jews and Their Neighbors in the United States," *Jewish Journal of Sociology* 3, no. 2 (Dec. 1961): 184.

19. Will Herberg, "The Integration of the Jew in Contemporary America," *Conservative Judaism* 25, no. 3 (spring 1961): 9.

20. Judith Kerman, "The Embarrassed Jew," *Jewish Currents* 20, no. 5 (May 1966): 24–26.

21. Solotaroff and Sklare, "Introduction," in Stember et al., *Jews in the Mind of America,* p. 8.

22. Lothar Kahn, "Another Decade: The American Jew in the Sixties," *Judaism* 10, no. 2 (spring 1961): 104.

23. Keller, "Jews and the Character of American Life since 1930," in Stember et al., *Jews in the Mind of America,* p. 270.

24. Stember, "Reactions to Anti-Semitic Appeals before and during the War," in ibid., pp. 121, 134.

25. Stember, "The Holocaust," in ibid., p. 147.

26. Stember, "The Recent History of Public Attitudes," in ibid., pp. 127–34. See also Shapiro, *The Jewish People in America,* vol. 5, p. 40.

27. S. M. Lipset, "A Unique People in an Exceptional Country," *Society* 28, no. 1 (Nov./Dec. 1990): 10.

28. Solotaroff and Sklare, "Introduction," in Stember et al., *Jews in the Mind of America,* pp. 3–4.

29. *New York Times,* 21 Jan. 1962, p. 14.

30. Ibid., 16 Jan. 1960, p. 7.

31. Ibid.

32. See Hertzberg, *The Jews in America,* who quotes Ben Gurion's rebuke of American Zionist leader Abba Hillel Silver's desire to "sit in Cleveland and give directions to Tel Aviv" (p. 342).

33. Shapiro, *The Jewish People in America,* vol. 5, p. 29.

34. Leonard Fein, *Where Are We?* (New York: Harper & Row, 1988), p. 11.

35. Dawidowicz, "A Century of Jewish History, 1881–1981," in *AJYB, 1982,* p. 42.

36. Fein, *Where Are We?* p. 5.

37. Ibid., p. 10.

38. Dawidowicz, "A Century of Jewish History, 1881–1981," in *AJYB, 1982,* p. 42.

39. Thomas B. Morgan, "The Vanishing American Jew," *Look,* 5 May 1964.

40. See Alvin Chenkin in *AJYB* for the years 1960–69.

41. Diamond, "A Reader in the Demography of American Jews," in *AJYB, 1977,* p. 289.

42. E. Rosenthal, "Jewish Fertility in the United States," in *AJYB, 1961,* p. 27. See also Goldscheider, "A Century of Jewish Fertility in Rhode Island," p. 336.

43. In 1970, the total fertility rate (TFR), which is the final number of children that women are expected to have on average if their current age-specific fertility performance persists, was 1.5. See Sidney Goldstein, "Jewish Fertility in Contemporary America," in Paul Ritterband, ed., *Modern Jewish Fertility* (Leiden: Brill, 1981). Uziel Schmelz recomputed this figure and estimated that the TFR was 1.7 or 1.8. See Uziel Schmelz, "Jewish Survival: The Demographic Factors," in *AJYB, 1981,* p. 79.

44. Diamond, "A Reader in the Demography of American Jews," in *AJYB, 1977,* pp. 302–3, based on research of Fred Massarik.

45. Goldscheider, "Demography and Jewish Survival," p. 130.

46. Ibid., p. 135.

47. Nathan Glazer, "New Perspectives in American Jewish Sociology," in *AJYB, 1987,* p. 8.

48. Rosenthal, "Jewish Intermarriage in Greater Washington," in *AJYB, 1963.*

49. Chenkin, "Jewish Population in the United States, 1957," in *AJYB, 1958,* p. 8.

50. Nathan Glazer, *New Perspectives in American Jewish Sociology* (New York: American Jewish Committee, 1987), p. 10.

51. This figure is a merged statistic for Baltimore, Boston, Cleveland, Dallas, Essex and Morris Counties in New Jersey, Providence, R.I., and Worcester, Mass., a population of just under 10 percent of American Jewry. See Peter Y. Medding, Gary A. Tobin, Sylvia B. Fishman, and Mordechai Rimor, *Jewish Identity in Conversionary and Mixed Marriages* (New York: American Jewish Committee, 1992), p. 41.

52. Goldscheider, "Demography and Jewish Survival," p. 122.

53. Ibid.

54. Ibid.

55. Of course, the ultra-Orthodox, for those who truly understood them, were actually making the same point, but most Americans missed the point. See Samuel Heilman, *Defenders of the Faith: Inside Ultra-Orthodox Jewry* (New York: Schocken, 1992).

56. Fein, *Where Are We?* p. 5.

57. Ibid., pp. 18–19.

58. Goldscheider, "Demography and Jewish Survival," p. 123.

59. Chaim I. Waxman, "The Fourth Generation Grows Up: The Contemporary American Jewish Community," *Annals of the American Academy of Political and Social Science* 454 (Mar. 1981): 72–73.

60. John Higham, "The Pot That Didn't Melt," *New York Review of Books*, 12 Apr. 1990, p. 12.

61. Arthur A. Cohen, *The Natural and the Supernatural Jew* (New York: Pantheon, 1963), p. 36.

62. Richard M. Merelman, *Making Something of Ourselves: On Culture and Politics in the United States* (Berkeley and Los Angeles: University of California Press, 1984), p. 30. See also Peter Y. Medding, "Segmented Ethnicity and the New Jewish Politics," in Ezra Mendelssohn, ed., *Studies in Contemporary Jewry* (New York: Arno, 1987), pp. 26–45.

63. Robert N. Bellah, "Competing Visions of the Role of Religion in American Society," in Robert N. Bellah and Frederick E. Greenspahn, eds., *Uncivil Religion: Interreligious Hostility in America* (New York: Crossroad, 1987), p. 228.

64. Medding et al., *Jewish Identity in Conversionary and Mixed Marriages*, p. 16.

65. Seymour Siegal, "Religion: Judaism," *Encyclopedia Americana Yearbook, 1969.*

66. Marshall Sklare and Joseph Greenblum, *Jewish Identity on the Suburban Frontier*, 2d ed. (Chicago: University of Chicago Press, 1979), pp. 57–59.

67. Goldscheider, "Demography and Jewish Survival," p. 125.

68. The comment belongs to Arthur Hertzberg and comes from the final page in his book *The Jews in America: Four Centuries of an Uneasy Encounter.* Although writing in 1989, he was expressing an anxiety that he and Jews like him have felt since the sixties.

69. That such a population exists has been documented in S. Heilman and S. Cohen, *Cosmopolitans and Parochials: Modern Orthodox Jews in America* (Chicago: University of Chicago Press, 1989). These are the people of whom the old joke spoke, the ones for whom the synagogue they *do not* go to is an Orthodox one.

70. Robert Gordis, "Religion," in *AJYB, 1950*, p. 149.

71. Morris Axelrod, Floyd J. Fowler, and Arnold Gurin, *A Community*

Survey for Long Range Planning (Boston: Combined Jewish Philanthropies of Greater Boston, 1967), p. 119; Bernard Lazerwitz, "Past and Future Trends in the Size of American Jewish Denominations," *Journal of Reform Judaism* 26, no. 3 (summer 1979): 77–82; Goldscheider, *Jewish Continuity and Change,* p. 154; Sklare, *Conservative Judaism.*

72. Data drawn from the NJPS 1970 and 1990 surveys.

73. Charles Liebman, "A Grim Outlook," in *The Quality of American Jewish Life: Two Views* (New York: American Jewish Committee, 1987), p. 38.

74. Kosmin et al., *Highlights of the CJF 1990 National Jewish Population Survey,* table 25, p. 33.

75. Sklare, *Conservative Judaism,* p. 255; Axelrod, Fowler, and Gurin, *A Community Survey for Long Range Planning,* p. 143.

76. Remarks at the Rabbinical Assembly Convention in 1959 reported by Jacob Neusner, "Communal Affairs: Religion," in *AJYB, 1960.*

77. Sklare, *Conservative Judaism,* p. 264.

78. Goldscheider, "Demography and Jewish Survival," p. 128.

79. Kosmin et al., *Highlights of the CJF 1990 National Jewish Population Survey,* p. 3.

80. For the extent of their non-Jewish behavior, see Sylvia Fishman, Mordechai Rimor, Gary Tobin, and Peter Medding, "Intermarriage and American Jews Today: New Findings and Policy Recommendations," distributed by the Cohen Center for Modern Jewish Studies, Brandeis University, Oct. 1990.

81. Goldscheider, "Demography and Jewish Survival," p. 126.

82. See Frank Newport, "The Religious Switcher in the United States," *American Sociological Review* 44 (1979): 528–52.

83. Martin Marty and R. Scott Appleby, *Fundamentalisms Observed* (Chicago: University of Chicago Press, 1992).

84. Paul Weinberger, "The Effects of Jewish Education," in *AJYB, 1970,* pp. 230–49.

85. Leora W. Isaacs, "What We Know about Enrollment," in S. Kelman, ed., *What We Know about Jewish Education* (Los Angeles: Torah Aura, 1992), p. 64.

86. Schappes, *A Pictorial History of the Jews of the United States,* p. 271.

87. Weinberger, "The Effects of Jewish Education," in *AJYB, 1970,* p. 233.

88. Massarik, "Trends in U.S. Jewish Education," in *AJYB, 1977,* p. 242.

89. B. Lazerwitz, "The Ethical Impact of Jewish Identification," *Judaism* 18 (fall 1969): 421.

90. Isaacs, "What We Know about Enrollment," p. 65.

91. Liebman, "A Grim Outlook," p. 37.

92. Walter Ackerman, "Jewish Education—For What?" in *AJYB, 1969.*

93. G. Bock, "Does Jewish Schooling Matter?" in *Jewish Education and*

Jewish Identity (New York: American Jewish Committee, 1977); and Harold Himmelfarb, "Jewish Education for Naught," *Analysis* 51 (1975).

94. Fein, *Where Are We?* p. 12.

95. Goldscheider, "Demography and Jewish Survival," p. 143.

96. Medding et al., *Jewish Identity in Conversionary and Mixed Marriages*, p. 12.

97. Engelman, "Jewish Education," in *AJYB, 1960.*

98. *New York Times*, 16 Jan. 1960, p. 7.

99. Joseph H. Lookstein, "The Goals of Jewish Education," *Tradition: A Journal of Orthodox Jewish Thought* 3, no. 1 (fall 1960); reprinted in Jeffrey Gurock, ed., *Ramaz* (Hoboken: Ktav, 1989), pp. 199, 198.

100. Mission Statement for the Ramaz School, 4 Mar. 1992. The articulation dates to 1992, but the attitude was already very much in evidence in the 1960s.

101. Weinberger, "The Effects of Jewish Education," in *AJYB, 1970.*

102. Waxman, "The Fourth Generation Grows Up," p. 76.

103. Stuart E. Rosenberg, *America Is Different: The Search for Jewish Identity* (New York: Nelson, 1964), p. 252.

104. Seymour M. Lipset and Everett C. Ladd, "Jewish Academics in the United States: Their Achievements, Culture, and Politics," in *AJYB, 1971,* pp. 92–93.

105. Dawidowicz, "A Century of Jewish History, 1881–1981," in *AJYB, 1982*, p. 56.

106. Eli Ginzberg, "Jewish Welfare in America," *Menorah Journal* 39, no. 2 (autumn 1951): 191.

107. Quoted in Shapiro, *The Jewish People in America*, vol. 5, p. 95.

108. Chiswick, "Labor Market Status of American Jews," in *AJYB, 1985*, p. 145. The exact figures are given below:

	M.D., D.D.S., health fields	Law	All professions
Jews	6.10	3.58	27.2
Non-Jews	1.35	0.72	15.3
Ratio (Jews/non-Jews)	4.5	5.0	2.8

109. Cohen, "Economic Status and Occupational Structures," in *AJYB, 1950*, p. 67.

110. See Schappes, *A Pictorial History of the Jews of the United States*, p. 265.

111. *Encyclopedia Judaica*, vol. 15, p. 1639.

112. Hughes, *The Sociological Eye*, p. 332.

113. Ibid., p. 334.

114. Ibid., p. 332.

115. Steven M. Cohen, "Trends in Jewish Philanthropy," in *AJYB, 1980*, pp. 33–34.

116. In point of fact, as Charles Liebman has pointed out ("A Grim Outlook"), for all the wealth of Judaica on campus, "we have no data on the number of Jewish college students enrolled in courses in Judaica" (p. 37).

117. Dawidowicz, "A Century of Jewish History, 1881–1981," in *AJYB, 1982*, p. 67.

118. *Menorah Journal* 43, nos. 1–2 (1955): 3.

119. Inaugural address, 20 Jan. 1961.

120. Arthur Goren, *The American Jews* (Cambridge: Harvard University Press, 1982), p. 98.

121. Shapiro, *The Jewish People in America*, vol. 5, p. 223.

122. Jonathan Kaufman, *Broken Alliance: The Turbulent Times between Blacks and Jews in America* (New York: Scribners, 1988), pp. 86–88.

123. Shapiro, *The Jewish People in America*, vol. 5, p. 54.

124. See S. M. Cohen, *The Dimensions of American Jewish Liberalism* (New York: American Jewish Committee, 1989), p. 35.

125. See Hillel Levine and Lawrence Harmon, *The Death of an American Jewish Community* (New York: Free Press, 1992), for a full elaboration of a case study: Boston's blacks and Jews.

126. Cohen, *The Dimensions of American Jewish Liberalism*, p. 3.

127. Jerry Rubin, *We Are Everywhere* (New York: Harper & Row, 1971), pp. 74–76.

128. Reuven Kimmelman, "A Jewish Peace Demonstration," *Judaism* 18, no. 3 (summer 1969): 354–57.

129. Higham, "The Pot That Didn't Melt," p. 13.

130. Jack Nusan Porter and Peter Dreier, eds., *Jewish Radicalism* (New York: Grove Press, 1973), p. xi. See also Richard J. Israel, "Jewish Students and the Jewish Community: The Hillel Conference of Jewish Students," *Judaism* 18, no. 3 (summer 1969): 469.

131. Israel, "Jewish Students and the Jewish Community," p. 470.

132. Ibid., p. 465.

133. S. M. Cohen, "American Jewish Feminism," *American Behavioral Scientist* 23, no. 4 (1980): 524.

134. Israel, "Jewish Students and the Jewish Community," p. 468.

135. Edward B. Fiske, *New York Times*, 23 Nov. 1969, p. L-65.

136. Porter and Dreier, *Jewish Radicalism*, p. xli.

137. Israel, "Jewish Students and the Jewish Community," p. 465; Paul Weinberger, "The Effects of Jewish Education," in *AJYB, 1970*, p. 246.

138. Levine and Harmon, *Death of an American Jewish Community*, p. 252.

139. Ibid.

140. Israel, "Jewish Students and the Jewish Community," p. 468. See also Joel Harris, "The Conference of the World Union of Jewish Students (May 1–4, 1969)," *Judaism* 18, no. 3 (summer 1969): 470–73, which reports on the spectrum of Jewish activism.

141. Arnold J. Band, "Jewish Studies in American Liberal Arts Colleges and Universities," in *AJYB, 1966*.

142. Cohen, "American Jewish Feminism," p. 532.

143. Ibid., p. 538; and Anne L. Lerner, " 'Who Hast Not Made Me a Man': The Movement for Equal Rights for Women in American Jewry," in *AJYB, 1977*, p. 7.

144. Quotation from a Jewish feminist, cited by Cohen, "American Jewish Feminism," p. 532.

145. Michael Novak, *The Rise of the Unmeltable Ethnics: Politics and Culture in the Seventies* (New York: Macmillan, 1972).

146. Daniel Bell, "Where Are We?" *Moment*, 1986, pp. 15–22.

147. Nathan Glazer, *American Judaism* (Chicago: University of Chicago Press, 1972), p. xii, italics added.

148. Rosenberg, *American Is Different*, p. 256. See also *Encyclopedia Americana Yearbook, 1960–62*; Cohen, "Trends in Jewish Philanthropy," in *AJYB, 1980*, pp. 32.

149. Goldin, "The UJA," pp. 70–71.

150. Cohen, "Trends in Jewish Philanthropy," in *AJYB, 1980*, p. 32.

151. Ibid., p. 33.

152. Ibid.

153. Gerald B. Bubis, "Jewish Dollars Drying Up," *Moment* 17, no. 6 (1992): 28–33.

154. Ibid., p. 32.

155. Cohen, "Trends in Jewish Philanthropy," in *AJYB, 1980*, p. 49.

156. Ibid., p. 43.

157. This point was originally made in Eli Ginzberg, "Jewish Welfare in America," *Menorah Journal* 39, no. 2 (autumn 1951): 187.

158. Steven M. Cohen, *Content or Continuity? The 1989 National Survey of American Jews* (New York: American Jewish Committee, 1991); Heilman and Cohen, *Cosmopolitans and Parochials*.

159. Cohen, "Trends in Jewish Philanthropy," in *AJYB, 1980*, p. 49.

160. Ibid., p. 37.

161. Ibid., pp. 37–38.

162. Rabbi Mordecai Waxman, personal communication.

163. Bubis, "Jewish Dollars Drying Up," p. 30; Jerry Winter, Aryeh Meir, and Lisa Hostein, *The High Cost of Jewish Living* (New York: American Jewish Committee, 1992).

3. Quality versus Quantity:
The Challenge of the 1980s and 1990s

1. Nathan Glazer, *New Perspectives in American Jewish Sociology* (New York: American Jewish Committee, 1987), p. 17.

2. Leo Rosten, *The Joys of Yinglish* (New York: McGraw-Hill, 1989).

3. Herbert Gans, "Symbolic Ethnicity: The Future of Ethnic Groups and Cultures in America," *Ethnic and Racial Studies* 2 (Jan. 1979): 1–20; Richard Alba, "Intermarriage and Ethnicity among European Americans," *Contemporary Jewry* 12 (1991): 16; and Richard Alba, *Ethnic Identity: The Transformation of White America* (New Haven: Yale University Press, 1990).

4. Sergio DellaPergola, "New Data on Demography and Identification among Jews in the U.S.: Trends, Inconsistencies, and Disagreements," *Contemporary Jewry* 12 (1991): 79.

5. Cohen, *Content or Continuity?* pp. 72, 5.

6. Percentages given in parentheses are from the 1990 National Jewish Population Survey. See Kosmin et al., *Highlights of the CJF 1990 National Jewish Population Survey.* For the most part, the numbers refer to proportions among the entirely Jewish portion of the sample. The percentage of Thanksgiving celebrants is from Cohen, *Content or Continuity?* p. 62.

7. S. M. Cohen, *Ties and Tensions: An Update, the 1989 Survey of American Jewish Attitudes toward Israel and Israelis* (New York: American Jewish Committee, 1989), p. 5.

8. The "core Jewish population" includes those who were born Jews and still claim to be Jews, those born Jews who currently claim no religion, and those who are Jews by choice (see the section entitled Population Growth and Fertility for more details). Sidney Goldstein, "Profile of American Jewry: Insights from the 1990 National Jewish Population Survey," in *AJYB, 1992,* pp. 172–73; S. M. Cohen, "The 1981–1982 National Survey of American Jews," in *AJYB, 1983,* pp. 89–110; Bethamie Horowitz, *The 1991 New York Jewish Population Study* (New York: UJA-Federation, 1993), p. 52.

9. Cohen, *Content or Continuity?* p. 66.

10. All these figures come from Kosmin et al., *Highlights of the CJF 1990 National Jewish Population Survey.*

11. Ibid., p. 28.

12. Nathan Glazer, "On Jewish Forebodings," *Commentary* 8 (1985): 36.

13. S. M. Cohen, *The Dimensions of American Jewish Liberalism* (New York: American Jewish Committee, 1989), p. 31.

14. Peter Steinfels, "Beliefs," *New York Times,* 3 Apr. 1993, p. 8.

15. Cohen, *Content or Continuity?* p. 70.

16. Ibid., p. 57.

17. Ibid., p. 59.

18. Kosmin et al., *Highlights of the CJF 1990 National Jewish Population Survey.*

19. S. M. Cohen, "Reason for Optimism," in S. M. Cohen and Charles S. Liebman, *The Quality of American Jewish Life: Two Views* (New York: American Jewish Committee, 1987), based on the 1981 Greater New York Jewish Population Survey (4,500 respondents), p. 9.

20. DellaPergola, "New Data," p. 84.

21. Charles Liebman, "Leadership and Decision-Making in a Jewish Federation: The New York Federation of Jewish Philanthropies," in *AJYB, 1979,* pp. 3–76.

22. On the strength of Orthodox Jewish commitment to Jewish continuity, see Cohen, *Content or Continuity?* pp. 22–23.

23. See Samuel Heilman, "The Ninth Siyum HaShas at Madison Square Garden: Contra-acculturation in American Life," in N. Cohen and R. Seltzers, eds., *Americanization of the Jews* (New York: New York University Press, 1995), pp. 311–38.

24. See Steven M. Cohen and Leonard Fein, "From Integration to Survival: American Jewish Anxieties in Transition," *Annals,* July 1985, pp. 75–88.

25. Fein, *Where Are We?* pp. 128–49.

26. Goldscheider, "Demography and Jewish Survival," p. 124.

27. Goldscheider, *Jewish Continuity and Change,* p. xiii; S. M. Cohen, "The American Jewish Family Today," in *AJYB, 1982,* p. 137.

28. Goldscheider, *Jewish Continuity and Change,* p. 4.

29. Glazer, *New Perspectives,* p. 19.

30. See Goldscheider, "Demography and Jewish Survival," p. 127. See also Goldstein, "Profile of American Jewry," in *AJYB, 1992,* p. 108.

31. DellaPergola, "New Data," p. 72.

32. Goldscheider, "Demography and Jewish Survival," p. 130.

33. Ibid., p. 133.

34. Goldscheider, *Jewish Continuity and Change,* p. 80.

35. Kosmin et al., *Highlights of the CJF 1990 National Jewish Population Survey,* p. 15.

36. Goldscheider, "Demography and Jewish Survival," p. 133.

37. Ibid., p. 131.

38. Kosmin et al., *Highlights of the CJF 1990 National Jewish Population Survey,* p. 15.

39. See the cover story, by J. J. Goldberg, in *Jerusalem Report,* 5 Nov. 1992, pp. 28–32.

40. Kosmin et al., *Highlights of the CJF 1990 National Jewish Population Survey,* p. 17.

41. Goldscheider, "Demography and Jewish Survival," p. 137.

42. Ibid.

43. Heilman and Cohen, *Cosmopolitans and Parochials.*

44. *The High Cost of Jewish Living* (New York: American Jewish Committee, Apr. 1992).

45. Horowitz, *The 1991 New York Jewish Population Study*, p. 41. These well-to-do counties where the people feel comfortable are, not incidentally, the counties with the fewest Orthodox Jews.

46. See Samuel Heilman, *Making Connections and Contact: Two Programs for Jewish Affiliation*, Report for the Memorial Foundation for Jewish Culture (1990), p. 14.

47. DellaPergola, "New Data," p. 69, italics added.

48. Alan Fisher, "The National Gallup Polls and American Jewish Demography," in *AJYB, 1983*, p. 120.

49. Glazer, *New Perspectives*, p. 9. See also Bureau of the Census, *Statistical Abstract of the United States* (Washington, 1981), p. 26.

50. Goldstein, "Profile of American Jewry," in *AJYB, 1992*, p. 105; Bureau of the Census, *Statistical Abstract of the United States* (Washington, 1991), p. 19.

51. Cohen, "The American Jewish Family Today," in *AJYB, 1982*, p. 138.

52. Cohen, "Reason for Optimism," p. 20. See also Cohen, *Content or Continuity?*

53. DellaPergola, "New Data," p. 79.

54. Cohen, "The American Jewish Family Today," in *AJYB, 1982*, p. 147.

55. Ibid., p. 149.

56. Kosmin et al., *Highlights of the CJF 1990 National Jewish Population Survey*, p. 18. Of course, Jews were in some measure reflecting changes in American family patterns. The 1990 census reported that nearly a quarter of the nation's unmarried women become mothers, an increase of almost 60 percent during the past decade. Moreover, the increase was particularly steep among educated and professional women, the segment of the population from which most Jewish women of childbearing age come (see *New York Times*, 14 July 1993, p. 1).

57. S. M. Cohen, *Alternative Jewish Families in the Jewish Community: Singles, Single Parents, Childless Couples and Mixed-Married* (New York: American Jewish Committee, 1989), p. 1.

58. S. M. Cohen, "Will Jews Keep Giving? Prospects for the Jewish Charitable Community," *Journal of Jewish Communal Service* 55, no. 1 (autumn 1978): 66.

59. Cohen, "Reason for Optimism," p. 17.

60. DellaPergola, "New Data," p. 81.

61. Cohen, "Reason for Optimism," p. 17.

62. Cohen, "Will Jews Keep Giving?" p. 69; and Cohen, "Trends in Jewish Philanthropy," in *AJYB, 1980*, p. 37.

63. See Horowitz, *The 1991 New York Jewish Population Study*, p. 86.

64. Cohen, "Reason for Optimism," p. 18.

65. Cohen, *The Dimensions of American Jewish Liberalism*, p. 11.

66. *Newsday,* 17 Nov. 1992.

67. See ibid., p. 7.

68. Cohen, *Ties and Tensions,* p. 41.

69. Ibid., p. 11.

70. Ibid., p. 3.

71. Ibid., p. 11, italics in original.

72. See Goldstein, "Profile of American Jewry," in *AJYB, 1992,* pp. 119–20.

73. Glazer, *New Perspectives,* p. 19.

74. Cohen's scale of Jewish activity includes synagogue membership (49 percent of his polled population), Jewish organization membership (46 percent), devoting at least "some time" to a Jewish organization (28 percent), serving on a board or committee of a synagogue or Jewish organization (20 percent), contributing at least $100 to the UJA or a federation (19 percent), and contributing to an American pro-Israel candidate or committee (14 percent). Those who did four or more of these things, he defined as actively Jewish Jews. Orthodox Jews score high in this scale. See Cohen, *Content or Continuity?* p. 9.

75. Heilman and Cohen, *Cosmopolitans and Parochials,* p. 197.

76. See Samuel C. Heilman, *Jewish Unity and Diversity: A Survey of American Rabbis and Rabbinical Students* (New York: American Jewish Committee, 1991).

77. Cohen, "Reason for Optimism," p. 17.

78. Goldscheider, "Demography and Jewish Survival," p. 132.

79. Cited in Tom W. Smith, *What Do Americans Think about Jews?* (New York: American Jewish Committee, 1991), p. 52.

80. Goldscheider, *Jewish Continuity and Change,* p. 78.

81. Kosmin et al., *Highlights of the CJF 1990 National Jewish Population Survey,* p. 27.

82. For the population figures, see Horowitz, *The 1991 New York Jewish Population Study,* pp. 1–43. The 1991 Jewish population proportions for certain parts of New York are even higher: Brooklyn and Nassau are at 16 percent, and in Manhattan Jews make up 21 percent of the total population—or one out of every five citizens.

83. Goldscheider, "Demography and Jewish Survival," p. 133.

84. Goldstein, "Profile of American Jewry," in *AJYB, 1992,* pp. 95–96.

85. Cohen, *Alternative Jewish Families in the Jewish Community,* p. 7. See also Horowitz, *The 1991 New York Jewish Population Study,* p. 104.

86. Peter Y. Medding, Gary A. Tobin, Sylvia B. Fishman, and Mordechai Rimor, *Jewish Identity in Conversionary and Mixed Marriages* (New York: American Jewish Committee, 1992).

87. Goldscheider, *Jewish Continuity and Change,* p. 32.

88. Goldscheider, "Demography and Jewish Survival," p. 132.

89. Cohen, "Reason for Optimism."

90. Ibid., p. 22.

91. Gary Tobin and Alvin Chenkin, "Recent Jewish Community Population Studies: A Roundup," in *AJYB, 1985*, pp. 154–78.

92. Horowitz, *The 1991 New York Jewish Population Study*, pp. 49, 52.

93. Glazer, "On Jewish Forebodings," p. 34.

94. Kosmin et al., *Highlights of the CJF 1990 National Jewish Population Survey*, p. 14.

95. N. D. Glenn, "Interreligious Marriage in the United States: Patterns and Recent Trends," *Journal of Marriage and the Family* 44, no. 3 (1982): 555–66.

96. Cohen, *Alternative Jewish Families in the Jewish Community*, p. 7.

97. DellaPergola, "New Data," p. 87. See also Sylvia Fishman et al., *Intermarriage and American Jews Today: New Findings and Policy Implications* (Waltham, Mass.: Cohen Center for Modern Jewish Studies, Brandeis University, Oct. 1990).

98. Cohen, *Content or Continuity?* p. 58.

99. Jonathan Sarna, "The Secret of Jewish Continuity," *Commentary* 98, no. 4 (Oct. 1994): 55.

100. Goldscheider, *Jewish Continuity and Change*, p. 10.

101. Egon Mayer, *Love and Tradition* (New York: Plenum Press, 1985); U. O. Schmelz, "Jewish Survival: The Demographic Factors," in *AJYB, 1981*, p. 89; Sergio DellaPergola and U. O. Schmelz, "Demographic Transformation of American Jewry: Marriage and Mixed Marriage," *Studies in Contemporary Jewry* 5 (1989): 192.

102. The first statistic comes from DellaPergola, "New Data," pp. 76–77, based on the 1990 NJPS. The last comes from the 1988 national survey by Cohen (*Content or Continuity?* p. 73).

103. Marshall Sklare and Joseph Greenblum, *Jewish Identity on the Suburban Frontier* (New York: Basic Books, 1967).

104. Glazer, *New Perspectives*, p. 12.

105. Cohen, *Content or Continuity?* p. 64.

106. Kosmin et al., *Highlights of the CJF 1990 National Jewish Population Survey*, p. 16.

107. Goldscheider, *Jewish Continuity and Change*, p. 28.

108. Lisa DiCerto, "Passover Essay," *America*, 6 Apr. 1991, pp. 380–81.

109. Adam Dikter, "Queens Synagogue Home to Unconventional Families," *Jewish Week*, 23–29 July 1993, p. 14.

110. Glazer, *New Perspectives*, p. 13.

111. Sarna, "The Secret of Jewish Continuity," p. 55.

112. Goldscheider, "Demography and Jewish Survival," p. 128.

113. See, e.g., Daniel Bell, "Where Are We?" *Moment*, spring 1986, pp. 15–22; and Cohen, *Content or Continuity?*

114. DellaPergola, "New Data," p. 77.

115. The comment comes from Rabbi S. Hecht, a Lubavitcher Hasid from Crown Heights, Brooklyn, quoted in *Newsday*, 9 Aug. 1992, p. 6.

116. Heilman and Cohen, *Cosmopolitans and Parochials*, p. 123.

117. Cited in Cohen, *The Dimensions of American Jewish Liberalism*, p. 2.

118. *New York Times*, 9 Nov. 1994, p. 6.

119. Glazer, "On Jewish Forebodings," p. 36.

120. Goldstein, "Profile of American Jewry," in *AJYB, 1992*, p. 94.

121. Cohen, *Content or Continuity?* p. 66.

122. Glazer, *New Perspectives*, p. 18.

123. Goldstein, "Profile of American Jewry," in *AJYB, 1992*, p. 119.

124. Ibid., p. 120.

125. Alan Fisher, "The National Gallup Polls and American Jewish Demography," in *AJYB, 1983*, p. 115.

126. Goldstein, "Profile of American Jewry," in *AJYB, 1992*, p. 138. Since over half of the Jews by choice identify themselves as affiliated with the Reform movement, and about a third with the Conservative, chances are the synagogues in which Jews by choice are members are either Reform or Conservative (see ibid., p. 170).

127. Horowitz, *The 1991 New York Jewish Population Study*, p. 66.

128. Cohen, *Content or Continuity?* pp. 56, 74.

129. See Cohen, "Reason for Optimism," pp. 6–7.

130. See S. M. Cohen, "The 1981–1982 National Survey of American Jews," in *AJYB, 1983*, pp. 89–110; and Kosmin et al., *Highlights of the CJF 1990 National Jewish Population Survey*, p. 31.

131. Cohen, *Content or Continuity?* p. 56.

132. See R. Cohen and Sherri Rosen, *Organizational Affiliation of American Jews: A Research Report* (New York: American Jewish Committee, 1992).

133. Goldscheider, *Jewish Continuity and Change*, p. 3.

134. Glazer, "On Jewish Forebodings," p. 35.

135. Smith, *What Do Americans Think about Jews?* p. 43.

136. See, e.g., ibid.

137. *Newsday*, 17 Nov. 1992, p. 7. See Smith, *What Do Americans Think about Jews?* pp. 41–42.

138. Allan Nadler, "Tremblers," *Commentary* 96 (Aug. 1993): 56.

139. Cohen, *Content or Continuity?* p. 71.

140. Goldscheider, *Jewish Continuity and Change*, p. 104.

141. See Medding et al., *Jewish Identity*, table 17, p. 52.

142. Cohen, *Ties and Tensions*, p. 16.

143. Medding et al., *Jewish Identity*.

144. Heilman and Cohen, *Cosmopolitans and Parochials*, p. 134. Wherever not specifically cited, the statistics provided in the following pages about American Orthodox Jews come from this book.

145. Cohen, *Content or Continuity?* p. 58.

146. See C. Jaret, "The Impact of Geographical Mobility on Jewish Community Participation: Disruptive or Supportive?" *Contemporary Jewry* 4 (spring/summer 1978): 9–20.

147. Marshall Sklare, *Conservative Judaism: An American Religious Movement*, 2d ed. (New York: Schocken Books, 1972), p. 43.

148. Goldstein, "Profile of American Jewry," in *AJYB, 1992*, p. 129.

149. Horowitz, *The 1991 New York Jewish Population Study*, p. 59.

150. Goldstein, "Profile of American Jewry," in *AJYB, 1992*, p. 132. My augmented count of Orthodox Jews suggests less of a drop than the approximately 731,000 adherents, or 73 percent, Goldstein finds.

151. Jacob Sloan, "Religion," in *AJYB, 1955*.

152. Goldstein, "Profile of American Jewry," in *AJYB, 1992*, p. 170.

153. Heilman and Cohen, *Cosmopolitans and Parochials*, p. 197.

154. See Heilman, *Jewish Unity and Diversity*.

155. Gary Tobin and A. Chenkin, "Community Population Studies," in *AJYB, 1985*, p. 171. See also Horowitz, *The 1991 New York Jewish Population Study*.

156. Kosmin et al., *Highlights of the CJF 1990 National Jewish Population Survey*, p. 33.

157. Chaim Waxman, "The Family and the American Jewish Community on the Threshold of the 1980s: An Inventory for Research and Planning," in Marshall Sklare, ed., *Understanding American Jewry* (New Brunswick, N.J.: Transaction, 1982), p. 179.

158. Quoted in J. J. Goldberg, *Jerusalem Report*, 5 Nov. 1992, p. 32.

159. The U.S. census, cited in *Times Herald*, 14 July 1992, p. 8.

160. Heilman and Cohen, *Cosmopolitans and Parochials*, p. 78.

161. These estimates are drawn from a variety of sources; see ibid., esp. pp. 131–36.

162. Horowitz, *The 1991 New York Jewish Population Study*, p. 41.

163. See Heilman, *Jewish Unity and Diversity*, p. 28, which shows that, at least among rabbis, majorities of the non-Orthodox saw these terms as accurately characterizing the Orthodox.

164. DellaPergola, "New Data," p. 90.

165. Quoted in "Faith's Anchor in a Western Diaspora," *New York Times*, 26 July 1993, p. A9.

166. Cohen, "The 1981–1982 National Survey of American Jews," in *AJYB, 1983*, p. 95.

167. Arthur Hertzberg, *The Jews in America: Four Centuries of an Uneasy Encounter* (New York: Simon & Schuster, 1990).

168. Charles Liebman, *The Ambivalent American Jew* (Philadelphia: Jewish Publication Society, 1978).

169. Cohen, "The 1981–1982 National Survey of American Jews," in *AJYB, 1983*, p. 95.

170. Liebman, "A Grim Outlook," pp. 40–41.

171. Glazer, *New Perspectives*, p. 14.

172. Liebman, "A Grim Outlook," p. 45.

173. Goldscheider, "Demography and Jewish Survival," p. 126.

Index

acculturation, 8, 22–25, 28–30, 35, 60–62, 88, 101, 110, 115
actively Jewish Jews, 62–64, 78, 88, 90, 92, 95, 107, 110, 116, 118, 119, 124, 125, 143, 144, 150
African-Americans, 64, 87, 123. *See also* civil rights
Agudath Israel of America, 153
aliyah, 56, 155. *See also* Israel
American Jewish Committee, 54, 56, 108–10, 116, 140, 141, 143
Americanization, 27, 61, 79. *See also* acculturation
anti-Semitism, 5, 18, 32, 37, 45, 54–57, 86, 123, 129, 137, 138. *See also* Dartmouth
asemitism, 54
assimilation, 5, 16, 18, 22, 23, 25, 27, 29, 31, 47, 48, 50, 56, 60, 61, 65, 67–69, 82, 88, 131, 144, 146, 159, 161, 162
Association of Orthodox Jewish Scientists, 153
Auschwitz, 167n26
authentic Jew, 51

baby boom, 8, 42, 58, 114
bar mitzvah, 34, 101, 104
Blacks. *See* African-Americans
B'nai B'rith, 81, 123
B'nai B'rith Hillel, 81, 89–91

census, 18, 20, 21, 42, 44, 59, 131, 154, 166n22

charitable giving, 95, 97–99. *See also* philanthropy
Chenkin, Alvin, 9, 42, 43, 172n5, 174n40,n49, 186n155
City College of New York, 39
civil rights, 15, 17, 73, 84–88, 101, 102. *See also* African-Americans
Cohen, Steven M., xvi, 82, 98, 103–10, 121, 125, 140, 145, 149, 175n69,n142, 178n124
collective consciousness, 19
college, 8, 12, 32, 33, 36, 37, 39, 40, 48, 49, 60, 61, 80–83, 85, 90, 92, 94, 97, 99, 108, 126, 158
Commentary magazine, 5, 23, 47
Conference of Presidents of Major Jewish Organizations, 109
Conservative Jews, 28, 51, 62, 70–73, 78, 86, 93, 116, 134, 139, 147
core Jewish population, 104, 105, 113, 114, 119, 122, 139, 141, 148
cultural drift, 131–34, 158
cultural pluralism, 10, 22, 64, 79, 103, 107–8
culture shock, 8

Dartmouth, 81. *See also* anti-Semitism
Denver, Colorado, 127
dietary laws. *See* kosher food
divorce, 17, 93, 138, 145
dual loyalty, 101, 110

economic stability, 146, 152

Eichmann, Adolf, 64
Eisenhower, Dwight D., 28, 48
ethnic diversity, 15, 63, 101,
    108, 109

family, 4, 10–13, 17, 21, 22, 24, 25,
    42, 53, 59, 66, 68, 99, 105, 113–
    16, 121, 123, 126, 131, 133, 134,
    138, 145, 153, 155, 156, 160, 164
Farrakkhan, Louis, 87. See also
    anti-Semitism
feminism, 89, 92, 94, 108
Ferguson, Max, xiv
fertility, 41–43, 58, 59, 68, 104, 111,
    114, 115, 125, 128, 144, 152, 162

generational variations, 119,
    120, 124
ghettoes, 22, 29, 32, 51, 79, 126
ghettoization, 20, 65
Goldscheider, Calvin, xv, 26, 43,
    61, 74, 110, 125, 133, 142
Goldwater, Barry, 48, 112, 173n9

Habad, 61, 109, 143, 145, 151, 157
Hadassah, 141
halacha, 70, 146, 150
Ha-Levi, Yehuda, 163
Hanukkah, 53, 65, 102–4, 128, 129,
    131, 162
haredim, 136, 144, 147, 150, 154,
    156, 158
Hasidim, 62, 75, 109, 143–45, 157
havurot, 88, 90, 94
Hebrew, xv, 6, 32, 34–38, 52, 53,
    63, 68, 70, 72, 77, 78, 91, 94,
    109, 118
Herberg, Will, 28–30, 51, 68
Hertzberg, Arthur, 50
Hillel. See B'nai B'rith Hillel
Holocaust, xiii, 3, 5, 17, 18, 32, 54,
    55, 59, 64, 69, 72, 75, 97, 102,
    104, 113, 138, 162, 167n26

immigration, 4, 17, 39, 47, 59, 113,
    114, 149
income, 11, 47, 48, 60, 96, 98, 99,
    116, 117, 122, 141, 154–56, 158
institution building, 45, 146, 152–54
intermarriage, 6, 17, 26, 43, 44, 59,
    60, 89, 102, 104, 128, 130–34,
    144, 146, 162. See also outmar-
    riage
intimacy with non-Jews, 122
Israel, xiii, xvi, 3–6, 17, 23, 45, 53,
    56, 61, 63, 64, 66, 69, 72, 74, 75,
    79, 87–91, 96, 99, 101, 104, 107–
    9, 116, 118, 119, 123, 124, 137,
    143, 144, 146, 149, 153, 154, 156,
    159, 162, 163. See also aliyah;
    Zionist

Jerusalem Report, 114
Jewish
    activists, 88
    birthrate, 42, 43, 114
    charities, 63, 98, 99, 122, 153
    continuity, 20, 26, 71, 103, 106,
    109, 113, 119, 127, 129, 144, 150,
    157, 160
    day school, 32, 33, 37, 67, 78,
    79, 116, 125, 149, 152, 153, 155,
    157–59
    demography, 18, 26, 43, 59, 60,
    103, 110, 111, 113, 139
    fertility, 41–43, 58, 59, 114
    heritage, 32, 53, 61, 62, 65–67, 74,
    75, 86–88, 95, 102, 103, 106, 124,
    125, 133, 138, 160, 162
    household size, 59, 114, 155
    identification, 77, 119
    identity, 13, 16, 18, 22–24, 28, 30,
    32, 35, 39, 41, 45, 51, 52, 54, 56–
    58, 60, 61, 64–68, 70, 74, 75, 77,
    81, 87, 89, 91, 94, 95, 100–103,
    105, 107–11, 115, 117, 118, 120,
    121, 123–25, 135–38, 144, 149,

150, 153, 160, 163
particularism, 75, 79, 131
periodicals, 105, 122, 139
summer camp, 116, 155
superiority, 22, 23, 52
tribalism, 82, 161
voluntary associations, 140
wealth, 6
women, 42, 49, 92–94, 114, 142
Jewish-Americans, 65–67, 72, 75,
    76, 78, 79, 81, 84–88, 96, 98, 99
Jewish Heritage Week, 102
Jewish studies, xi, 1, 6, 32, 37, 38,
    61, 63, 81, 83, 89, 91, 108, 139,
    140, 158, 170n91
Judaica, 6, 41, 82–83, 162
Judenschmerz, 31, 32

Kennedy, John F., 14, 48, 84
King David, 26
Kiryas Yoel, 154
kosher food, 69, 103, 109, 145,
    156, 162

landsmanschaftn, 56
liberal, 22, 23, 65, 67, 71, 72, 83–87,
    89, 90, 93, 137, 144, 161
Liebman, Charles, 71, 161, 162
life cycle, 121
Lipset, Seymour M., 45, 55, 80
Look magazine, 16, 28, 58–60, 64,
    67, 114
loyalty, 14, 17, 56, 61, 101, 110
Lubavitch. *See* Habad

marriage, 17, 41, 42, 52, 59, 60, 78,
    79, 93, 113, 127–32, 151
McCarthyism, 14, 15, 18, 55
medical schools, 81
melting pot, 15, 22, 50, 63, 64,
    101–3, 107
meritocracy, 16, 43, 45, 62, 79
migration, 111, 126, 141, 149

mitzvot, 30, 70, 79
mobility, 9, 12, 19, 22, 24, 27, 41,
    43, 47, 65, 82, 114, 126, 127, 145

National Council of Young
    Israel, 153
New Jersey, 60, 117, 127
New Rochelle, N.Y., 21, 160
New York, xvi, 3, 4, 9–11, 15, 18,
    20–22, 25, 26, 28–30, 33, 37, 39,
    41, 44, 47, 49, 50, 54–57, 59, 62,
    65, 66, 71, 77, 78, 80, 82, 86–90,
    92, 93, 95, 102, 104–6, 109, 110,
    113, 116, 117, 122, 126–29, 134,
    139, 147, 148, 150, 151, 154, 156
nuclear family, 10–13, 66

occupations, 40, 43, 82
organizational life, 111, 138
Orthodox Jews, 6, 23, 25, 28, 33,
    53, 56, 58, 61, 62, 66, 70, 71, 73,
    78, 79, 88, 109, 115–17, 124, 125,
    127, 136, 137, 140, 143–59, 163
outmarriage, 44, 69, 78, 111, 129–
    32. *See also* intermarriage

Passover, 53, 65, 68, 69, 128,
    131, 133
philanthropy, 82, 96–98, 118
Phoenix, Arizona, 127, 128
pluralism. *See* cultural pluralism
polarization, 65, 68, 73, 79
    of Jewish life, 68
political influence, 100, 123, 140,
    142, 143, 145, 146, 161, 162
poverty, 39, 43, 98
Presbyterians, 50
professionalization, 40, 41, 60, 79,
    82, 96, 97, 158

Rabbinical Assembly, 70, 72, 93
rabbis, xv, 17, 70, 73, 86, 88, 94,
    106, 109, 125, 150, 157

Ramaz, 78, 79
Reconstructionist Jews, 94, 134, 147
Reform Jews, 53, 58, 62, 70–73, 78,
  94, 116, 117, 134, 139
religious elites, 70
religious switch, 75
residential patterns, 24, 25, 111, 125
ritual practices, 120
Rosenthal, Erich, 22, 44
Rubin, Jerry, 87

Seattle, Washington, 160, 163
second generation, 18, 31, 113, 120
secular education, 32, 38, 40, 41,
  60, 79, 88, 158
secular Jews, 119, 131, 138
seder, 53, 65, 68, 69, 103, 104, 106,
  128, 129, 131, 133, 160
segregation, 19, 23
shrinking middle, 68, 71
Six Day War, 97
Sklare, Marshall, 21, 67, 132, 147
social equality, 66, 137
socialization, 22
Soviet Jewry, 61, 74, 75, 89, 107
Starr, Joshua, 38
student deferments, 83
suburbs, 9–13, 19–28, 32, 38, 42,
  44, 49, 50, 59
supplementary schools, 77, 140
survivalist Jewish attitudes, 109

symbolic heritage, 68, 95, 120
synagogue, 18, 28–36, 38, 51–53,
  65–68, 70, 86, 93, 99, 104, 105,
  107–9, 116, 117, 121, 122, 128,
  129, 134, 139–41, 145, 147, 152,
  155, 169n67

television, 12–14
Thanksgiving, 69, 103, 104
Torah U'Mesorah, 78
transformation of American Jewry,
  134, 162

UJA (United Jewish Appeal), 3–4,
  96, 147
ultra-Orthodox. See haredim
Union of Orthodox Jewish Congregations of America, 143, 153

vanishing American Jew, 58, 60,
  67, 114
Vietnam War, 73, 87, 88

Yeshiva College, 32, 33, 80
Yiddish, 38, 63, 70
Yom Kippur, 18, 64, 69, 97, 104,
  117, 128, 129, 166n22

Zionist, 3, 4, 52, 56, 63, 139. See
  also Israel